SHATTERED AIR

SHATTERED AIR

A True Account of Catastrophe and
Courage on Yosemite's Half Dome

BOB MADGIC
with Adrian Esteban
ILLUSTRATIONS BY WILLIAM L. CRARY

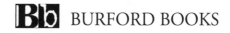

BURFORD BOOKS

Printed in the United States of America.

10 9 8 7 6 5 4 3 2 1

Library of Congress Cataloging-in-Publication Data

Madgic, Bob.
  Shattered air : a true account of catastrophe and courage on Yosemite's Half Dome / by Bob Madgic with Adrian Esteban ; illustrations by William L. Crary.
    p. cm.
  ISBN 1-58080-130-7 (hardcover)
  1. Rock climbing accidents—California—Half Dome. 2. Search and rescue operations—California—Half Dome. I. Esteban, Adrian. II. Title.

  GV199.42.C2M34 2005
  796.522'3'028'9--dc22
                                    2005001763

This book is dedicated to Robert Frith and Brian Jordan.

CONTENTS

MAIN CHARACTERS

ESTEBAN AND RICE'S PARTY
Adrian Esteban
Tom Rice
Bob Frith
Bruce Weiner
Bill Pippey
Brian Jordan
Bruce Jordan
Karl Buchner
Steve Ellner

MIKE HOOG'S PARTY
Mike Hoog
Linda Crozier
Rick Pedroncelli
Dan Crozier
Jennie Hayes

BRIAN CAGE'S PARTY
Brian Cage
Zip Cotter
Clu Cotter
Paul Kolbenschlag
Monroe Bridges
Steve White

OTHER HELPERS
Renee Miller
Brutus

THE ROCK CLIMBERS
Ken Bokelund
Rob Foster

YOSEMITE PERSONNEL

Colin Campbell
(first ranger to arrive on the summit of Half Dome)

Steve Jackson
(trail maintenance individual who accompanied Campbell)

John Dill
*(search and rescue technician who used a bullhorn
to communicate with the helpers on the summit)*

James Reilly
(supervising ranger throughout the episode)

Gary Colliver
(ranger who accompanied Medi-Flight to the summit)

Dan Horner, Mike Mayer, Paul Ducasse
*(park medics who left the Valley on horses
en route to Little Yosemite Valley)*

Ron Mackie, Scott Emmerich
(rangers who carried out the rescue in Tenaya Canyon)

Evan Smith, Dan Dellinges, J. R. Tomasovic, Jim Tucker
(rangers who prepared the bodies for removal on Sunday morning)

MEDI-FLIGHT AIR AMBULANCE SERVICE
Al Major, pilot
Bill Bryant, paramedic
Maggie Newman, nurse

AUTHOR'S NOTE

———◄○►———

THE EPISODE ON HALF DOME in 1985 was extraordinary. But lightning itself can impact anyone, anywhere in the world. This universality distinguishes it from more regional natural forces such as cyclones, hurricanes, and earthquakes. As a result of my own unforgettable experience, its dangers have been long imprinted on my mind. It went like this. In the late 1970s, I planned a one-day, fifteen-mile round-trip hike to the Mokelumne Wilderness canyon in the Sierra Nevada. Joining me were my wife, Diane, and our three children: Jennifer, sixteen; Kirk, fourteen; and Doug, twelve. The trek first involved a three-and-a-half-mile ascent up to the bare summit of Mount Reba at 8,750 feet in elevation. From there it was a four-mile drop down to the canyon floor and the Mokelumne River.

It was the return hike that proved most memorable.

After a picnic lunch and fishing the river, we headed back up the steep trail. As we approached Mount Reba in late afternoon, what had been a sparkling blue sky with a few billowy cumulus clouds was now covered by dark thunderheads. At the summit we were greeted by rain, while vicious streaks of lightning and sharp thunderclaps rocked the heavens to the east. We should have retreated down to tree level and waited for the storm to end. We didn't, mainly because I foolishly thought that as long as the lightning stayed to the east of us, two to three miles away at most, we'd be okay.

As the storm grew in intensity, with jagged spears of lightning striking nearby treetops and ground, accompanied by earsplitting thunder, my wife, who is rightly terrified of lightning, started running down the bare mountain slope, quickly joined by our three children. I, too, broke out into a run when a bolt struck to the west, placing us in the middle of the inferno. Fear drove us, our exhausted, wobbly legs gaining strength where none existed moments earlier. Up ahead Diane shrieked and fell down. Kirk, running alongside her, thought she was struck by lightning. Fortunately she only stumbled on loose rocks, but it was a hard fall. With scraped hands and knees, she got up and continued running.

Panic-stricken, we raced down the open terrain, frantically trying to outrun the next lightning bolt. The rain turned torrential, drenching us as we half ran, half stumbled, desperate to reach tree line a mile down from the ridge. Once there, we pushed our way through dense woods until we arrived at the meadow where our small yellow Honda was parked. Bomb blasts of lightning continued to rock heaven and earth. Likening this to a World War I battlefield, I sprinted across the naked field and threw myself into the car.

Never before or since have I experienced such raw, fearsome power. Never have I felt so vulnerable. What's so terrorizing is lightning's randomness—that at any moment a killing bolt can come from anywhere and strike you.

We were extremely fortunate that day. My judgment and actions were irresponsible to the extreme. If anyone had been struck, perhaps killed, I would have had to live with the tragedy for the remainder of my life, if indeed I survived. Yet it wasn't until I started writing this book and dissecting the Half Dome disaster that I fully internalized the reckless and uninformed leadership I carried out and which placed my family in that enormously high-risk situation. My daughter pointed this out to me when I was discussing with her the actions of the Half Dome leaders. It was a sobering realization.

Another reason why the 1985 Half Dome incident stayed etched in my mind was that I indirectly knew one of the participants—the son of a woman who worked in my office. He was one of four hikers (out of nine) who blessedly did not reach the summit that day. I have told this story often, how with different circumstances, he would have been there at the top when lightning struck and possibly killed. When I ended my career in education and looked to writing to keep me engaged, I quickly concluded that a broad audience might exist for the Half Dome story, which at the time received wide media attention. I placed a phone call to my co-worker's son, and now seven years later, the book is published.

I had great luck in tracking down almost all of the people who contributed one way or another to that 1985 episode. Out of over forty participants, I failed to locate only one key person. (That's Renee Miller, one of the main helpers that night. Perhaps she'll contact me if she sees this book.) College alumni offices proved key in two critical cases. So, too, was the Internet for a few others. Once I contacted a person, he or she usually was able to provide information on someone else. One connection was extremely fortuitous. There were only two rock climbers on the face of Half Dome at that time, and one just happened to be the son of my college classmate. He read about this project in the *Amherst Alumni Journal* and thought it sounded like the very time his son was there. Amazingly, it was.

Yosemite National Park was exceptionally responsive to my requests, as indeed were all national park personnel whom I contacted. Without park reports I would not have been able to complete this project. The National Park Service heroically carries out its multifaceted responsibilities, albeit with insufficient resources. Our parks deserve more from our nation.

Medi-Flight Air Ambulance service personnel were also all fully cooperative and helpful.

Nothing takes the place of on-site research. I hiked to Half Dome's summit twice since I began this project (I had been up there years earlier as well). Adrian Esteban and Bill Pippey—two primary players in the 1985 event—joined me on one of the excursions. I also went to Kings Canyon National Park and retraced the steps of the individual who was killed by lightning the same day as the Half Dome incident. It took a little doing, but my wife and I found the rock enclosure in which he took cover and where his body was discovered. I also hiked to Paradise, located on a small tributary off the Merced River. I didn't jump from the ledge into the pool. (The reader will understand this reference shortly into the story.)

Not everyone involved one way or another in the story supported its telling, including one central participant. The text will identify who he is. Fortunately, a wide range of participants enthusiastically embraced the project, including most of the main characters. Adrian Esteban's recollections, insights, and voice are central to the book throughout.

To present as accurate rendition of the story as possible, I used quotation marks in the text only for a direct statement from an individual, either as presented to me or as quoted in a newspaper account or other formal documents. When individuals I interviewed recalled statements and conversation, they appear without quotation marks if I included them.

Lastly, a word about lightning injuries and treatments. After becoming acquainted with this complex field, I've learned that much of the terminology and reports on the medical aspects of lightning as presented in 1985 do not accurately convey what is known today. New findings are being uncovered each year. For the most part I retained the 1985 language, for example with coroner and medical reports, even though it may be inaccurate according to current information. On a very limited basis I attempted to bring the field up to date in chapter 10—Aftermath.

Bob Madgic
Anderson, California
June 2005

INTRODUCTION

*The great Tis-se-yak, or Half Dome, rising at the
upper end of the valley to a height of nearly a mile, is
nobly proportioned and lifelike, the most impressive of
all the rocks, holding the eye in devout admiration,
calling it back again and again from falls or meadows, or even the mountains beyond. . . .—John Muir*

I N THE FALL OF 1849, two men tracked a grizzly bear deep into
the central Sierra Nevada in the hope of shooting it. They got
lost. Trying to find their way back to camp, the men followed an
Indian trail that led instead to "a valley enclosed by stupendous
cliffs." Not far off, a waterfall dropped from a cliff below three
jagged peaks into the valley. The hunters also noted "a rounded

mountain . . . which looked as though it had been sliced with a knife as one would slice a loaf of bread." They called it the Rock of Ages.

This is the first recorded description of Yosemite Valley and Half Dome.

Native Americans probably visited Yosemite Valley, which is only one-half to one mile wide and less than seven miles long, as far back as ten thousand years. People of Miwok lineage most likely took up residence in the valley about a thousand years ago, living peacefully among its natural riches and beauty, and drawing water from a river that Spanish explorers named the Merced, in honor of the Virgin Mary.

◄○►

ONE EXPLANATION OF THE NAME *Yosemite* holds that it was a corruption of *uzumati* or *uhumati*, Native terms for "grizzly bear." Apparently the Miwok had divided themselves into two clan-like social groupings, and one of them was generally identified with the grizzly bear. A second interpretation draws from the linguistic roots of the Miwok language: *Yo'hem-iteh* means "they are killers."

In time other Indians in the region began calling these valley dwellers "Yosemites." Grizzly bears were dangerous, and people beyond the hidden valley came to regard the Natives who lived there as equally ferocious. Outsiders may have referred to them as both grizzlies and killers.

Regardless of its origin, the name doesn't honor the now extinct California grizzly, *Ursus arctos californicus*. Rather, it venerates the Natives who once inhabited the lush green valley known as Ahwahnee—"the big mouth" or "place of the big mouth." They referred to themselves as Ahwahneechees. The Ahwahneechees called the strange mountain with the cutoff side *Tis-se-yak*. According to legend, a woman by that name entered the valley with a great conical gathering basket and slaked her thirst by drinking all of the water in the valley's only lake before her equally thirsty husband, Nangas, arrived. Upon seeing what Tis-se-yak had done, an angry Nangas beat her. She retaliated by throwing her basket at him. For their wickedness, both were turned into stone: She became what is now known as Half Dome, her husband became the Washington Column, and her basket became Basket Dome. The dark streaks on Half Dome's face are the tears that Tis-se-yak shed as she ran from Nangas, and the human profile seen from some vantage points is that of her in mourning.

◄o►

IN THE LATTER HALF of the eighteenth century, disease spread among the Ahwahneechees, forcing the survivors to leave the valley. Many trekked to the eastern side of the Sierra Nevada to the Mono and Kuzedika Paiute villages. There were no inhabitants in Ahwahnee for several decades. Living among the Monos was Teneiya, son of an Ahwahneechee chief and a Mono mother. The chief told Teneiya about the remote river valley where his people had lived. After his father died, Teneiya traveled there on foot. When he arrived in the valley, he knew at once it would be his home. Teneiya returned to the Mono village to gather followers—family, descendants of his father's people, and scattered Mono and Kuzedika Paiute tribe members. The group, numbering about two hundred, was an unpredictable and contentious lot that included many outlaws and malcontents.

Teneiya's band prospered in Ahwahnee, where the chief grew old and his three sons became men. These Native people had a passionate and spiritual attachment to Ahwahnee; their sense of place defined who they were. But a medicine man counseled Teneiya that intruders could threaten their survival. So he and his braves remained vigilant and were prepared to fight any encroachers.

◄o►

AFTER GOLD WAS DISCOVERED in California, miners flooded into the foothills. Native American tribes tried to defend their land and villages (called rancherias) from gold-seeking intruders, while Indian braves in turn plundered and pillaged the white man's camps. In one murky incident, a trading post on the Fresno River owned by a Major James D. Savage was raided. The settlers rightly or wrongly blamed the Yosemites, even though the post was quite distant from their normal range. Vengeful miners called for "wiping out the Indian savages."

To bring the Yosemites and other Indians to the treaty table, Savage organized the Mariposa Battalion, a volunteer military unit consisting of about two hundred mostly rough-hewn men. Accompanying the party on their first foray to Yosemite was Lafayette Houghton Bunnell, a twenty-seven-year-old educated and fair-minded medical adviser. He took extensive notes and later wrote an account of his experiences, *Discovery of the Yosemite*, that became a valuable historical record. Bunnell recalled that when he first entered the concealed valley, "a peculiar exalted sensation seemed to fill my whole being, and I found my eyes in tears with emotion."

Across two years, the Mariposa Battalion succeeded in killing, capturing, and driving the remaining Indians out of Yosemite. Chief Teneiya and a small group fled and took refuge with the Monos. After the soldiers left, they returned to Yosemite, intent upon living there in secrecy. But he and the others were ultimately vanquished one last time. Whether battalion soldiers or members of the Mono tribe produced their demise is not clear.

Bunnell and soldiers in the Mariposa Battalion named many of Yosemite landmarks: El Capitan, Mirror Lake, Clouds Rest, Little Yosemite Valley, Vernal Fall, Nevada Fall, Ribbon Fall, and Bridalveil Fall. A beautiful, high-country lake where the battalion captured a holdout band of Yosemites became Lake Teneiya. (The spelling of this and other namesakes evolved into *Tenaya* over time.) Tenaya Canyon and Tenaya Creek also honor the chief. Several names refer to incidents involving the Yosemites: Three Brothers, Lost Arrow, and Indian Canyon.

Half Dome originated from the first impression of a battalion soldier as he entered the valley. "I looked a good long while at that split mountain," he reportedly said, "and called it a 'half dome'"— a name that had become firmly established by 1865. Earlier it was known as Tis-se-yak and then, for a few years, as South Dome. (North Dome was on the opposite side of the valley.)

◄○►

IN 1860, YALE GRADUATE Josiah Dwight Whitney was appointed California state geologist and charged with studying the state's geology to locate mineral deposits in the Sierra. His influential *Report of the Geological Survey of California* was published five years later. Whitney described Half Dome as "a new revelation in mountain forms; its existence would be considered an impossibility if it were not there before us in all its reality . . . nothing even approaching it can be found except in the Sierra Nevada itself."

Despite his growing reputation as a geologist, Whitney proved way off the mark on two counts: first, his assumption that "Half Dome is perfectly inaccessible, being probably the only one of all the prominent points about the Yosemite which never has been, and never will be, trodden by human foot"; and second, his conclusion that Half Dome "had been split in two, one half having been engulfed at the time of the formation of the chasm at its base . . . the lost half having gone down in what may truly be said to have been the wreck of matter and the crush of worlds."

Another individual who came to Yosemite in the 1860s and who lived there on and off across fifty years was a Scotsman by the name of John Muir. Muir's conservation legacies have shaped the very character of America. Among his many accomplishments, he was instrumental in having Yosemite preserved as a national park. He also helped found the Sierra Club in 1892 and became its first president. In fighting many battles on nature's behalf, his sword was the written word. He wrote ten books and more than three hundred articles in some of the most eloquent and compelling language ever penned.

Although he was one of this country's greatest naturalists ever, John Muir incorrectly attributed Half Dome's shape to glacial forces. He correctly deduced that glaciers carved out the canyons and valleys of the Sierra, but he erred in concluding that glaciers sculpted the domes, at least those more than four thousand feet from the Valley floor. According to various studies, Half Dome protruded five hundred to nine hundred feet above the highest glaciers.

Exfoliation and erosion formed the rounded domes as forces, in a process also called sheeting, cast away successive thin, granite slabs called spalls over time, much like the peeling away of onion layers. Scoured by the weather—ice and frost wedging and heaving, and lightning strikes—the granite top progressively lost mass and hence weight. As the load decreased, the granite expanded outward, creating the spalls. Originally, the mountain may have been angular, but exfoliation shaved off the corners of the spalls.

Half Dome's sheer face extends twenty-two hundred feet from its base of jumbled rocks to the crest. It was formed by the progressive removal of thin rock sheets from a zone of nearly vertical joints. Indeed, this process shaped many of the landforms in Yosemite that glaciers didn't sculpt. (In Yosemite's high country, the jointing process is evident among other granite domes with partial vertical faces.) Much of a granite monolith like Half Dome consists of solid rock that is highly resistant to erosive forces. But often present in the rock are parallel cracks or fractures called joints. Weathering forces, especially ice, cause the jointed segments to break off eventually. In the case of Half Dome, the fractures are vertically aligned; that produced the mountain's distinctive vertical face. However, one prior form still remains, at the apex of this northwest side: the Visor, a prominent protrusion that resembles the beak of a giant bird or an observation booth.

To the surprise of many, there never was another half to Half Dome. Up to 80 percent of the famous northwest side may still be intact, despite references to the "missing half." Indeed, the Dome's appearance is more illusory than real. That shape prevails in views from the Valley floor, but a view of Half Dome from Glacier Point or Washburn Point reveals that only the top of the southeast side is rounded; the remainder is almost as vertical as the northwest face.

◄o►

AS IF ON A GRAND PEDESTAL, Half Dome stands at the far end of the Valley, on the divide between Tenaya Canyon and Little Yosemite Valley. At 8,892 feet in elevation, its summit juts almost one mile above Yosemite Valley. Of all the eminences in this part of Yosemite, only the lofty, two-mile-long granite ridge called Clouds Rest, with an altitude of 9,929 feet, surpasses it. Half Dome's location and height bestow upon it a visual prominence and allure that any visitor to Yosemite Valley takes in. They also account for yet another of this monolith's features—its susceptibility to weather systems to unleash their torrents there. Storms that build over Clouds Rest inevitably move down Tenaya Canyon and take aim at Half Dome. The same holds true for ones that develop in lower Yosemite Valley.

If there is any such thing as a "granite lightning rod," Half Dome is it.

◄o►

EVERY MOUNTAIN BECKONS to climbers for a host of personal reasons. And contrary to Whitney's assessment that Half Dome would never be scaled, its summit lured the adventurous early on. Several first attempts ended in failure. But on October 12, 1875, George Anderson—a former sea captain, carpenter, blacksmith, and one of Yosemite Park's early trail builders—set his sights on the top and would not be denied. The challenge: ascending a rounded slope of polished granite with a grade of forty-five to sixty degrees. First, Anderson tried applying pine pitch to the bottoms of his bare feet as an adhesive. That didn't work. Then, summoning his trade skills, he drilled a six-inch-deep hole into the granite slope every five to six feet and drove in an iron bolt, which he used as a foothold to drill the next hole. The Scotsman thus painstakingly proceeded up the six-hundred-foot incline over several days. When he finished, he descended on the same bolts and spliced together sections of rope to connect them. That enabled Anderson to pull himself back up to the top of Half Dome.

What he found was a vast, mainly flat surface covering about thirteen acres (the equivalent of approximately seventeen football fields), with a higher knoll in the middle of the dome. The side overlooking the Valley had a sheer edge; the other sides had rounded slopes before they, too, became almost vertical.

Delighted with his accomplishment, Anderson returned to the Valley. He thought about constructing a staircase to the summit.

Within a week, six men and a woman wearing a skirt successfully made the ascent using Anderson's rope. The woman, Sally Dutcher from San Francisco, a twenty-eight-year-old assistant to the famous photographer Carleton E. Watkins, demonstrated that mountaineering was not strictly a man's sport. On November 10 of the same year, right after a snowstorm that would have discouraged anyone else, John Muir became the ninth person to accomplish this feat.

Muir described his first view from the summit of Half Dome as "perfectly glorious. . . . A massive cloud of pure pearl luster . . . was arched across the Valley from wall to wall. . . . My shadow, clearly outlined, about half a mile long, lay upon this glorious white surface with startling effect. I walked back and forth, waved my arms and struck all sorts of attitudes, to see every slightest movement enormously exaggerated." The German word for this rare optical illusion, in which a vast shadow or apparition is projected on the mists of a mountain, is *Brockengespenst* or the "specter of the Brocken" (Brocken is the highest of the Hartz Mountains in Germany). Atop Half Dome, Muir identified plants such as spirea, cinquefoil, alpine daisy, buckwheat, goldenrod, Sierra onion, penstemon, and three species of "repressed and storm beaten" pine—white-bark, western hemlock, and lodgepole.

Since Muir's time, the rare Mount Lyell salamander, a lungless amphibian that sustains itself on a diet of spiders and other insects, has been spotted on the summit. The only mammal living there before the arrival of humans was the golden-mantled squirrel, often referred to as a "chipmunk." It still exists there, along with other small furry creatures that undoubtedly followed the parade of humans to the top.

Anderson's rope trail attracted only those willing to pull themselves up a perilous slope using a system that could fail at any time. In fact, snow and ice during the winter of 1883–84 broke the rope and ripped out spikes. A new rope broke in 1895 and again in 1901. In 1908, a climber inserted new pegs. Such patchwork repairs continued until a more permanent trail could be built. Anderson, who died of pneumonia in 1884, never realized his dream of constructing a staircase.

◄O►

TO ASCEND ANDERSON'S ROPE, of course, you had to reach the base of Half Dome. The effort then and now typically begins on the renowned Mist Trail, built in the late 1850s. Consisting largely of granite steps, it starts at Happy Isles at the far end of the Valley and winds alongside the Merced River up a narrow canyon. The trail leads hikers first to Vernal Fall, where crashing water sprays off rocks, creating swirling mists—hence the trail's name—that engulf those who pass by at the closest point. Vernal Fall drops only 317 feet, but the sheet of water is unbroken from top to bottom and as wide as 80 feet when the Merced is full, thus making it one of the most symmetrical falls in the world.

Mist Trail continues up the steep ravine to the top of Nevada Fall, not quite three and a half miles from the trailhead. Nevada Fall, like Vernal Fall, plummets over a granite platform, one of many steps in the "Giant Staircase." The full staircase, encompassing less distinguishable platforms, reaches from the Valley floor to the base of Mount Lyell—a distance of twenty-one miles and an altitude gain of seventy-six hundred feet. Glaciation quarried away the massive vertical joints of granite formations at roughly right angles, leaving stair-like platforms in its wake. Trail builders tried to duplicate nature's work, although on a much smaller scale, in the tight canyon below Nevada Fall. Using only manpower, they placed more than two thousand granite steps; some of the risers are nearly fifteen inches, others barely one.

At the lip of Nevada Fall, the Merced River surges through a narrow opening in the granite and plummets 594 feet to a projecting ledge that splays the massive falls slightly outward. Nevada Fall, unlike Vernal's even drop, begins as a constricted blast of water and then widens dramatically as it drops, resembling a giant horsetail.

From Nevada Fall, the Mist Trail follows the river to Little Yosemite Valley, which is slightly less than four miles from Half Dome's shoulder—a steep, six-hundred-foot hump that had to be surmounted on somewhat perilous footing before one reached the base of Half Dome's eastern side and the start of Anderson's rope trail. For decades, the shoulder was informally called quarter dome, a designation that conflicted with that of nearby formations formally called Quarter Domes. (Today the shoulder is referred to as Sub Dome, a name that some people find less than endearing.) In 1919, the Sierra Club funded the construction of more-permanent climbing aids up Half Dome. A train of about a dozen mules carried two coils of connected steel cable from the Valley to the base of Sub Dome. There a civil engineer named Lawrence Sovulewski took over; his crew manually hauled the coils to the top of the hump, then up the slope of Half Dome.

The revamped pathway consists of a cable handrail on each side and wooden footholds, a design that hasn't changed much since 1919. The cables are thirty inches apart—close enough to grip with both hands yet far enough apart that hikers can squeeze past each other—and above average shoulder height to accommodate the steep incline, which obliges climbers to lean forward as they pull themselves up. The cables are attached to steel posts set in sockets drilled into the granite every ten feet and fortified by heavy chains bolted into the rock every hundred feet. Two-by-fours secured to the steel posts provide a foothold—and frequent opportunities to rest.

In 1934, a crew from the Civilian Conservation Corps, an outgrowth of President Franklin Roosevelt's New Deal, replaced the cables as part of trail-building projects nationwide. The National Park Service did the same in 1984. Most of the steel posts with the exception of those along the very upper part are removed each fall and laid on the granite in order to prevent destruction from snowslides. They are then returned to their holes in early spring.

The early trail builders also constructed a granite stairway up Sub Dome. The "Rock Stairway," as some publications refer to it, has roughly 600 steps, most of which are manmade. Then the trail descends a short distance to the beginning of the cables.

The trail from the Valley floor to the summit—the Half Dome Trail—has been recognized in the National Register of Historic Places since 1988. Thousands of people from around the world hike to the top every year.

◄○►

Among those who made regular pilgrimages to Half Dome's summit were Adrian Esteban and Tom Rice. For them and a coterie of companions, the Dome took on a meaning far beyond that of other outdoor adventures.

YOSEMITE NATIONAL PARK

Thunderheads eclipsed the lowering sun as it dipped toward the western horizon. The storm had swept down from Clouds Rest past Tenaya Canyon and was now massed over Half Dome, where arrows of lightning pierced the darkening gloom and caused the air to smell as if it were burning. While thunderous detonations rocked the heavens, rain began pounding Half Dome's granite slopes and raced downward in ever-thicker rivulets.

Nothing in the experience of the frightened backpacker who was caught out on Half Dome's summit had prepared him for this. Lashed by sheets of rain, barely able to make out the surrounding ridges between lightning flashes, he was growing desperate when he stumbled upon a human-made rock enclosure. He scrambled inside, spread out a sleeping pad, and scrunched himself on the ground against one of the low walls. Clutching a tarp around him, he prayed he'd survive. His imagination, perhaps stoked by the thunder blasts and rushing wind, conjured the voices of vengeful demons.

Then he thought he heard a different sound.

Amid the reverberations ripping through the sky and rolling off Yosemite's domes and spires, he could have sworn he heard laughter.

Human laughter.

He raised his head and peered cautiously over the wall. In a sustained flash that lit the surrounding terrain, he saw a pale figure a few hundred yards off, toward the area atop Half Dome known as the Visor. His brain, in shocked disbelief, registered the image of a dancing man. A dancing naked man, head thrown back, arms spread wide, hooting up into the rain.

The light died away but the shouting did not.

The backpacker rubbed his eyes. He hadn't hallucinated because, in fitful illumination from successive bursts of lightning, he saw the figure again, his skin chalk-white in the eerie light, spinning and bending with reckless grace on the exposed rock as if it were a dance floor. Another patch of darkness, then a new shock: Four figures now circled the naked man. They were sodden, dark, clothed shapes, slapping at each other and seemingly exchanging high fives, weaving like drunken acolytes of some mountain Bacchus, their disregard a mockery of the deadly forces playing around them.

But in the next dark interval, they all vanished.

The observer stared. It was as if they had dropped into the mountain. Or never been there at all. Yet he was certain that he'd seen and heard them. What mortals would dare expose themselves on the bare summit of Half Dome, which, in a fierce storm, was essentially a gigantic lightning rod?

At the first sign that the storm was dissipating, he rose to his feet, troubled. He quickly stuffed his gear into his pack and hurried toward the cables, his lifeline to a safer refuge below. As he dropped down the granite incline, the cables burning his hands from his swift descent, the image of the dancers remained with him.

Who were they?

Where had they come from?

Where had they gone?

—AN ANONYMOUS OBSERVER ON HALF DOME, JULY 27, 1985

1

THE LEADERS

*A large granite mountain cannot be denied—it speaks
in silence to the very core of your being.*—Ansel Adams

FOUR YEARS EARLIER
MAY 23, 1981

ADRIAN ESTEBAN FOLLOWED TOM RICE on a hillside path edging
a tributary feeding the Merced River, a spring-fed creek that
tumbled down from high in the rugged foothills outside Yosemite
National Park. Yellow oak, foothill pine, chaparral, and poison oak
formed dense clusters in the ravine below. Half a mile up the narrow trail, just before the open terrain steepened abruptly and

where the distant top of the mountain was visible, Rice stopped. Through erosion, the creek had created beds of polished red stone here, their hue the result of oxidized iron deposits. The particular pool they were looking at was set within a rock grotto, one side vertical and slick. It was known as Paradise. On the hot summer days common in the Sierra foothills, local residents were fond of jumping from the surrounding rock platforms into the cold water, sliding otter-like down a natural chute into the pool, and sunbathing on the smooth stones.

Which was fine for the locals. But Esteban knew very well that Rice had not brought him here for restful play.

There it is, Rice said. Up there.

Shading his eyes from the morning sun, Esteban peered where Rice was pointing to a ledge high above. With a rising sense of unease, Esteban shrugged free of his army-surplus rucksack and removed the green bandanna from his head. He unbuckled the military belt that held his metal canteen—Esteban's outdoor wardrobe was greatly influenced by Vietnam combat films—then pulled off his boots and, finally, his camouflage pants with multiple pockets. The tank top he liked to wear to show off his sharply defined muscles stayed on, as did his shorts. Rice, meanwhile, had stripped off his pack, old low-cut sneakers, and mandala-emblazoned T-shirt and was moving up toward the ledge.

It was morning on their first trip together to Half Dome. Rice had already informed Esteban that he had to complete a test before they would do the Dome. It was to jump from the ledge here at Paradise into the pool. To Rice, this initiation ritual was an integral part of the Half Dome experience. It would demonstrate that a companion was able to overcome his fears—a central piece in Rice's beliefs about how to reap life's rewards.

When they stood on the ledge together, Rice told Esteban it was exactly forty-four feet to the surface of the pool. He knew this because he'd previously measured the distance with a rope. The pool's depth was fifteen feet—plenty deep for their purposes.

As Esteban looked down, his stomach felt queasy, his legs weak. The swimming hole, which had seemed about the size of a small backyard pool when he stood near it, looked considerably smaller from up here. He felt himself recoiling inwardly at the thought of leaping from the ledge. In fact, he couldn't remember ever feeling so intimidated. He glanced sideways at Rice but found no reprieve in the other's set features.

He would have to do it.

Forty-four feet is higher than a four-story building. The high-diving platform in diving competition is ten meters, or roughly thirty-eight feet, above the water. Jumps of twenty to twenty-five feet challenge most thrill-seekers. To throw yourself into a small pool forty-four feet below requires extraordinary nerve—there's little margin for error. As soon as you jump, the gravitational force generated by accelerating thirty-two-feet-per-second-per-second sends your stomach upward, causing a sudden constriction of the chest and lungs, and a loss of breath. When your body reaches the water 1.7 seconds later, it's traveling about fifty-three feet per second, or thirty-six miles an hour. At that speed, water becomes a hard surface, especially if you don't slice into it just right. (Increase the height to 120 feet and you hit the concrete-like plane three seconds later at sixty mph, which explains why suicidal leaps from high bridges are mostly successful.) Impacting the water at the wrong angle could snap your neck or back.

To conquer personal fear, Rice liked to say, you had to believe in yourself. As if to prove it, he assumed a diver's stance, arms at his side, toes curled over the edge. He took a leisurely breath, raised his arms, and sprang. He wrapped himself into a tight ball in midair, spun one and a half times as he descended, uncoiled just above the water, and neatly broke the surface in a headfirst finish.

Rice paddled to the pool's edge and looked up questioningly.

Esteban's feet remained anchored to the rock. Jump or fail. As the minutes passed, his right leg started to tremble uncontrollably. Rock climbers call this sewing-machine leg. It's caused by fear.

Jump or fail. He would not—*could not*—back down.

Rice yelled up, You can do it. Trust me!

Esteban made a move to jump. Then stopped. He peered down at the water. More minutes passed.

Rice shouted, Just do it!

Esteban realized that was the key, the only solution. Just do it! With a gulping inhalation, he jackknifed his legs, then thrust himself outward. Bellowing as he plunged (good for releasing air and thus reducing pressure on the lungs), arms overhead to prevent them from smacking the surface, he felt the soles of his feet slam, stinging, into the water. Gravity drove him to the bottom, the water slowing and cushioning the impact. The late-spring, fifty-degree water seemed to clutch at his chest and squeeze his lungs. He pushed hard off the bottom and shot to the surface, emerging in a watery explosion. Looking straight at Rice, he raised his arm in triumph.

Rice nodded and smiled. Esteban had passed his qualifying test and proved himself worthy.

From this point on, Esteban knew what it took to make the leap: Just do it!

Now they could tackle Half Dome together.

As they gathered their gear, Esteban hesitated. He pointed to the mountaintop overlooking Paradise and said he wanted to go up there before they left this place; he felt this mountain calling to him.

Rice gave him a questioning glance, wondering what was going on with his buddy. Then he nodded again, pleased with the words and seeming to attune himself to Esteban's exhilaration after making the jump.

Rice told him to lead the way.

As they neared the crest, Esteban spotted something white on the ground.

Stop! he called out.

Rice froze, thinking he was about to step on a rattlesnake.

Then, looking where Esteban pointed, he composed himself with a sheepish look—Rice tried never to show fright—and bent down to pull a partial set of antlers from the thick grass.

After a quick examination, Rice handed over the antlers, the left side of a young buck's rack. He told Esteban to keep the trophy; after all, he'd spotted it first.

They were the first antlers Esteban had seen in the wild. He studied them appreciatively, then tied the prized find to his pack. Moments later, when they reached the summit, Rice discovered the other half of the rack—the carbon-copy right side—at the mountain's very highest point. To the two young men, these finds held great meaning. The buck had needed to shed his old antlers before he could grow new ones. He'd visited the hill's apex to make a symbolic passage into a new phase—adulthood—and it struck Esteban and Rice that, with this initial trip to Half Dome together, they, too, were entering a new phase in their lives. The antlers seemed to signify their deepening bonds of friendship.

There on the crest, they made a pact: Each would keep his half of the antlers, thus linking them forever.

After they descended and were driving toward Half Dome, Esteban told Rice with quiet intensity that he felt the mountain had been beckoning him the whole time; he'd needed to go to its summit to answer the call.

Rice offered a one-word explanation: *Karma.*

◄○►

ADRIAN ESTEBAN AND TOM RICE HAD met five years before, when Rice was a senior and Esteban a sophomore at Peterson High School in Santa Clara, about forty miles south of San Francisco. On the surface, the two teens hardly could have been more different.

Rice was the youngest of four children in a well-to-do, supportive family. His father was a Chevron Corporation executive. Two of Rice's siblings were considerably older, which may have accounted for the lack of parental supervision he'd received while growing up. Although intelligent, Rice was hardly a dedicated student. Nor was he a dedicated athlete. Very much his own man, he mostly avoided team sports, preferring instead to concentrate on his diving abilities, which he pursued on the school swim squad. At five foot nine and 160 pounds, with a diver's lithe and well-honed body, dirty-blond hair, and striking blue eyes, he looked like the quintessential California surfer. Slightly prominent teeth gave the appearance of a constant smile. Rice was amiable, outgoing, and charismatic—traits that gave him a wide circle of friends.

But at heart, Tom Rice marched to his own beat. He resisted any hint of constraint placed on him by "the system" or anyone else. Much of his free time was spent hanging out, both with the athletes or "jocks," and with the drug users or "stoners." (Such stereotyped groupings were of course typical of high school campuses.) Rice was one of those rare kids who could comfortably mix with either group. It was at parties that he and Esteban first got together, with drugs and alcohol a standard connector. As uncontested holder of the "killer stash," Rice was a fixture at all the so-called best ones, which prompted some of his friends to call him The Legend and led his classmates to designate him "most likely to party" in their yearbook. Often the first thing Esteban asked him—even before "How ya doin'?"—was "What's going down this weekend?" To Esteban, Rice was indeed the man to know, his "in" to the social world that mattered most to him.

Unlike Rice, who enjoyed all the upper-middle-class advantages and could fit in wherever he chose, Adrian Esteban was a disadvantaged minority in the mainly white schools around Silicon Valley. His grandparents had left the Philippines in the 1920s for Hawaii, where they worked in the pineapple fields and where Esteban's mother and father met and married. Believing the mainland offered more opportunity, the couple moved to San Francisco in 1957. The first of their five children, Adrian, was born in 1959. Mr. Esteban worked as a materials handler at Hunters Point Naval Shipyard in South San Francisco. When it closed, he moved his

family south to Sunnyvale and took a job at the Mare Island Shipyard across the Bay. His modest income, coupled with a gambling
addiction, often left the family financially strapped.

To Adrian, his peers always seemed to have more money, better clothes, and, long before he had one, their own cars. His parents never saw college as a worthy goal, so they didn't push their
children academically. Mr. Esteban seldom showed love or emotional support; nor did he provide much in the way of positive
guidance or discipline. Mainly he pressured his son to be an outstanding athlete, to adopt a *win-at-all-costs* mentality. Adrian also
could not connect with his mother on a very deep level because
in their culture it was considered less manly for a son to be too
close to his mom; he didn't want to have an image of being a
momma's boy.

As the eldest son, Adrian felt particularly harassed. He rebelled
against his father's badgering early on. At age thirteen, he drank
some beer. And he liked it—a lot.

Despite little parental encouragement, Esteban managed to
earn outstanding grades. He also demonstrated impressive physical gifts. At five foot six, he was small for an athlete, but he packed
160 solid pounds on his frame and had powerful legs. He worked
out religiously, pumping weights and using resistance machines to
build leg strength. In his junior year, he led the football team in
rushing and was a standout in baseball, with strong potential to
play at the next level.

But by then, Esteban had added marijuana to his growing alcohol intake—a combination that, increasingly and inevitably, mud-
dled his judgment. Entering his senior year, thinking he had it
made as an athlete, he didn't bother to train or work out over the
summer in preparation for football. He partied most of the night
before the first practice. Then, in a mile run with others to test
their fitness, he could barely finish. The coach chastised him for
his poor physical condition and lack of dedication, a rebuke that
only fueled Esteban's rebelliousness. Although he'd been heralded

at the start of the season as one of the league's best running backs, he consistently failed to produce.

Outside football, things weren't any better. Esteban's parents were divorcing, which heightened his anger and sense of isolation. He cut classes excessively, causing his academic performance to plummet. He found solace—and escape—in beer and pot. His main objective in life was to go to the best parties.

With the approach of spring, the baseball coach lectured Esteban on his lack of discipline and bad attitude. Seeing Esteban goofing around in the batting cage at one of the first practices, he warned him to shape up or risk being a flop on the diamond.

Esteban, stung and resentful, waved contemptuously at the field and told the coach this was all a crock of shit.

The coach replied that if he kept up that attitude, he may as well not stick it out.

Fine, snapped Esteban. I quit.

So much for baseball.

Joining the U.S. Marines after graduation seemed like a promising option. Military images had long fascinated Esteban. His favorite entertainments involved war movies, books, and games, and he fantasized about being in combat himself. But Esteban was not yet eighteen. His father refused to give the necessary consent and instead threatened to disown him if he tried to enlist. With Korea and Vietnam in mind, Mr. Esteban didn't want his son killed. But somehow that concern got lost in the fray. A shouting match erupted. Enraged at being denied, Esteban stormed out of the house.

In following months, apart from working at a gas station, he mainly hung out. He had moved his bed and belongings to a room in his parents' garage and spent much of his time partying with buddies who congregated there. His life became increasingly aimless.

At age nineteen, Esteban bought a "crotch rocket"—a gleaming new Yamaha 350 racing motorcycle engineered for top speed. The very next week, a car pulled in front of him on a sharp turn.

Esteban hit the brakes hard, causing them to lock, and slid under the car, his head banging the pavement. Had he not been wearing a helmet due to cold weather, he would have been totaled like his mangled Yamaha. Nonetheless, undaunted and seemingly uncaring, he seldom bothered with a helmet thereafter.

Two more bike spills followed, which he again survived with no major injuries. Then, driving a car home late one night from a party while drunk, he foolishly dared himself to cover the intervening two miles without disturbing the cruise control. On a curve where he should have braked, the vehicle sped straight ahead, slammed through a fence, and crashed into a house under construction. Mrs. Esteban reported herself as the driver to protect her son's insurance and driving record.

Deep down, recognizing the fatal course his life was taking, Esteban longed to change. At age twenty, he saw an ad for a free personality assessment and mailed in a questionnaire. The Church of Scientology invited him weeks later to come to a meeting and discuss his personal needs. Esteban enlisted in the program soon after. He liked Scientology's emphasis on uncovering the roots of behavior patterns and its technique-oriented strategies for dealing with his problems: a dysfunctional family, self-destructive actions, reliance on drugs and alcohol. What he didn't like was the escalating cost of this help and oddities such as using a meter to gauge his reactions to stress.

Esteban eventually dropped Scientology. He still found meaning in religion and the concept of a supreme being. Esteban often looked to such an outside force—"the gods"—to account for happenings in his life. Moreover, he had long believed he possessed paranormal powers, a sixth sense. Once, on deck in a ball game, Esteban suddenly just "knew" he would hit a home run. At the plate, on the second pitch to him, he blasted the ball over the centerfield fence, the longest drive he'd ever hit. During that experience, he felt an unusual clarity, as if he were looking down on it all from an astral plane. On another occasion, after he suspected an object had been stolen from him, he somehow sensed that it was still in his house—and "saw" it in the attic hidden beneath a pile of boxes. That's precisely where it proved to be, to the astonishment of his housemates. Esteban was also convinced he'd had more than one brief, out-of-body experience.

◄o►

AS HE MATURED, Esteban's interest in psychic phenomena and metaphysics grew. Movement in that direction was catalyzed by Tom Rice, who bluntly questioned Esteban's attachment to Scientology and encouraged him to look inward to deal with problems. *Trust yourself, trust your own instincts,* he argued incessantly. Rice himself embraced a Buddhism-tempered philosophy, which held that *the real god is within the self;* every individual controls his own destiny.

"I'm my own church," Rice was fond of saying. He espoused a strict moral code from which he seldom strayed. He openly shared his judgments with those around him and didn't mince words or try to shade the truth—Esteban and others knew they would always get the "full Tommy." In purely practical matters, Rice could be equally inflexible. For example, he insisted on driving only Volvo sedans because they were the safest cars around—a concern that must have amused some of his companions, given Rice's extreme risk taking in other respects.

Esteban and Rice shared a passion for pondering these and numerous other topics, generally under the influence of marijuana. Characteristically, Rice used only "natural" drugs such as pot or mushrooms. If it didn't come from the ground, he proclaimed, he couldn't be sure what was in it; even in a drunken state, he shunned LSD and other synthetic concoctions. "Sez Buds" (sensimilla) from Humboldt County frequently were their drug of choice. Also popular was the cheaper, generic, more readily available "skunk weed" from Mexico. Anything especially effective was respectfully dubbed Buddha Bud.

Rice had access to it all.

Their minds thus frequently in altered states, Esteban and Rice spent long hours together musing about the nature of humankind. Central to Rice's beliefs—his close friends referred to these as "Tommy's philosophies"—was the idea that fear prevented people from achieving their potential. In order to live life to the fullest and gain bountiful rewards, you had to overcome inhibitions and mental blocks. Only by taking risks and regarding all obstacles as tests of character could you conquer personal fear. Rice summarily rejected negativity, excuses, and rationalizations. If a companion struggled, if he faltered and grew discouraged, Rice tried to buoy him by saying, "Conquer it—it's all in your mind." *Face your fears* was his constant litany. *Only by so doing can you achieve your full potential.* In his view, because fear was created by the mind, it could also be discarded by the mind. That was life's challenge.

A tall order for most—but one that carried tremendous appeal for Esteban. Such discipline and self-reliance seemed to address a void he had long sensed in his own world. From his older friend, Esteban received the sort of guidance he had never gotten—or been able to swallow—from his father or coaches. Rice saw life as akin to a military mission, too—an element extremely potent for Esteban.

The men engaged in long discussions, usually with Esteban sharing his innermost thoughts and feelings, while Rice listened and offered advice. And Rice proved able to get beyond his dogma while offering his friend comforting personal advice.

Esteban: "When I had questions about life, Tom was someone whom I could talk with on a deep level, about women and relationships, about problems that I had at home like the bad communication between me and my parents and my father's gambling addiction, things that I was learning in Scientology that were giving me some interesting and different perspectives on life. I also sensed that he was able to relax his guard around me when it was just the two of us. He had this image of always being tough and unafraid, and able to handle any situation. To people who knew him just casually he could come off as arrogant and standoffish. But when we were by ourselves Tom could be very kind and sensitive. He told me that of all his friends he trusted me the most and that I was the most honest. With Tom it was all about truth. He did not like people who were 'plastic,' people who were fakes and not true to themselves. He did not like liars and people who did not respect themselves or others. He always told me to be true to my heart, to be honest to myself and my true feelings, no matter if everyone else wanted something else. This is the greatest attribute that I admired about Tom—the ability to always be true and honest to oneself no matter what other people thought."

◄○►

ENHANCING RICE'S AUTHORITY was his aura of mystery. Few won entry into that private, inner world—not even Esteban, who by this time was probably his closest friend. To all, Rice remained an enigma, and that was the way he wanted it. He didn't discuss his innermost feelings, his personal struggles, his many relationships with women. He spoke about human issues mostly in the abstract. To those who knew him best, he seemed unattached on a deep emotional level—a closed person. The more you hung out with Rice, some claimed, the less you knew about him.

Yet it could be argued that Tom Rice craved attention and feedback. Although he seemed to respond little, if at all, to external influences, his attire—outrageous tie-dyed garments favored by acidheads; T-shirts with logos of obscure rock bands—and his extroverted persona seemed to cry out for attention. More than one of his peers suspected that beneath Rice's veneer of flamboyant confidence was insecurity.

Whatever the case, Rice above all sought to control—*expected* to control—his and friends' agendas and whatever physical challenges he took on. Rice believed that he alone was always in charge.

Increasingly, he and Esteban took their personal quests to natural settings, especially those offering unique vistas. At night, they often climbed a towering tree and sat on a high limb, fueling their talk with beer or tequila. One time Rice chose a tree in the middle of a cemetery at midnight to put them in the presence of spirits; relating to the dead, he figured, was an excellent way to confront fear. Another night found them high up in a century-old oak, the tallest in San Jose. Esteban had played in it while growing up and carried a scar on his chest from where one of its branches had broken his fall and saved his life after he lost his grip higher up. The interior of this grandfatherly oak was hollow, burned out from a lightning strike. At the time, they gave its charred black surfaces no particular thought.

Years later, they would have abundant cause to.

Another favorite place was "Acid Rock" in the foothills above the Bay Area, a huge formation rounded on one side and with a steep vertical cliff on the other. A "mini Half Dome," Esteban called it. The top provides a panoramic view of South San Francisco, the South Bay, and even much of the East Bay and Oakland. The two often went up there at night to enjoy the necklace of shimmering lights surrounding the dark bay waters, all of it encapsulated by star-filled heavens. Sometimes they stayed until sunrise.

For larger social gatherings, usually on the beach in Santa Cruz and often involving women, Rice prepared his "famous guava juice," a potent blend of fresh cantaloupe, honeydew, watermelon, oranges, lemons, limes, seedless green grapes, mangoes, pineapples, nectarines, peaches, and a "sacred" guava, all submerged in massive amounts of Hansen's Natural Soda in a huge ice chest and laced with at least two bottles of Bacardi rum 151 proof. After a caveat from Rice that the "inspired chef" was not responsible for any actions that might result after downing two glasses of this concoction, the juice was duly imbibed and the "enriched fruit" eaten. The recipe's natural sugars tended to keep everybody up all night; happily, few got sick. It was, in Rice's lexicon, "the original nectar of the gods."

Rice often provided an enormous chuck steak as well. To properly prepare the meat, he first elevated it above his head and then walked into the ocean until both he and the steak were submerged. This "sacrifice to the gods," he claimed, also seasoned the meat with spices from the sea.

The ocean figured in another of Rice's rituals. With Esteban, he would swim out to the quarter-mile buoy in apparent disregard of the frigid water and its powerful riptides and undertows—not to mention the possible presence of sharks—while each swimmer held a joint above his head. At the buoy they smoked the joints, then swam back stoned—a good test of their basic manhood and survival abilities, Rice believed.

Their thrill seeking sometimes bordered on insanity. Once, en route to Santa Cruz on Highway 17—aka Blood Alley—Esteban sped his motorcycle perilously close to Rice's car so they could pass a joint back and forth. The road is a winding, treacherous, two-lane speedway (center dividers would be installed years later) where few weekends passed without a major accident. On another occasion, Rice misjudged and strained his back diving off a cliff. On yet another, he damaged his teeth when his truck slammed into a telephone pole. Esteban suffered mishaps of his own but accepted them as the price for being an outdoor soldier: Minor wounds were inevitable and should be disregarded or serve as proud emblems of missions during which fear had been conquered.

Esteban came to believe that, together, he and Rice were invincible.

Eventually, Rice focused on the grandest of all locations—Yosemite and its crown jewel, Half Dome. He himself already had hiked to its summit several times. Now Rice, twenty-four, judged Esteban, twenty-two, ready for the granite monolith.

◄○►

WHEN THEY ARRIVED IN Yosemite Valley on that Saturday afternoon of Memorial Day weekend in 1981 and saw Half Dome, its striking image reflected in the Merced River, the moment was a defining one for Esteban. Still exhilarated from the leap into Paradise and the discovery of the antlers, he now felt an irresistible new power tugging at him.

The two had decided to backpack four miles into Little Yosemite Valley and spend the night above Nevada Fall, braving the company of insatiable mosquitoes and pesky bears. The next day they would hike the remaining four miles to the top of Half Dome. Leaving the Valley floor, Rice set off at a fast pace. He and Esteban took pride in their fitness, the drinking and drugging notwithstanding. They swam vigorously, hiked long distances, scaled heights. Esteban lifted weights. On all such adventures, each tried to outdo the other, and neither would admit weakness or back away from a challenge. Once, on a backpacking trip in the rugged Big Sur coastal region, Esteban had fallen way behind. Rice told him his fatigue was mental, something he could overcome if he wanted to. He branded Esteban a puss, gutless, a laggard, all of which inflamed Esteban, who then somehow pushed his spent legs in an effort to exceed Rice's pace.

And so it went between them.

On this day in Yosemite, the two sped up the easiest part of the Mist Trail to the bridge, where they savored Vernal Fall in its full spring glory. Then it was up the constricted canyon, where they attacked the high granite risers, sucking in ever-larger quantities of ever-thinner air as they ascended. A two-thousand-foot elevation gain in that narrow ravine was a push even for someone without a backpack. For Rice and Esteban, the physical demands and muscle burn added zest to the experience.

Above Vernal Fall, Rice tried to climb faster yet. More steps had to be navigated, but most of them were low and graduated. For Esteban, the tramp up what they called staircase canyon was more than just a test of stamina and strength. He felt his spirit absorbing powerful energy from some distant source.

Atop Nevada Fall, their hearts pounding, they stretched their legs out for long minutes to ward off cramping. Their quadriceps ached and their inner thighs were as taut as bass fiddle strings.

But pain was transmuted by a heady sense of conquest. "Doing the staircase" would thereafter become one of their mandatory rituals.

At midmorning on Sunday, they struck out for the Dome.

As he marched upward for what seemed like unending miles, it became evident to Esteban he was not prepared for the hike's relentless demands. Without a sports regimen to keep himself in top shape, he had allowed his body to deteriorate. The constant partying, done to mask his many failings, was now taking its toll. To escape the pain his body was experiencing, he turned inward, contemplating things going on in his life.

By this time he deeply regretted his lapses in high school, mainly his not fulfilling his potential in sports. He knew he should have repeated his all-league performance in football his senior year, and that he could have played baseball at the college level, perhaps even professionally. His self-destructive ways ultimately had robbed him of success in the most important area of his life, and nothing else offered that sense of personal worth and accomplishment. A huge vacuum now existed, which he filled by hanging out with a bunch of alcoholics and drug addicts, and even a criminal element.

He realized that he had accomplished nothing of real worth or importance in his life. And he had no clue on what he would do next.

But this trek to Half Dome felt right.

Rice paused halfway up at a stream bubbling out of the hillside, a tiny flow in a gully off the trail. The water was refreshing and cold, tasting like the granite rock of Yosemite. As the only source of fresh water along the trail, the partly concealed outflow attracted many hikers. But for Esteban and Rice it was their secret good-luck spring of artesian water, an obligatory pause to quench thirst and replenish spirit. On the descent, Rice would refill his canteen and carry the precious contents home, a gift of nectar from the gods to cleanse and sustain his body between quests.

The trail took them to Half Dome's shoulder (then informally called quarter dome, and now known as Sub Dome). The steepness of the abrupt hump surprises most first-timers. Traversing it required climbing the nearly six hundred steps put in place by Yosemite trail crews over the years.

Beside the stairway at the base of Sub Dome was a metal sign in both English and Spanish in bold red letters:

DANGER
IF A THUNDERSTORM IS ANYWHERE ON THE HORIZON
DO NOT PASS BEYOND THIS SIGN.
LIGHTNING HAS STRUCK HALF DOME DURING EVERY
MONTH OF THE YEAR.

PELIGRO
SI ESTA EMINENTE UNA TORMENTA
NO PASE ESTE PUNTO.
EL RELAMPAGO CAE SOBRE HALF DOME
CADA MES DEL ANO.

Esteban and Rice, preoccupied with their push to the top, proceeded up the stairs with nary a glance at the sign. In any case, the sky was clear. By this point Esteban's physical condition was nearing its limits. With his stamina exhausted and legs that both ached and felt like butter, it was as though he were pushing against an immovable wall. He didn't think he could continue up this steep grade, never mind the final push to the top of Half Dome. After taking a few steps he stopped and leaned on his legs, his hands pressing against his knees to support his upper body, all the while gasping for breath.

Rice looked at him and told him that he didn't have what it took to do the Dome with him; he was weak.

Once again, Esteban had to dig deeply to meet Rice's challenge. He forced his legs to move, one step at a time, fighting back the muscle burn, and made it to the top of Sub Dome where Rice waited.

There the two looked across a low saddle at cables running high up the granite slope of Half Dome. The daunting sight usually triggers an adrenaline rush in newcomers. Esteban was no exception. It was the last hurdle, now only six hundred feet away, and when he surmounted it he would stand at the apex of that wondrous pinnacle that had stared down on him just the prior day. At that moment, Esteban felt powerful vibrations emanating from Half Dome and resonating deep inside. He knew that this mountain would change his life. What he couldn't know was the extent to which this granite temple would affect not only his life, but also that of the companion who'd brought him here this day, and those of others who'd follow in their footsteps.

◄○►

AFTER CROSSING THE SADDLE and now at the base of Half Dome's final steep slope, Esteban and Rice stared at the parallel steel cables leading skyward. Most mountain trails—Mount Whitney's, for example—have switchbacks to maintain a fifteen-degree gradient. The typical home staircase rises at an angle not exceeding forty degrees. But Half Dome's incline from that point is around forty-five degrees for the most part, and up to sixty degrees along certain portions. More intimidating are the steep, rounded slopes off to the sides of the cables; without something to hold on to, a hiker would likely slide to oblivion. So the cables provide essential grip. Gloves help, both to protect climbers' hands and to enhance their grasp.

But even with the cables and gloves, the prospect of pressing on is simply too fearsome for some; they go no farther. Some who do proceed suffer leg cramps or muscle strains from the high leg lifts that are necessary; they quit, too. Still others lack the upper-body strength to pull themselves up the cables, which, strung on metal poles, are above the heads of many hikers bent forward to counteract the incline. Despite the rigors, most who get as far as the cables manage to complete the ascent by pushing their bodies in a last supreme effort. Waif-like women shorter than five feet complete the climb, as do hikers in their sixties, in a few hardy cases seventies, and even on occasion eighties.

The usual climbing mode is an accelerated driving of the legs coordinated with determined pulling on the cables, a rest at one of the horizontal two-by-four boards affixed at ground level to the vertical iron poles at ten-foot intervals, and another spurt up the grade to the next board, followed by another rest. Sometimes, if there's a traffic jam, faster climbers go outside the cables, gripping just one of them. Even when the way is clear, only the strongest and fittest attempt nonstop ascents.

Arriving at the top of Half Dome is a memorable achievement, and those who climb the rock are quick to congratulate themselves. But the looming journey back down casts a shadow over the minds of many, particularly those who have even the slightest fear of heights. The mountain climber's credo, *Going up is optional, coming down is not,* applies in this case, too. In practice, though, the descent doesn't live up to the dread of it. Again, the cables are key. Although some hikers go backward down the mountain so they don't have to look at the frightful depths just beyond the granite curvature, many others, emboldened by their success up until then, slide down rapidly, allowing the cables to whiz through their gloved hands.

With the successful descent comes relief and a strong feeling of fulfillment, but there's still that eight-plus-mile trek back to the Valley floor. By this time, the legs of all but the best conditioned of hikers are wobbly. The trail's unrelenting downward course stresses your knees, and if your footwear lacks room to absorb the pounding, you may end your outing with painful and blackened toenails.

Esteban and Rice attacked the granite incline with resurgent energy. As if the duo were racing—which, in a sense, was true— they bulled their way up along the cables without halting. Esteban found strength that he didn't know he had. Whatever fatigue he had previously felt was now overcome by his resurgent motivation to get to the top.

In a final burst, Esteban pulled at the last of the cables and eclipsed the final rock barrier before arriving at the summit where Rice waited. There a sign—tucked among the rocks and easy to miss—read:

DANGER

IF A THUNDERSTORM OCCURS WHILE YOU ARE HERE,
THESE ARE THE SAFEST THINGS TO DO:

1. STAY AWAY FROM THE CABLES.
2. GET RID OF ANY METALLIC OBJECTS.
3. STAY AWAY FROM CAVES, OVERHANGS, AND
   LARGE CRACKS IN THE ROCKS.
4. GO TO THE LOWEST PLACE ON TOP AND SIT
   ON ANY NONMETALLIC OBJECTS YOU HAVE TO
   INSULATE YOU FROM THE ROCK.

WAIT. STAY THERE UNTIL THE STORM HAS PASSED.

The two men barely glanced at the sign, as though such warnings didn't apply to them.

Once on the summit, the broad expanse of the mostly flat surface surprised Esteban, as it does most. From down in the Valley, he hadn't grasped how large an area would greet him here. As expected, the summit was barren other than for a single gnarled, weather-beaten pine tree clinging to the rock and half a dozen or so low rock enclosures that previous climbers had constructed as shelters from the wind. Over toward the edge overlooking the Valley, the surface was covered by stone slabs resembling giant pancakes. The section known as the Visor jutted out about twenty feet from the edge.

What consumed Esteban, however, was not what he found on the summit. It was the 360-degree vista that greeted his eyes.

To the west towered El Capitan, the earth's largest granite mass, its three-thousand-foot face double the height of Gibraltar. Across the Valley—native Ahwahneechees called it "the place of the gaping mouth"—Yosemite Falls stumbled down the canyon wall in two majestic spills. The Upper Fall registered 1,430 feet, the Lower Fall 320, the intermediate cascade 675—a total of 2,425 feet, which makes it the highest waterfall in the United States and the eighth highest worldwide. Just then, the tumultuous torrent was swollen to its greatest volume from spring runoff.

Across the narrow Valley, lower than Half Dome, rose the polished granite of North Dome. To the east lay vast Tenaya Canyon, where glaciers in past eons emerged and sculpted Yosemite Valley. Jutting above the canyon, two miles long and one mile tall, rose the mammoth exposure of granite bluffs known as Clouds Rest. Nearby, to the south, stood Mount Starr King, among the park's tallest domes. Finally, nearly a mile directly below Rice and Esteban, lay the floor of Yosemite Valley, where lush meadows, dark groves, and the sun-sparkled river, with massive canyon walls as a frame, teased the senses like a real-life masterpiece.

Now Esteban realized beyond any doubt why Rice had wanted to bring him here. *We are on top of the world here*, he thought. *The gods are talking to us.*

Rice wasn't finished with his exhibitions for the day. As Esteban stared in fascination at the Valley floor far below, Rice approached a stone slab known as the diving board* that extended some five feet out from the Dome's sheer face. Not only does the projection bank ten degrees, but its width narrows from four feet at the cliff face to a scant fifteen inches at the tip.

Beneath this lies twenty-two hundred feet of empty space.

---

*Not to be confused with the formally designated Diving Board, a Yosemite rock formation shown on maps. The latter is a craggy rock tower extending from the west shoulder of Half Dome midway between the Valley floor and the summit. Here, two thousand feet up the steep granite, a twenty-five-year-old by the name of Ansel Adams unloaded forty pounds of photography gear in 1927 to get a shot of Half Dome's face. The striking result, *Monolith: The Face of Half Dome*, changed Adams's understanding of his medium and launched his career as one of America's most innovative photographers. Things might have gone differently had he not, with only one plate remaining, used a deep red filter to darken the sky and shadows dramatically. The result gave him what he wanted—"not the way the subject appeared in reality but how it *felt* to me." Thereafter, photography became for him a supremely creative process that transcended mere recording.

Esteban watched in horror as Rice, barefoot now, stepped onto the small slab. He inched his way backward to the tip, paused to intensify his focus, then slid his heels carefully over the edge until only the front half of his feet remained on the rock, his body leaning forward and arms extended before him. He held this position, his balance perfect, as if he were preparing to dive backward into the depths behind. Then, still balanced and with breathtaking composure, he slowly lifted a foot and stood on one leg.

After several seconds, Rice lowered his foot and walked calmly back. Esteban, transfixed, felt limp and nearly sick with relief when Rice ended his stunt. Rice's theatrics also had mesmerized others on the Dome that day, many of whom at first gaped at Rice's outrageous act and then shut their eyes in dread. His performance on that gargantuan stage suggested that, given a ready audience, there was no risk he was unwilling to take.

About then, a premonition began haunting Esteban.

He feared that someone he knew would fall from Half Dome.

2

THE DOME

Was there ever so venerable, majestic, and eloquent a minister of natural religion as the grand old Half Dome?—Joseph LeConte, *A Journal of Ramblings Through the High Sierras of California*, 1875

E STEBAN AND RICE RETURNED to Yosemite later that summer, and again over Labor Day. Their agenda was literally carved in stone: Hike to the top of Half Dome.

For both men, treks to the Dome were far from routine events. It was as if some mystic force kept luring them back time and time again. Each year, they returned faithfully on the Memorial Day and Labor Day weekends—and whenever the urge struck. Sometimes Rice phoned Esteban out of the blue and said, "Let's go do the Dome." Esteban would drop everything, no questions asked, to join his buddy for yet another odyssey to that granite monolith.

Yosemite's natural wonders and the invigoration that came from immersing themselves in the wild made these outings a rebirth of sorts for Esteban and Rice. They always returned from Half Dome with their "karma batteries" recharged, their spirits rejuvenated, their ties with each other and the natural world more securely fastened.

However, a complication arose in Esteban's budding love affair with the granite mistress: marriage. In the spring of 1981 at age twenty-one, he had met a nineteen-year-old waitress and immediately fallen in love. Within a month, they had eloped to Reno. Unfortunately, she lacked any interest in the outdoors, preferring to stay at home. She also wanted to start a family. Neither of these priorities squared with those of Esteban, who wanted to do what he pleased, mainly with Rice.

As the months passed, it seemed to her that Esteban valued Rice and their forays together more than he valued her and their marriage. She was right. Esteban ultimately concluded that marriage had been a mistake—he just wasn't ready to commit. After a mere eighteen months together, he and his wife separated and, a year later, divorced.

◄o►

A FAILED MARRIAGE was only one of Esteban's woes. He had been attending San Jose Community College on and off since graduation from high school in 1977, taking a class or two each semester with the goal of earning an AA degree. After he and his wife split, Esteban dropped out of college in order to "get my stuff together mentally." He also considered quitting his job as a laser tech—mainly because he felt he didn't measure up—and launching a new career. The marriage fiasco made him wary about diving into another intimate relationship.

The one solid entity in his drifting life was Half Dome.

Each time Esteban arrived in Yosemite and peered up, his life took on meaning and direction. Half Dome rendered no judgments about who was worthy to scale its flanks. It asked nothing of anyone but gave everything—the universe on a platter. Deep down, Esteban knew this was something he could fully commit to. He also knew the Dome would always be there, beckoning. There were few guarantees in his erratic, stale world, but Half Dome was one of them.

On the trail in Yosemite, Esteban absorbed the air's crispness, which cleared his mind. The everyday demands and entanglements weighing down his life seemed less burdensome. He lost himself in the natural surroundings as physical pain from the unrelenting push upward stirred an inner dialogue. Initially, the mundane problems—work, college tests, and the like—roiled his brain. But with each passing mile, they melted away. His thoughts became more dream-like, and fantasies bubbled up. He imagined himself a bear, an eagle, a deer. What, he wondered, do these creatures sense? Or he imagined himself a Navy SEAL assaulting a great fortress. It was all part of the mental cleansing, the flushing out of trivial stuff, that freed his mind to ponder bigger issues: What's life? What does it all mean? How do I fit in?

Marveling at the beauty and power of waterfalls he passed, Esteban pictured himself crawling to the edge of one of these tumbling chutes and peering over the edge. One small slip and he'd be fatally swept down. Such intense, frightful images of death had a hypnotic effect on him.

He felt a bond with strangers on the trail, most of whom radiated a spirit of engagement and humanity. When he looked into their eyes, a mutual understanding flowered. Out here, masks weren't necessary; rank vanished. Everyone was on equal footing as they pressed toward the summit.

Esteban's confidence grew with each journey to and from Half Dome. He saw these outings as a blueprint for life: Identify a goal, lay plans to achieve it, then execute the plan. The treks required both physical and mental preparedness. That meant no late partying the night before; rising at dawn; apportioning his time, food, and water on the trail; avoiding cramped or pulled muscles by taking breaks in proper sequence and of appropriate length; and overcoming bodily pain. The payoff: million-dollar views at the top, the camaraderie of fellow hikers and rapt discussion of life's many unanswered questions, a storehouse of adventures to share with others, and that sweet sense of success.

Accomplishing this agenda energized Esteban. It made him feel good about the world and was a powerful antidote for his low self-esteem. It also helped him conquer the demons within, to get past his travails.

On return hikes to Yosemite Valley and gazing back up from the Valley floor at that majestic rock face as it held the day's last rays of sun, Esteban felt that he belonged here. He was both exhilarated and let down about leaving. But the brief respite from nagging reality stoked his enthusiasm. He was recharged and ready for life back home again. The image of Half Dome remained fixed in his mind long afterward. When difficulties arose, he could simply recall the Dome and find peace.

Esteban knew Rice harbored similar feelings. If anything, Rice revered the Dome more than anyone, though, unlike Esteban, he chose not to verbalize his sentiments. Rice let his actions do the talking.

Over the years, traveling to Yosemite evolved into pilgrimages for these best of friends. The Dome became their mecca, a sacred place. They called it "our mountain."

◄○►

ESTEBAN AND RICE COMPETED fiercely to see who could go the farthest and fastest. But they took even more pride in their accomplishments together. Leaping off the ledge at Paradise, scaling the staircase up Nevada Fall, driving their legs up Sub Dome and the cables . . . each of these achievements testified to their personal well-being but also cemented the bond between them. Rivalry melded into deep loyalty and trust once they arrived on Half Dome's summit.

Up there, camaraderie is magnified and spreads widely. For many climbers and hikers, something intangible happens on a mountaintop—what John Muir described as the "mysterious enjoyment felt there, the strange calm, the divine frenzy." Human frailties—prejudice, envy, selfishness, egotism—tend to dissipate in the thinner air, and all human emotions boil down to the joy of the moment. Many people feel infused by a spirit of kinship and kindness. They are more apt to touch someone else, provide assistance, share. Much of this fellowship flows from the energy everyone had mustered to reach the summit. In collective consciousness, they savor this special place.

That feeling of connectedness may also stretch into Yosemite's past. You can almost sense the many American giants—Chief Teneiya, John Muir, Joseph LeConte, Teddy Roosevelt, and Ansel Adams, among others—as well as countless foreign dignitaries and notables from all walks of life and nations who have visited its hallowed grounds. Place-names, plaques, photos, exhibits, and the captivating scenery call attention to individuals who helped preserve Yosemite and contributed to what it is today. Esteban often remarked that he felt the presence of the original Native dwellers. He envisioned them making one last stand in Yosemite Valley, where their souls elected to stay. That, in his view, explained the sacredness permeating the site.

At least initially, Rice was much more attuned than Esteban to the outdoors. He knew about poisonous snakes, bears, and poison oak, and how to filter water, tie knots, and navigate by the stars. He was familiar with campground etiquette, fishing techniques, survival strategies, and a host of other things related to the natural world. He taught Esteban many outdoor crafts and skills. And he respected the environment. His family had taken him camping and read books about John Muir, Ansel Adams, and other conservationists. As an adult, Rice practiced good environmental ethics in the wild, picking up trash left by others, leaving each campsite cleaner than he'd found it, and urging his companions to do the same. He railed against stinky horsepack trains in the high country and ugly pizza stands, hamburger joints, and housing units on the Valley floor, "one of the most beautiful places on earth."

John Muir's penchant for taking risks in the wilderness and his seeming invincibility probably resonated with Rice. Indeed, Muir had an insatiable lust for learning and a relentless desire to probe the inner depths of the natural world—in effect, to be part of it. In his quests, he had numerous brushes with death. To sense the immense power of whitewater rushing over Yosemite Falls, Muir crawled perilously close to its brink. He ventured behind a small waterfall between Upper and Lower Yosemite Fall at night to "see the glory of moonlight through the meshes of the denser portions of the fall"— and almost got trapped there. He clambered up a four-hundred-foot ice cone at the base of the falls, formed by plunging water, so he could look down inside. He was caught in a snow avalanche while trying to study it. Muir also provoked a bear into chasing him so he could see how it ran; took refuge in a hollow tree trunk to observe a forest fire; rushed outside when a "noble earthquake" shook Yosemite, hoping to learn something; climbed a hundred-foot ponderosa pine during a fierce thunderstorm and clung "like a bobolink on a reed" to the slender top, which swung wildly in the wind; was stranded for more than thirteen hours on the summit of Northern California's Mount Shasta in a driving hailstorm, where temperatures plunged below zero; and, while exploring a bay in Alaska, fell into a glacial crevasse that immersed him in icy water.*

Muir pursued most of his adventures alone.

----

*The Muir Glacier in Glacier Bay honors him as its discoverer.

-◄○►-

PART OF THE TOTAL EXPERIENCE for Esteban was reciting the wonders of the Dome and recounting his adventures to workmates and buddies. These included Bill Pippey, who was always up for a challenge. To his friends, "Bip," who had brown hair and hazel eyes that were more blue than green, seemed bigger than his five feet, ten inches, and 155 pounds, probably because of his outgoing personality and high excitability. He often spoke loudly to compensate for deafness in one ear; that and his high, raspy voice got others' attention. Everyone liked Bip.

Born in 1958 and a single child, Pippey was only six years old when his mother died. From then on, his father neglected him, often disappearing for days. Pippey had spent weekends with his grandparents from the time he was nine until his grandmother died when he was twelve. His grandfather then moved into Pippey's house and looked after him. He died two years later—so the young teenager had to learn to fend for himself. He reached out to others in his East Bay neighborhood, particularly the nearby Jordan family. The Jordans, who had three daughters and two small twin sons, watched over Pippey, took him on family vacations, and treated him as one of their own. Still, the young teen lived mainly alone. His father came and went at whim.

About this time, while Pippey and his best friend were walking together on the way to a bowling alley, his companion was hit and killed by a car when he tried to cross the street. This tragedy—the death of another loved one, this time witnessed firsthand—almost destroyed him.

Pippey worked odd jobs to support himself and to partly cover his share of house payments, as his father demanded. In high school, he succumbed to drugs—mainly pot—and often was truant. An insensitive school dean told him in his sophomore year that before he could return to school, a parent conference would be necessary. Pippey's problems worsened. In the eleventh grade, the dean expelled him and sent him to a continuation program for problem students. There he enrolled in a technical course and found he had good skills. He earned straight A's. But the program didn't prevent him from dropping out of high school for good by the end of his junior year. To Pippey, it seemed the entire world was aligned against him. He didn't have any close friends, was extremely shy, never went on a date, and had little hope of success.

In 1976, Pippey read *The Power of Positive Thinking* by Norman Vincent Peale. It changed his life. "For the first time," he recalled, "I felt as though I could succeed." He worked diligently, paid his bills, saved money, and got a girlfriend. In 1976, he began working as an assembler at Quantra-Ray, a laser manufacturer across San Francisco Bay in Mountain View.

But two days before Pippey's twenty-second birthday, his father split for good, taking money he had been hoarding from his son's contributions, including three months of back rent and cash for other bills. That same day his girlfriend also broke up with him. Pippey hit another low. He began drinking and abusing drugs even more heavily than before, abetted by co-workers and others. It wasn't unusual for him to consume four shots of liquor at lunchtime and half a pint of bourbon in the evening—just enough, he said, "to still be able to function at work the next day." Plus he regularly used pot, methamphetamine, acid, and coke. By this time, he had moved into an apartment with a Quantra-Ray co-worker in Sunnyvale, near Mountain View.

Pippey took his first backpacking trip in the summer of 1982 and discovered the power of the mountains. He began backpacking frequently. It was an activity he quickly came to value and respect, and one that provided an energy outlet. Time in the outdoors reduced the stress in his personal life and the workplace. It helped heal wounds. To get in top shape for these outings, he initiated a physical conditioning regimen, which included jogging ten to twenty miles on most days.

Pippey's life had turned the corner.

—◄○►—

AFTER HIS FIRST TRIPS WITH RICE, Esteban recruited Pippey for a trip to Half Dome the following summer. In addition to Rice, Esteban's three younger brothers, Alan, Andrew, and Alex, and two of his young cousins, Sean and Eric, joined them. Esteban wanted as many of his family and closest friends as possible to "gain the magic of a Dome expedition." To him, it was a rite of manhood and an initiation into the "Dome brotherhood."

When the party of eight arrived at a small camping area called Red Bud on Highway 140 near the town of El Portal just outside of Yosemite, at midnight on a Friday in midsummer, they consumed two six-packs of beer while relaxing after the long, tiring drive. Then, instead of bedding down in the campground, they loaded their gear and took off in pitch darkness for Paradise. Esteban and Rice, always quick to fantasize, likened this nighttime foray to a "midnight assault in 'Nam requiring total silence."

With only one flashlight among them, no one could see more than two feet ahead on the narrow, hillside pathway. At one point, Esteban lost his footing and went rolling down the slope, crashing through brush and almost landing in a stream. Although uninjured, he lay there motionless in the dark to see how his companions would react. Pippey started shouting in panic, until Rice punched him to hold him to the code of silence of their military fantasy. Satisfied with his charade, Esteban eventually made his way back up to the trail, and the group marched on.

At Paradise, Sean, a scrawny young teenager who carried a sleeping bag under each arm, slipped on the polished rock and fell into the water. He reemerged without the bags, which rested at the pool's bottom. Although they retrieved them, the bags were soaked. Esteban's two cousins had to pass the night without them.

The next morning, they all watched as Rice climbed up to the ledge resting forty-four feet above the pool.

Esteban: "To see Tom on a rock, perched high like an eagle, waiting for the exact right moment to dive into the wind and execute perfection . . . that's what Tom was all about. He would wait until all eyes were keyed on him, for this was what his ego demanded. Then he would delay, as though he were part of the stone itself, seeking the perfect vibration that resonated from his inner universe. Only then would he launch into his beautiful, flawless dive."

Rice spun his tightly compacted body two and a half times on the descent, straightening out just in time for his hands and head to break the water.

It was Esteban's turn. He knew what he had to do. He climbed to the ledge and leaped off without hesitation. By this time, however, he had adopted a new approach when jumping: He kept his arms close to his sides to protect them from slapping the water, all the while cupping his groin area to thereby "protect the family jewels," as he put it. No one else wanted any part of this exercise. However, Rice expected Pippey to jump. None of them knew that Pippey was terrified of heights.

Pippey realized he couldn't refuse Rice. He climbed up to the ledge but, paralyzed by acrophobia, couldn't even go near the edge. For more than fifteen minutes, he dawdled up there, frozen with fear, while everyone waited. Pippey finally clambered down to a lower, twelve-foot ledge and jumped.

Returning to the high perch, he told himself, Whatever it takes to throw myself off this ledge, I'm going to do it. Rice gave him a thumbs-up, Pippey sucked in a full chest of air, launched himself, and hurtled down into the pool.

Pippey was ecstatic—he nearly came out of his skin with glee. It was a great personal victory.

Rice was impressed. Pippey had gazed into those frightful depths and conquered his terror. He had passed Rice's test. From that time on, Rice referred to Pippey as one of the bravest people he knew.

After the sleeping bags had dried in the sun, the eight packed up, returned to their vehicle, and left for Yosemite.

On the Mist Trail, Rice set his usual fierce pace up the granite stairs. Pippey was close behind and Esteban held his own, while the others lagged. The men were sweating profusely by the time they reached the top of Nevada Fall, where they performed another ritual that marked their Half Dome excursions: plunging into the Merced River to cool off. In mid-July, the river's flow was not strong, but it was a very cold fifty-six degrees.

◄◦►

THE MERCED RIVER BEGINS on the glacial slopes of Mount Lyell, Yosemite's highest peak at 13,114 feet. After crashing down Nevada and Vernal falls, the river meanders through Yosemite Valley where the current remains strong, especially in spring and early summer. That and its frigid water have accounted for several drownings over the years. With additional volume from Yosemite and Bridalveil falls and a host of smaller cascades, the Merced surges again by the time it leaves Yosemite, tumbling down steep chutes and cascading for several miles over and around boulders the size of cars and houses. Then it drops more modestly—a long run of swift current, intermittent rapids, and deep pools that attract kayakers, whitewater rafters, swimmers, and anglers. From Happy Isles in upper Yosemite Valley to the Lake McClure Reservoir, the Merced flows 135 unobstructed miles.*

Swimming in the Merced's chill water and treacherous current can be exceedingly dangerous at any time. The risk is many times greater above a waterfall. From 1975 through 2000, there were 37 drownings in Yosemite, which made up 22 percent of the park's 166 accidental deaths during that period. Twenty-nine of the thirty-seven occurred in and around waterfalls. Five happened in the Merced River directly above Nevada Fall, and four of those individuals were carried over the falls. Ten drownings took place

---

*The natural beauty and assets of the Merced River were given added protection when its upper seventy-one miles from Yosemite to the town of Briceburg, and the forty-three-mile-long South Fork of the Merced, were designated National Wild and Scenic Rivers in 1987. The lower part of the main stem was given this federal designation in 1992, thus preserving the free-flowing state of this spectacular waterway.

near Vernal Fall—three of those victims went over. Another three people lost their lives at Yosemite Falls, while one got swept over Bridalveil Fall and another over Ribbon Fall. Hidden Fall was the scene of four deaths.

Several common denominators characterized the drownings in and around Yosemite's rivers and waterfalls. People who misjudged the current may have been swept off their feet or unable to swim out of it. Some may have lost their footing in the water or slipped on a rock and fallen in, only to be carried downstream. In other cases, the force of the current pinned them under a downed tree, rock, or other obstruction in the river. Hypothermia as a result of the Merced's frigid temperature can quickly sap a person's strength and make it almost impossible to escape the current. (Hypothermia is a drop in body temperature caused by exposure to cold conditions. Depending on the circumstances, it can set in slowly or rapidly. You lose your ability to function and, without countermeasures, can die from hypothermia itself or from the loss of bodily function that leads to drowning, a fall, or other fatal mishap.)*

◄O►

RICE AND PIPPEY STRIPPED off their clothes and dove into the icy water fifty yards upriver from Nevada Fall. Esteban and three others joined them but kept their shorts on. Given the gentle, midsummer flow, this exercise wasn't too risky. They all swam the few feet out to a large, flat boulder and sunbathed. Despite other hikers and campers nearby, Rice and Pippey weren't the least self-conscious

---

*A classic example of misjudging river hazards is the twenty-nine-year-old man who parachuted illegally from El Capitan on June 9, 1999. He was BASE jumping, one of the most dangerous of all sports, which entails parachuting from Buildings, Antennas, Spans, and Earth. It has been illegal in Yosemite since 1980, mainly because jumpers violated the rules when it was legal. In this case, the jumper had planned his escape in advance. He landed safely, quickly removed his gear, and, before the authorities could snare him, dove into the Merced River in the hope of reaching a getaway vehicle on the other side. But the man disappeared, surely overcome by hypothermia and the current's strength and turbulence. His body was found nearly a month later three or four hundred yards downstream, pinned horizontally in the upstream undercut of a large boulder and out of view.

about being naked. Rice seldom hesitated to flaunt his body; for him, it was all part of overcoming inhibitions and gaining freedom. On Half Dome's summit, he regularly strolled about and sunbathed in the nude.

Returning to the riverbank, thoroughly cooled and refreshed, the men got dressed and ate lunch.

They left for Half Dome after eating. At the bottom of the cables, Pippey totally freaked when he saw the steep grade and cable handholds, which looked perilous. He kept his fear to himself, though, hoping he could make it up by focusing on the stone at his feet. He waited until the others were ahead before starting. One hundred feet up, he glanced to his right and saw nothing but emptiness. Panic seized him. His body trembling, his face ashen, he retreated inch by inch, unable to look left or right and gripping the cables with a steel hold. He collapsed at the base of the cables, still trembling as he embraced the ground.

Esteban and Rice retreated down the cables to check on Pippey. They encouraged and cajoled him, but Pippey, convinced he'd never reach the top, told them to go on ahead. After a few minutes, Rice lit a joint, inhaled deeply, and passed it to Pippey, who took a couple of hits and then several more. Soon stoned, eyes glazed, he bounced to his feet raring to go—anywhere. He tackled the cables again, with gusto, bellowing the *Batman* theme song all the way up the granite slope.

Pippey survived his first journey up the Dome and, his dues paid, was henceforward a Dome regular. Being with close and supportive comrades filled a longtime void in Pippey's life. He became Esteban's housemate. He also was swayed by Rice's leadership and charisma, and counted him among his best friends, though he tended to be more cautious than Rice about taking risks.

Pippey: "To me, taking risks is like confronting a fence. Some individuals stop when they see an obstacle and stay safely on their side. Others might go to the top of the fence, to at least see what's on the other side before deciding. And then some just jump over the fence without knowing what's on the other side. I saw myself as the second type, one who looks first and, if things appear too dangerous, stops. Rice was the latter type, one who is willing to plunge into something without sizing up the possible consequences if anything should go wrong."

◄O►

PIPPEY OFTEN DROVE his outlandish, souped-up truck on these trips, including that first one to Half Dome. After purchasing it in 1981, he invested more than seven thousand dollars and much of himself in creating what everyone called the "Bip Mobile," totally reconstructing the half-ton, extra-long-bed '72 Ford inside and out. Pippey disassembled the cab, then built a frame from half-inch steel tubing and covered it with sheet metal rippled with dents. He painted the metal blue, interweaving stripes of silver, gold, and copper. He fashioned a wedge-shaped and tilted front end with a big hood scoop, including fenders and radiator, that all opened as a unit, like a big-rig truck. He installed two square headlights and a square fog light below each to form a triangle. The cab interior had gold-colored, diamond-tucked crushed velvet on the headliner, side panels, sun visors, and seat, which also sported foot-long strips of brown- and gold-patterned crushed velvet. Brown shag carpeted the floor. A T-shaped console on the interior ceiling housed four lighted switches for dual gas tanks, dual fuel pumps, dual batteries, fog lights, and a stereo. There were eight speakers in the cab and two in the customized aluminum camper shell Pippey had installed. Inside the shell were side paneling, brown- and gold-patterned crushed-velvet strips where the sides and headliner intersected, gold crushed-velvet headliner with a 110-volt outlet in the center and two lights, and more brown shag, beneath which lay a four-inch-thick foam-rubber mattress pad. To rev up performance, Pippey overhauled the 302-horsepower, V-8 engine and converted the manifold to four barrels from two. He raised the compression ratio to 1.5:1, balanced and blue-printed the short block, and installed a new carburetor, recreational vehicle camshaft, headers, dual exhausts, power brakes, power steering, and automatic overdrive transmission.

When he finished, the truck weighed a hundred pounds less than the original and was more efficient, enabling him to cruise at a hundred miles an hour and get twenty-three miles to the gallon. Pippey often drove that fast late at night on Highway 395 in the eastern Sierra Nevada en route to Mount Whitney, another of his favorite haunts. The Bip Mobile could accommodate eight people—three in the cab and five in back. Including the many trips to Yosemite and Mount Whitney, it logged more than two hundred thousand miles. The truck's roar and dual exhausts caused heads to turn in Central Valley towns—and drew the attention of police, who sometimes pulled him over, mostly out of curiosity.

In the spring of 1984, Pippey proposed to Pam Skog, his girlfriend of three years. He and his buddies drove to Paradise for a bachelor party, for one last fling before that big leap to the altar. Pippey urged his best man, Tom Rolf, to jump from the high ledge. Just before Rolf hit the water, he assumed a sitting position—a common technique for creating a huge splash in a swimming pool, but not a smart maneuver while plunging thirty-six miles an hour into a creek pool. According to Pippey, Rolf "banged himself up pretty good" and, for weeks afterward, including at the wedding ceremony, suffered from a sore and bruised underside.

◄o►

RICE AND A HALF DOME expedition were inseparable in everyone's eyes. He was the organizer, the motivating force, the one who planned everything down to the last detail, including the timeline and all logistics. He even prepared the menu, which emphasized good nutrition: veggie sandwiches, gorp, PowerBars, fruit, and lots of water. Plus beer, especially a choice microbrew when the guys could afford it. Everyone else had only to show up and pay his share.

Sometimes, instead of stopping at Red Bud after their long drive from the Bay Area, the men ditched at Camp Curry in Yosemite, where they slept behind a big rock so park personnel wouldn't see them. Or they broke into an unoccupied tent-cabin, occasionally with help from an employee whom Rice had befriended and perhaps partied with. Rice knew a woman who worked in the cafeteria; she prepared custom-made sandwiches for the gang, filling them with avocado, sprouts, tomatoes, peppers, onions, lettuce, and cheeses, and plastering them with mayo, mustard, and black pepper. The men referred to these as Dome-wiches. A gallon-sized mini keg of imported beer they lugged into the backcountry was a Dome keg.

Every trek had an element of competition and challenge: Who could race up the staircase, Sub Dome, and cables the fastest? Who could pack the heaviest load? Who could get closest to the edge? There was little tolerance for the timid—slackers were taunted. And Rice always tried to set the highest bar.

Esteban: "Tom was one of the most competitive persons I've ever known. He would make everything into a game of competition, and he always had to win. If he could not be better than you physically and athletically, then he would try to be tougher than you mentally, which included not showing any emotional signs of weakness."

On the trail, Rice scrambled way ahead, stopped, and waited for everyone else to catch up. Then he set another killer pace to the next milestone. He drove everybody to keep on schedule so they could ascend the summit and descend before dark, if they weren't camping on the top. Rice knew what it took to motivate Esteban: question his courage. He prodded others differently. If anybody questioned him, he just growled and said, "Eat shit and die."

His own personal frailties lay beyond anyone's reach.

On the summit, Rice typically gravitated to the diving board. There, occasionally wearing only his briefs, he assumed the diving position and inched backward until he stood at the end of that naked rock pedestal. The more people who watched, the more fearless he seemed to be. Sometimes his companions refused to look, either out of terror or to deprive him an audience.

Esteban: "Every time we climbed the Dome, you knew Tom would do it. It always scared the shit out of us and yet we were drawn to it, and it was inescapable, his closeness to death and sheer will to overcome his fear of it."

In this and his other stunts, Rice was betting as always that he controlled the outcome.

◄○►

TYPICALLY, RICE CONCEIVED a plot to make each Dome outing special. It became part of the ritual.

Once, on a "nighttime assault," they drove to Glacier Point and hiked in the dead of night to Little Yosemite Valley. Pippey brought his wife. She slowed the group down considerably, which enraged Rice, who didn't hide his displeasure or mince his disapproving words. Rice was adamant about excluding females from these forays into the wilderness. On this trip, they unwittingly placed their sleeping bags next to a steep drop-off and didn't realize their peril until daylight.

For their Memorial Day trip in 1984, accompanying Rice and Esteban was "Half Dome Jerome," a summer employee in Yosemite National Park and friend of Rice, who bestowed the moniker. Half Dome Jerome was built like a shotputter. The three-some brought a case of San Miguel, a premium Filipino beer. The twenty-four bottles weighed just over thirty-three pounds, and to avoid breakage they carried the case in a separate backpack. Each hiker took a turn hauling it along with all his other food and gear—akin to adding a sack of bricks to an already oppressive load.

When they reached the summit and saw unmelted snow in shaded areas, Esteban interpreted this as a "great message from the gods." The snow guaranteed ice-cold beer.

Part of their routine on top was to circulate among other campers, strike up conversations, and share stories and tangibles.

On this overnight outing, the three men indeed had something special to share: cold beer, a few bottles of which they sold for five bucks each to some of the two dozen campers on the summit. With others, exchanges transpired. One camper, for example, invited everyone to peer through the giant lens of his telescope while he described the constellations. Elsewhere, a cheery fire stoked by wood that a camper had hauled up was attracting a friendly group. And there was a chef from a New Orleans restaurant who cooked up a killer stew and shared it with Rice and his buddies. They reciprocated with beer.

Esteban met a camper who offered him LSD. In the drug world, this particular acid—"Orange Sunshine"—allegedly was the best, concocted by the Harvard professor and drug guru Timothy Leary. Esteban downed it and soon was tripping. Lying on his back, he watched the flaming stars twirl about the moon in a gargantuan pinwheel pattern. He jumped to his feet and sauntered toward the western horizon, along the Dome's surface that sloped ever downward. As Rice and others watched, Esteban, playing a game of chicken with himself, disappeared below the skyline as though he would continue into the abyss. Just before gravity started to overcome the grip of his hiking boots, Esteban stopped and turned back.

Then he strolled toward the Dome's sheer face. The full moon cast Half Dome's image over the Valley. To Esteban, the shadow on a distant wall was an eagle, symbolizing his own powers, and the silhouette of Clouds Rest a giant pyramid. He tight-walked along the mountain's edge feeling totally in control, invincible. He stepped down to a three-foot-wide ledge and walked along it with only a dark void on his left. He dropped to another narrow ledge. In front of him a rock structure jutted out, like the beak of a giant bird. On its facing side was a black hole—an opening in the granite, the eye of the bird. He climbed to this mysterious cleft, peered in, and saw a rock chamber.

Later that night, after midnight, Esteban showed Rice and Jerome the cave he had discovered. They accessed it through an opening amid the jumble of rock slabs that covered this part of the summit. The chamber's interior was conical: fifteen feet long, three to four feet wide, and six and a half feet at its highest point, close to where they stood. It dropped to four and a half feet in the middle and to four feet at the farthest end. There Yosemite Valley was visible through the small portal Esteban had stumbled upon.

In the chamber's outer side—actually its own separate cubicle, which extended still farther out—was another four-foot-wide, five-foot-high opening that looked out to the upper Valley and Tenaya Canyon. Just beyond the gap was a ledge about four feet wide and thirty inches deep. You had to clamber over a two-and-a-half-foot boulder, then lower yourself down, to reach it. Esteban, Rice, and Jerome each slid over the boulder in turn and eased himself into a sitting position on the ledge, which conveniently tilted back slightly. A stone slab provided back support. Sitting there was like occupying the open cockpit of an airplane with only empty space in front of and below your legs.

Squeezed together, legs dangling over the edge, each swigging beer, the trio took in Yosemite's northern ridges and domes, all bathed in moonlight. The stars danced above, and a vast empty space loomed immediately before them.

They dubbed this bench-like perch the King's Chair.

◄○►

KARL BUCHNER WAS ANOTHER Dome compatriot whom Esteban recruited from Spectra Physics, a company that had bought out Quantra-Ray, where Esteban, Pippey, and Buchner still worked. Although an outdoorsman, Buchner wasn't a regular on Esteban's and Rice's outings. He and Esteban had met while playing together on a softball team. Buchner's friends called him Beach Boy or Surfer Dude. He looked and acted the part—blond hair, blue eyes, almost six feet tall, a muscular 185 pounds, laid-back. He did in fact surf and was active in a variety of other sports as well.

Esteban's descriptions of Half Dome and the King's Chair persuaded Buchner to join him and Rice on a Memorial Day weekend trip in 1985. On the summit, they smoked pot, mingled with other campers, and swapped stories. Buchner likened the communal spirit to that of a cult gathering, a mini Woodstock. As the sun disappeared beyond the granite pinnacles to the west and darkness settled in, Rice and Esteban led him to the cave, where they wedged together on the King's Chair and passed around a jug of "bug juice"—Gatorade and vodka. "Totally awesome" was how Buchner described this experience. The three men talked about returning later that summer. They would invite others and somehow make the outing really special. Buchner wanted his best friend, Steve Ellner, to join them and experience what he had. Esteban would invite his new supervisor at work, Bob Frith, whose passion for the outdoors was just getting ignited. Pippey would surely join them. He'd likely recruit the young Jordan twins, whom he had wanted to include on a Dome journey for quite some time.

They set the date for the same weekend as Rice's twenty-eighth birthday: July 27–28.

3

THE HIKERS

*I was lying in a great solemn cathedral, far vaster and
more beautiful than any built by the hands of man.*
—Theodore Roosevelt, Yosemite, May 1903

AMONG THE MULTITUDE attempting to reach Half Dome's summit
on Saturday, July 27, 1985, were three parties, their fates
destined to merge there on the top.

Rice and Esteban headed their contingent. Esteban had recruited
his work supervisor, Bob Frith, a recent East Coast transplant. Frith,
in turn, had enlisted his best friend, Bruce Weiner, also from the

East Coast and newly arrived in California. Bill Pippey brought along sixteen-year-old twin brothers, Bruce and Brian Jordan. The boys were drifting into chronic substance abuse, and Pippey hoped that exposing them to nature would redirect their lives in more promising directions. Rounding out the group were Karl Buchner and Steve Ellner. Buchner had persuaded a skeptical Ellner, his closest buddy, to join the outing. The group would backpack to the top, camp there, and celebrate Rice's birthday the next day in style.

Leading the second group was Mike Hoog of Santa Rosa, a town one hour's drive north of San Francisco. His party included Linda and Dan Crozier, Rick Pedroncelli, and Jennie Hayes. A Half Dome veteran himself, Hoog wanted the others—all of them Dome first-timers—to spend the night up there so they could experience its full impact.

The third group consisted of six men in their twenties from San Jose, five of whom worked for high-tech companies and lived in the same apartment complex. Their experienced leader and organizer, Brian Cage, had logged at least ten journeys to Half Dome's summit.

The leaders of all three groups shared deep ties to this granite temple—feelings of wonder and devotion that would infuse their companions as well. Staring up at that stone mass and realizing you'll be trekking to one of the most remarkable places on earth is enough to jump-start anyone, even veteran outdoorsmen.

There were twenty hikers in all, eighteen of them men who, to varying degrees, were risk-takers and self-styled outdoor warriors. They all had the same agenda: spend the night on Half Dome.

◄o►

IN 1985, FOLLOWING two decades of upheaval, the nation was mostly unruffled. It had returned to conservative values in politics, education, entertainment, and social affairs. The 1960s began with high hopes and idealism inspired by a young president, John F. Kennedy. But his assassination in 1963 and then the assassinations in 1968 of two other revered public figures—Martin Luther King Jr. and Senator Robert F. Kennedy—mired the country in prolonged grief and despair. The escalating war in Vietnam, moreover, ignited more protests than ever before. Intense demonstrations rocked college campuses, where students took control of administrative offices and, in some cases, shut down all operations. Police brutality sparked race riots and fires in several cities. Trust in government and institutions spiraled downward.

Questioning authority and convention became de rigueur. Individualism and alternative lifestyles flourished, symbolized in part by male hairstyles—shoulder-length manes, ponytails, Mohawks. Use of marijuana spread among the young. The advent of birth control pills in the 1960s liberated women and led to greater sexual license and promiscuity. The credo of the times was *Do your own thing.* These and other newfound mores coalesced at Woodstock in upper New York State in August 1969, a mammoth throng devoted to rock and roll, drugs, sex, and lawlessness.

At the dawn of the 1970s, anti-establishment activities—fueled by the Nixon administration's Watergate shenanigans—gathered even greater momentum. Drug use soared—not only of pot, but also of LSD and cocaine, the drugs of choice among the rich and famous. Violent underground movements took form. The Black Panthers, the Charles Manson cult (which murdered actress Sharon Tate), the Symbionese Liberation Army (which kidnapped and brainwashed newspaper heiress Patty Hearst), and other radical groups lashed out against what they saw as a corrupt system, but did so mainly to wreak destruction for its own sake. America's withdrawal from Vietnam and the resignation of President Nixon didn't immediately reverse Americans' cynicism. Slowly, however, extremism ebbed. Even some of the most radical protesters realized they still had to earn a living.

By 1980, an across-the-board retrenchment of mores was under way. Many people heralded conservative family values. And many in the new generation aimed to earn lots of money. Meanwhile, men's hair got shorter and inflammatory words and phrases like *pig, racist, anarchist,* and *burn, baby, burn* faded from the lexicon. *Cool, awesome, gnarly,* and *dude* reflected the more laid-back times. In schools, it was "back to the basics"; innovations from the '60s—flexible scheduling, individualized learning, inductive and problem-solving curricula—were curtailed. The spread of sexually transmitted diseases decelerated sexual promiscuity. Patriotism once again came into vogue. Spearheading this conservative movement was the new president, Ronald Reagan, elected in 1980 and reelected in 1984.

◄○►

ESTEBAN, RICE, AND CREW at mid-decade were among the era's "upwardly mobile" crowd, the original "twenty-somethings," the "me generation." Succeeding in their Silicon Valley high-tech jobs and making money were important, but enjoying life came first. For these guys, parties, drinking, drugs, and raucous gatherings were a way of life. Theirs was a true-life *St. Elmo's Fire* sans Demi Moore.*

The big ritual for Rice's crowd was attending the happy hour that most major nightclubs in the area—the Baja, The Rodeo, Terrace, Saint James Infirmary, P. J. Mulligan, D. B. Cooper's—held on Friday evenings. To entice customers, the clubs served up not only cheap drinks, but also free food. The group hit several venues every week, an activity they called upper hoboism.

The upwardly mobile were cool and had that *Miami Vice*/Don Johnson look—designer jeans, sport coat, casual dress shirt, no tie, tennis shoes, no socks. The exception was Pippey, who often

---

*Interestingly, the film's title refers to a type of lightning discharge. When the buildup of opposite charges is insufficient for lightning to form, a coronal discharge, a circular bluish glow, or even a mass of sparks may appear over a high, sometimes pointed object. The phenomenon, first noted at the top of ships' masts, is called St. Elmo's fire, for the patron saint of sailors. The movie's title connotes the turbulent energy of the characters as they approach adulthood.

showed up with ripped or stained clothes, sometimes both. Those who frequented the clubs were mostly singles, the last of the baby boomers. AIDS had not yet stormed into public awareness, so the pursuit of casual sex was still mainstream; booze and pot remained rampant; and smoking indoors was not only legal but hip.

By this time, the frenzied disco beat of the '70s was giving way to '80s pop. Culture Club, Prince, Dire Straits, and the sassy, unconventional Madonna hit the airwaves and distributed their music in a newfangled format, compact discs. Radio tunes in 1985 were likely to include Madonna's "Like a Virgin," "Material Girl," and "Crazy for You." Nevertheless, hard rock persisted and a guy needed to know how to dance to have a chance with the free-spirited young women who frequented local clubs.

Rice's charisma and often outrageous behavior attracted many followers, including a parade of females. Pippey, who often shouted across a crowded room to snare someone's attention, was loud and boisterous. Esteban, on the other hand, was usually laid-back and low-key. However, his hair-trigger temper could erupt if anyone annoyed him or he sensed disrespect, especially after a few beers, giving rise to the occasional parking-lot brawl. The group's other members were the more sedate Buchner and Ellner.

A newcomer was Bob Frith. He had moved to California that April to work as a laser tech supervisor at Spectra Physics. The youngest of eight children, with six older sisters, Frith had grown up outside Arlington, Virginia. He held a bachelor of science degree in engineering from the University of Rochester in New York, with a major in optical engineering. Only twenty-four years old in 1985 when he took the supervisory job at Spectra Physics, Frith was bright and had good business and people skills—definitely a young man on the move.

Frith charmed everyone he met with his sparkling personality and good looks accentuated by a strong chin, clean-cut features, and rich dark hair. A happy-go-lucky type who was always ready with a quick joke, Frith loved life and having a good time. He plunged enthusiastically into everything he did and always with a smile. He could arrive at a party not knowing a soul and, by night's end, be friends with everyone there. Plump at 190 pounds for his five-foot, eight-inch height, he nevertheless had a way with women. Between his and Rice's charm and good looks, the other guys would, as Esteban put it, "hover around like vultures waiting for scraps!"

—◄o►—

EXCEPT FOR THE MORE culturally inclined Ellner, the main bond among these men was sports. They competed fiercely in pickup basketball and touch football contests. After each game of the high-flying San Francisco 49ers, Esteban typically hosted a barbecue bash on the pool deck at his apartment complex that often blared long past midnight. In January 1985 Coach Bill Walsh and quarterback Joe Montana led the team to their second consecutive Super Bowl title by shutting down Dan Marino and the Miami Dolphins.

The men tracked most other sports as well. In the National Basketball Association, Larry Bird was voted the most valuable player for the 1984–85 season and a young player, Michael Jordan, was crowned rookie of the year. And in a rarity for major-league baseball, two Missouri teams, the St. Louis Cardinals and Kansas City Royals, were riding high and would later meet in the World Series.

Rice, Esteban, and company paid little attention to politics and international affairs, which were fairly low-octane at the time. There was no hint of a warming trend in the Cold War when Mikhail Gorbachev took the Soviet helm in 1985, but subsequent events—the fall of communism and the Berlin Wall, and the dissolution of the USSR—would make Gorbachev one of the most significant political figures on the twentieth-century world stage.

Aside from *St. Elmo's Fire*, movie hits included *Back to the Future* and another youth flick, *The Breakfast Club. Out of Africa*, starring Robert Redford and Meryl Streep, won Best Picture for 1985. Redford also launched the Sundance Institute that year and organized the first Sundance Film Festival in Park City, Utah.

The Half Dome crew may have read Tom Clancy's blockbuster *The Hunt for Red October*, but most likely didn't pick up two other big sellers that year: *The Color Purple* and *Lonesome Dove*. Treasure hunters located the *Titanic* on September 1, sparking renewed interest in the tragedy seventy-three years earlier and culminating in the monster film hit *Titanic* in 1997. Another tip of the iceberg that shocked the nation was the announcement on July 25 by movie star Rock Hudson that he had AIDS. This revelation and Hudson's death six weeks later generated big headlines. In recognition of the unfolding AIDS plight in Africa, music stars convened to record "We Are the World," which won a Grammy.

◄○►

IN THEIR QUEST for adventure at Yosemite, Rice, Esteban, and compatriots probably didn't realize that beneath the beauty and splendor of this famed national park simmered many long-standing sociopolitical issues.

Ever since the first national park—Yellowstone—was established in 1872, questions had swirled regarding the proper mission of national parks. Did America want them to be preserves for nature? Havens for tourists and recreationists? Resources for both private and public consumption? As much as any park, Yosemite reflected the conflict of priorities that buffeted these national treasures.

Yosemite was first designated a national park in 1890 (the state of California managed Yosemite Valley and the Mariposa Grove until 1906 when those land grants were receded to the federal government and made part of the national park around them.) Despite this protection from exploitation, powerful pressures to accommodate tourists and develop recreational amenities seethed. The Curry Co.—and other lodging and food operations—got

started in 1899. In 1903, state officials reinstituted a nightly entertainment spectacle that began almost thirty years earlier: an
evening bonfire at Glacier Point followed by hot embers dumped
over the edge, which created a flaming firefall to the Valley floor.*

The elegant, stone Ahwahnee Lodge opened in 1927, offering
a golf course, tennis courts, and a swimming pool. The park's
Badger Pass Ski Area began operating in the winter of 1935–36.
Over the subsequent three decades, gas stations, motels, gift shops,
apartments, restaurants, houses, garages—all told, more than a
thousand buildings, a few thousand campsites, and thirty miles of
roads and parking areas—sprouted in the Valley, resulting at times
in suffocating human and automobile congestion.

The surge of environmentalism that swept the nation in the
1960s and '70s carried over to the nation's parks.** The preservation of nature became the National Park Service's chief mission.
Increasingly, science rather than recreational values directed the
efforts of park managers. Their new philosophy was to let nature
exist on its own terms to whatever extent possible in these high-
use public settings.

That put an end in 1968 to Yosemite's nightly firefall, a small
but symbolic change. To reduce congestion, park managers closed
the upper end of the Valley to automobiles, built a one-way road
system, and introduced shuttle buses to transport visitors throughout the Valley. The main parking area at the visitor center was converted to a pedestrian mall.

In addition, certain meadows in the Valley became off-limits in
order to allow restoration of natural habitats, while in others, board-
walks were installed to accommodate walkers. The Ahwahnee golf

---

*The firefall was ended by an Assistant Secretary of the Interior in 1913 and reinstated
by the Secretary in 1917.
**This era produced the Federal Wilderness Act (1964), the National Wild and Scenic
Rivers Act (1968), the Federal Clean Air Act (1970), the Federal Clean Water Act
(1972), and the Federal Endangered Species Act (1973).

course was removed. Stocking Yosemite's historically fishless streams and lakes with hatchery-reared trout would eventually be phased out.

A General Management Plan for Yosemite was established in 1980 with five broad goals: reclaim Yosemite's priceless natural beauty, allow natural processes to prevail, promote visitor understanding and enjoyment, markedly reduce traffic congestion, and ease crowding. But by July 1985, little progress had been made. Too many groups had vested, often conflicting interests in the park's future. For example, those whose livelihoods depended on the arrival of millions of tourists each year, businesses both inside and outside the park, opposed restrictions on cars and any reductions in lodging and other visitor amenities. Environmental groups wanted the priority on preservation, while others insisted that the resources existed primarily to be used by the public.

Although the management plan favored letting Mother Nature take her course in Yosemite, shifting political climates and disagreements in subsequent years impeded timely progress toward that end.

◄○►

IN THE SUMMER OF 1985, backpacking and extreme outdoor sports such as hang gliding, aerial skiing, and BASE jumping were riding a wave of popularity. Few aficionados were as intense in their quest for adventure as Esteban, Rice, and especially Pippey, whose newly discovered love for the outdoors was toughening his body and spirit. Pippey liked nothing better than a grueling backpacking trip. He set a fierce pace way ahead of others, as if he were leaving behind years of family neglect and abuse. Pippey's favorite destination was Mount Whitney, offering one of the most spectacular hikes in the country.

Summiting Mount Whitney—at 14,494 feet, the highest peak in the lower forty-eight states—involves eleven uphill miles and an elevation gain of more than six thousand feet, mainly on a steady, 15 percent grade. Fortunately, there are countless switch-backs—a hundred of them just between Trail Camp at twelve thousand feet, where backpackers overnight, and the crest of the ridge at fourteen thousand feet.*

In early July, three weeks before the upcoming Half Dome event, Pippey organized a backpacking trip to Mount Whitney with Esteban and Frith. The plan was to hike to the summit, which is located in Sequoia National Park, then descend the other side and camp at the eastern end of the Park. It would be a major test for Frith, who had been in California less than three months, and who was overweight and a smoker. Frith may not have been in the best of shape, but his boundless enthusiasm usually carried the day.

En route to Mount Whitney, the Bip Mobile cruised east across the Central Valley, through Tuolumne Meadows in Yosemite, over Tioga Pass, and south down Highway 395 for a hundred miles. The three men crawled into sleeping bags alongside the parking lot at Whitney Portal (elevation: eight thousand feet) and slept. At sunrise, they set out for Trail Camp, where they spent the night before the final ascent.

Adding to the physical stress of lugging a fifty-pound backpack up more than six thousand feet are the risks posed by high altitude. As you climb higher, each breath contains fewer oxygen molecules due to decreasing barometric pressure; blood becomes increasingly inefficient as an oxygen supplier, so your body must work harder. Any exertion during the first couple of days at high elevation—even going up a typical staircase—causes shortness of breath, a normal response.

---

*Hulda Crooks is evidence that such an accomplishment requires more will than muscle. In 1962, at age sixty-six, after her doctor recommended that she begin exercising in the mountains to combat breathing problems caused by pneumonia, Crooks successfully hiked up Mount Whitney. She made the trek almost annually for the next twenty years, twenty-three times in all, climbing it one last time in 1987 when she was ninety-one. That same year she also scaled Mount Fuji in Japan. Crooks's feats earned her the nickname Grandma Whitney. One of Mount Whitney's needles is named Crooks Peak. She died in 1997 at the age of 101.

What isn't normal is altitude sickness, an unpredictable and imprecise affliction that generally can occur above five thousand feet. The first signs include headache and perhaps some dizziness or queasiness. Under the same conditions and regardless of age, gender, physical conditioning, or prior climbing experience, one hiker may experience altitude sickness while another feels nothing. Untreated, it can lead to acute mountain sickness (AMS), the body's intolerance of a hypoxic (low-oxygen) environment. AMS symptoms include headache, nausea or vomiting, fatigue or weakness, dizziness or light-headedness, confusion, and staggering gait. A hiker with these symptoms should stop and descend immediately. Practically speaking, ascending to eight thousand feet—the altitude at which Pippey, Esteban, and Frith launched their trek up Mount Whitney (and approximately the same elevation as the top of Half Dome)—shouldn't cause major problems. But above that level, and certainly above fourteen thousand feet, AMS becomes a serious, potentially life-threatening concern. If it occurs, you cannot get enough oxygen no matter how fast you breathe. That leads to brain swelling, a condition called cerebral edema, which can be fatal.

Hikers and mountain climbers usually can avoid AMS by acclimatizing over several days. The most stringent recommendation is one day of ascent for each thousand feet above eight thousand feet elevation. Pippey, Esteban, and Frith did acclimatize over two days on this particular journey; they spent one day at eight thousand feet and a second at twelve thousand. Nevertheless, thin air was still a threat.

Soon after the threesome left Whitney Portal and headed up the mountain, Pippey, a veritable hiking machine, was way out in front. The first three-and-a-half-mile leg meanders through a pine-scented forest of Jeffrey pine and red fir, and leads to Outpost Camp in a wildflower-filled meadow, the first of the two camping areas on the trail. From there, it is another three and a half miles to Trail Camp. Here backpackers have built low rock walls to ward off piercing winds, and resident marmots either beg for food or steal it from campers. The pica, a high-elevation-dwelling mammal that looks like a huge mouse but belongs to the rabbit family, also populates this area.

After Trail Camp, where the trio bedded down for the night, the trail becomes steep. But the vistas up ahead, to the left and right, more than compensate for the uphill grind. Tufts of sky pilot—one of the most beautiful and fragrant of alpine wildflowers—garnish the trailside. Then come the hundred switchbacks leading up to Trail Crest, a mountain pass that is still two miles from Whitney's summit. From this ridge is a view of the upper Kern River Basin to the west, a gigantic bowl beyond which lies another range of snow-covered peaks—the Great Western Divide and the Kaweah Range. To the east are sweeping vistas of lakes, the Owens Valley, and the Inyos Mountains beyond, home to bristlecone pine trees, some more than four thousand years old, maybe even six thousand.

Esteban and Frith struggled, their party lifestyle taking its toll. Ever the warrior and despite his fatigue and increasing light-headedness, Esteban pushed onward. So did Frith, who wore a bright red bandanna around his neck. At Trail Crest, Frith got a headache and nosebleed, but he trudged on, describing the adventure as "bitchin', bitchin'." (This was a standard phrase in Frith's vocabulary, one he applied to various marvels. He may have learned it from "Bob Bitchin'," a popular character on the TV show *Saturday Night Live*.)

When they finally reached the summit, as many as fifty other people were milling about, smiling, holding hands, and a few just meditating. Esteban felt very woozy—all he wanted to do was lie down. An instant later, or so it seemed, Pippey was shaking him awake. Actually, Esteban had been out for about thirty minutes, oblivious to the sheer drop-off just a few feet away.

The three men departed down the other side of Whitney to a grassy meadow bordering Guitar Lake, so named because of its shape. During this long descent, Esteban sweated profusely. When they arrived at the small lake, it was in shadows and the temperature had dropped. Esteban began shivering uncontrollably—the first sign of hypothermia. Pippey and Frith stripped his wet clothes, put him in his sleeping bag, and heated soup for him. While Esteban dozed, they stripped off their own clothes and jumped into the ice-cold lake, which they could tolerate only for a few seconds.

That evening, they saw two other backpackers camped nearby. In his customary fashion, Frith sauntered over and struck up a friendly conversation. He later returned with freshly popped popcorn his newfound friends had given him.

Esteban, Pippey, and Frith met a solo backpacker named Joe the next day. He was, as Esteban characterized him, a "1960s hippie type." Joe and Frith hit it off right away, and soon the four were a band of brothers. When the group had settled down for the evening, Joe broke out a few joints and Esteban produced a bota bag containing 151-proof Bacardi rum, which served as not only refreshment but also antiseptic, mouthwash, and fire starter. Between shots of straight rum and hits of Joe's weed, the happy campers soon forgot all about their physical ailments. Still to come were a dinner of Top Ramen noodles augmented with salami and cheese, and then "killer cigars" that Esteban kept in a waterproof pouch. Evening passed into night.

They realized the next day there was little food left. Checking his topo map, Pippey pinpointed a stream five miles away—a ten-mile round trip—where they might catch fish. It was either that or go hungry, so off they went. Both Pippey and Frith loved to fish and had brought along telescopic rods. At the stream, they saw many smallish trout, but the fish weren't biting. Pippey, hiding behind a small waterfall, finally managed to coax out about a dozen wary little rainbows with salmon eggs, and the men snared their dinner.

The party arrived back at camp just as darkness settled. That night, amid breathtaking wilderness rimmed by snowcapped mountains, they savored the fish fried in butter and lemon. More Bacardi, more pot, more cigars, and a cozy fire and fabulous view of Mount Whitney's crest . . . all left the three men quite mellow and very appreciative of the great outdoors.

For Frith, this outing confirmed his love of the Sierra Nevada. He already was looking forward to Half Dome.

-◄o►-

FOR THE HALF DOME OUTING, Frith recruited Bruce Weiner. Not only did he want his friend to experience California at its best, but he expected the trip to reignite their deep friendship.

Frith and Weiner had met at the University of Rochester in New York, where both were optical engineering majors. They were the same age—twenty-four. In contrast to his friend's heft, the five-foot, nine-inch, Weiner was on the lean side, weighing 165 pounds. He had thick, curly black hair. After college, Weiner was employed for a little more than a year by Inspex Corporation in Waltham, Massachusetts, but he was less interested in career than recreation—skiing, biking, golfing, beaching, gambling, party-ing—and scouting for female companionship. He worked out with weights three times a week and played racquetball most days, so he was in reasonably good physical shape. Although not as extroverted as Frith, Weiner was easygoing and friendly, and had a subtle sense of humor.

In letters he wrote to Weiner after moving to California in April, Frith reported "lots of jobs, lots of sun, lots of women in bikinis here in the West." The report quickly persuaded Weiner to pull up stakes. He began job hunting in the Bay Area and accepted an engineering position at Lockheed Missiles and Space Corporation in Sunnyvale, near where Frith worked.

Weiner had just arrived in California in early July; he'd moved all his boxes into his new apartment the very day he left for the Half Dome trip, leaving him no time to unpack. The Yosemite outing would be Weiner's first mountain adventure—in fact, his first real hike of any substance.

Steve Ellner—a single child who, by his own admission, could be stubborn, opinionated, and uncompromising—was a greenhorn, too. Unlike the others, he had zero affinity for the rugged outdoors. But Buchner was certain that the beauty of Yosemite and Half Dome would captivate the twenty-seven-year-old Ellner, as they do most first-time visitors. Buchner wanted his pal to experience the summit "happening," particularly sitting in the King's Chair at night. Because Ellner was Esteban's roommate (Esteban had moved out of the house he shared with Pippey when Pippey's girlfriend moved in), the wonders of Half Dome had been already drilled into him.

He agreed to go, despite considerable misgivings. In the preceding days, Ellner's co-workers kidded him about lightning on Half Dome. Aren't you the tallest? You'll probably be the one who gets struck, they joked. Ellner, the only six-footer in the group and a self-avowed coward, would carry those thoughts with him throughout the trip.

An unlikely pair would accompany the seven men: the sixteen-year-old twins Brian and Bruce Jordan. Pippey hoped the mountain might work its magic on these two drifting teens, his "little brothers." The youngest of five children, with three older sisters, the Jordan twins were just six years old when Pippey, then fourteen, "adopted" the Jordan family as his own. Mr. Jordan was an easy-going, affable guy who wrestled with an alcohol problem. He and Pippey often sat in the garage until very late at night, talking and drinking. Sometimes Mr. Jordan passed out in a drunken stupor.

He and his wife neither closely supervised nor firmly disciplined their two sons, who attended school in a low-income neighborhood in the East Bay city of Hayward and were surrounded by drugs and other temptations. Of the two, Brian was more outgoing and assertive. He often spoke of becoming a big success someday. Unfortunately, some activities, such as using and selling marijuana, were just too tempting. Bruce, who had blonder hair than his brother, was more reticent and quiet. He also got into drugs early on, but, unlike the enterprising Brian, didn't sell them.

Both good-looking young men, Brian and Bruce were mainly interested in girls and cars, like many teenage boys. But smoking pot contributed to their excessive truancy, and that prompted the high school to drop both from classes and send them to continuation school—the same thing that had happened to Pippey when he was their age. Recalling his own troubled past, Pippey realized that Brian and Bruce were surely headed for trouble, so he tried to steer them back on course. In order to do that, he believed he had to gain their trust. The linchpin in this scheme was fishing, an activity the twins had taken up at ponds around the East Bay and truly loved.

Pippey first took them on a backpacking trip near Mount Whitney, where they camped and hooked golden trout, a beautiful native species. The twins themselves got hooked, and more outings followed. Pippey was heartened to see the boys soak up these experiences and get high on nature. When it came time for the July pilgrimage to Half Dome, Pippey seized the opportunity to bring them along. It would be another major step in their reformation.

◄o►

AT 2 P.M. ON FRIDAY, July 26, Weiner picked up Frith at Spectra Physics in his rental car, courtesy of Lockheed. They bought various camping supplies, freeze-dried meals, and trail mix, then drove to Rice's home near Santa Cruz, where he and Esteban waited.

Pippey and the Jordan twins would drive in the Bip Mobile and rendezvous with others at Red Bud that night. Buchner and Ellner planned to meet the group on Saturday somewhere on the trail or, later, at the top of Half Dome. First, Buchner wanted to show Ellner as much of Yosemite as possible.

The caravan from Santa Cruz—Esteban and Rice in Esteban's truck, Frith and Weiner in the rental car—left for Yosemite around

5 P.M. They headed east across the Central Valley—listening again and again to the number one hit at the time, "Brothers in Arms," by the Scottish group Dire Staits—and stopped at nine thirty in Merced for a Chinese dinner. Esteban couldn't get the song's lyrics out of his head. On a dark stretch of road somewhere between Merced and Mariposa, Weiner noticed that Esteban's truck, just ahead, started to swerve. He flashed his high beams and honked until Esteban, who was dozing off at the wheel, pulled over. They switched drivers; Frith drove the truck and Rice joined Weiner. At Mariposa, they cranked up on caffeine and quickly hit the road again, arriving at Red Bud around midnight.

The Bip Mobile pulled in thirty minutes later. Despite the late hour, everyone was pumped up about the forthcoming hike. Some drank beer, others smoked pot, and everyone jabbered about the coming day. Weiner turned in before the others. Lying there among the pines, listening to his friends' chatter and the incessant chirping of cicadas while watching shooting stars streak across the sparkling sky, he thought it was one of the most peaceful and relaxed moments of his life.

The others eventually rolled into their sleeping bags, too. For most of them, it would be their last peaceful rest for a long time.

◄O►

MIKE HOOG'S GROUP—Jennie Hayes, Rick Pedroncelli, and Linda and Dan Crozier, who was a year younger than his twenty-two-year-old sister—reached the entrance to Yosemite on Highway 120 just before midnight that same Friday. They continued a few more miles to the Crane Flat Campground and bedded down.

The group rose at six thirty the next morning, gobbled down breakfast, quickly packed up, and left for the Valley and their big day of hiking. They were on the trail to Half Dome two hours later.

Hoog, twenty-one years old, was a passionate outdoorsman, and a fitness buff. He ran marathons and competed in triathlons. A lithe, 160-pound man who stood five foot eleven, he sported shoulder-length blond hair often tied in a ponytail and boyish good looks. His easygoing and fun-loving manner belied an inner intensity that drove him to achieve. He had spent a lot of time with the Crozier family since the third grade, including vacation time. The youngest of five children, Hoog had at eighteen experienced his father's death, an event that deeply affected him. He saw firsthand how fragile life could be, so his attitude was, *Savor the moment.* He had gone to Half Dome on several earlier trips and become a self-described Dome freak.

Hoog had just earned an associate of arts degree in emergency medical services from Santa Rosa Junior College. His close friend Linda Crozier also had recently graduated—from the University of California, Davis—with a bachelor of arts degree in physical education and had enrolled in a master's program in exercise physiology. In 1974, with her father's encouragement, Crozier became one of the first girls in the nation to play Little League baseball. In 1982, the nineteen-year-old and her father rafted down the Snake River in Idaho. She fell in love with whitewater rafting and the outdoors.

Crozier, who had a close and supportive family, was a straight-A student in high school. She thought about becoming a doctor but chose sports medicine and physical therapy instead. At Davis, she earned certification as an athletic trainer and worked as a student athletic trainer for several teams, which exposed her to all kinds of injuries. She also joined the Outdoor Adventures program there, learning to guide a raft through whitewater and gaining the requisite skills and mental toughness for whitewater rescues.

At 115 pounds, she was slim for her five-foot, five-inch, height—and distinctively pretty, with shoulder-length, feathered dark brown hair, hazel eyes, and olive skin. Crozier was self-confident, extroverted, and content—qualities that accented her Eurasian attractiveness (her father was Caucasian, her mother Chinese). Most of the time her face held a smile.

Hoog and his troupe arrived at Nevada Fall shortly after noon. Several trails converge there, bringing together day visitors, backpackers, and hikers; more than fifty were sprinkled about. Hoog's upbeat and friendly group ate their lunches and joked with each other and those nearby, radiating good spirits. They stretched out on the rocks in their swimsuits to soak up sunshine and rest before the final leg of the trek.

Hoog and Crozier were alike in many ways. But one common trait would prove most serendipitous on that particular Saturday— each was a trained emergency medical technician.

—◄o►—

THERE ARE SEVERAL PROGRAMS that prepare people to handle medical emergencies. The most elementary is Basic First Aid, offered by the American Red Cross. It entails two hours of training in fundamentals—bandaging, cleansing wounds, treating burns, and the like. Another Red Cross course (six hours) teaches cardiovascular pulmonary resuscitation (CPR), or how to treat a victim whose breathing or heart function has stopped. The Red Cross also offers a more extensive, fifteen-hour Public Safety Program that includes CPR. It's designed for firefighters, lifeguards, and others who respond to public emergencies.

Courses leading to emergency medical technician (EMT) certification are much more extensive.

Three levels of EMT certification are available in California: EMT-I, EMT-II, and EMT-III (paramedic). EMT-Is complete 114 hours of classroom and clinical training on diagnosis, treatment, and quick transportation of victims to the nearest medical facility. They are not certified to administer medications—except, in certain locations, oral glucose and epinephrine autoinjectors— nor to administer intravenous substances. EMT-IIs train for at least 306 hours. This certification level is uncommon in California, however; EMT-IIs work mostly in rural counties where the case numbers do not justify using paramedics. EMT-IIIs undergo 1,032 hours of instructional and clinical training to become paramedics. The training is broad—how to take blood samples; how to perform emergency interventions, such as intravenous procedures; how to administer a large assortment of prepackaged drugs, such as morphine and nitroglycerin; and more.

After Hoog completed his EMT-I certification in Santa Rosa, he considered studying to become a paramedic. Linda Crozier also had undergone a rigorous EMT-I course that spring. Her teacher, Dr. Ben Shrifrin, was an expert in wilderness emergency medicine and rescue; he had lots of experience in outdoor-related medical emergencies and was an avid mountaineer. A co-teacher in Crozier's class was Bill Bryant, a good friend of Shrifrin's who had a similar background in mountaineering. Bryant and Shrifrin had served together on the Tuolumne County Search & Rescue Team.

Their instruction would be put to good use on Half Dome.

◄O►

AT RED BUD, Rice's group of seven awoke to a crystal-clear summer sky. A full day of hiking was on tap, ruling out a side trip to Paradise. They tossed their gear into the vehicles and left for Half Dome.

The caravan entered Yosemite Valley thirty minutes later. Accustomed to the low, rounded mountains of the East, Weiner was awestruck by Yosemite's granite spires and domes. Then, at the distant end of the park, there it was—Half Dome. He had difficulty visualizing himself atop that overpowering mountain, and wondered silently if he could really accomplish such a feat.

They gorged themselves on a buffet breakfast in the cafeteria at Camp Curry, then loaded their backpacks with gear, clothing, and food. It was a two-mile march to the trailhead at Happy Isles.*

The sky was blue when the group headed out except for a single cumulus cloud floating above Clouds Rest.

---

*In earlier years, hikers could drive to and park at Happy Isles at the far eastern end of the valley. The General Management Plan of 1974 established a shuttle-bus system to replace cars and reduce congestion in that area. The trade-off, however, was diesel fumes spewed by the buses.

Each hiker hefted a full backpack. The exception was Weiner, who carried the only pack he had, a book bag with two shoulder straps; it contained a few food and clothing items. Frith packed forty-five pounds of his and Weiner's gear, a load they would take turns shouldering. The seven hikers reached the trailhead and began their journey. Fifteen minutes later, they were at the bridge where Vernal Fall is first seen, and hoofed it up the Mist Trail, "doing the staircase."

By the time they eclipsed Vernal Fall, a few cumulus clouds had formed in the sky to the east.

Meanwhile, Buchner and Ellner were a good thirty minutes behind the others when they reached the trailhead after their quick tour of the Valley's sights. At the bridge, Buchner chose the John Muir Trail along the canyon's side. It was a longer but more scenic route, and not as steep as the Mist Trail, an important consideration for Ellner, who had become increasingly dubious about this undertaking.

Rice, Esteban, Pippey, and the Jordan twins arrived at Nevada Fall around twelve thirty. Frith and Weiner, struggling with the altitude and arduous ascent, showed up several minutes later. Rice greeted them at the top of the trail; he was standing on the rock right at the lip of Nevada Fall, his toes inches from the river before it careened over the edge in a torrent of whitewater. Weiner and Frith couldn't believe what their eyes were telling them.

Frith and Weiner joined the others on a sandy beach alongside the river. Rice and Pippey then stripped off all their clothes, dove into the chill water upriver from Nevada Fall, and swam out to a large flat rock. So did Brian and Bruce Jordan, and then Weiner, who thought, This skinny-dipping is cool! On the rock, the swimmers hooted, shouted, and yelled obscenities while tussling like schoolboys to push each other off. They returned to shore and, still nude, lounged about while eating lunch and drinking beer.

Several cumulus clouds in the eastern skies now had combined and were massing over and around Clouds Rest.

-◄O►-

BRIAN CAGE, CLU AND Zip Cotter, and Steve White left work in the Bay Area on Friday and drove east until they reached a popular campground off Highway 120 outside Yosemite National Park. The plan was to rendezvous the next day at Glacier Point with Paul Kolbenschlag and Monroe Bridges, who would depart from San Jose at 4 A.M. on Saturday and drive straight through. Cage had persuaded the group to take the Glacier Point route to Half Dome, explaining that because the trail starts at about seven thousand feet, there is less elevation gain. In fact, the 4.6-mile hike from Glacier Point (at 7,214 feet) to Nevada Fall (at 5,900 feet) isn't all downhill. The Panorama Trail does descend to Illilouette Fall at 5,850 feet, but then it winds back up to 6,600 feet before dropping down again to Nevada Fall. The distance from Glacier Point to Half Dome is just under nine miles, or more than half a mile longer than the Mist and John Muir trails.

In the summer of 1983, while hiking along the Little Sur River south of Carmel on the Pacific Coast, Cage had slipped, fallen into the river, and fractured his right patella. He was evacuated by helicopter. After that debacle, his knee always ached on long hikes.

How dangerous is hiking in Yosemite? It's quite safe on the trails. Nonetheless, falls—while hiking or climbing boulders and rocks—account for most of the park's accidental deaths. Some hikers are killed by rocks cascading from above. Others die when they leave the trail to command a better view. Many trails in Yosemite traverse steep terrain littered with loose rock, such that one misstep may lead to a slide and fatal plunge. Ironically, there haven't been any recorded deaths on Half Dome's heavily traveled trail, despite the hazards. For those who might lose their grip on the cables, the sloping granite apparently allows sufficient footage and time to recoup.

Cage's party assembled in the Glacier Point parking lot shortly before noon on Saturday. After they donned hiking boots and organized their gear, everyone gathered for a group photo, with a side view of Half Dome in the background. Five of the men wore shorts, one wore jeans, and they all sported ratty T-shirts. Steve White wore his signature bandanna on his head. To the east beyond Half Dome a mass of cumulus clouds blanketed the mountain ridges. Before they departed Glacier Point, Clu Cotter bought a postcard showing a lightning bolt striking Half Dome.

Within the first half mile on the trail, the six men spotted two five-foot rattlesnakes about ten feet off the path, writhing together in mating behavior.* Few things get the adrenaline flowing on a hike like seeing one of these creatures, which do their best to avoid humans and keep the peace. These reptiles were exceptionally huge. Much to the dismay of his companions, Kolbenschlag waded into the bushes to get a photo of these specimens, but he kept a safe distance.

And then the six hikers resumed their march toward Half Dome.

◄○►

HOOG'S GROUP PAID LITTLE attention when Rice and his buddies arrived at Nevada Fall. However, when Rice, Pippey, and others shed their clothes and began shouting vulgarisms, Linda Crozier and Jennie Hayes were stunned and offended, especially with families, young teens, and other females gathered at this popular hiking destination—the standard terminus for most Mist Trail day-trippers.

Let's get out of here—we don't need this, Crozier told her friends.

So they hoisted their backpacks and left. It was 1:30 P.M.

---

*The author experienced the first of his many rattlesnake sightings in California very near Glacier Point over forty years ago. Contrary to popular belief, rattlesnakes inhabit elevations of up to ten thousand feet—even higher in warm climates. That's probably their uppermost range in the Sierra Nevada around Yosemite. According to the Yosemite Medical Clinic, about two persons suffer a rattlesnake bite in the park each year; there has been one known snakebite death in Yosemite, in 1931.

By that time, a thick, dark cloudmass hovered above Clouds Rest. The first rumbles of thunder could be heard off in the distance.

The threatening weather prompted Rice and his companions to pack up. Rice and Esteban assured the others that once they were on the summit, they would be safe and dry in the cave if a thunderstorm hit. That's where we're heading, Esteban said as his fellow hikers prepared to move out.

It would be a race to the top of Half Dome: Who could get there first? Pippey and Bruce Jordan didn't wait for the others; they hefted their packs and pounded up the trail, with Esteban, Rice, and Brian Jordan not far behind. Frith and Weiner brought up the rear again.

After the surprise encounter with rattlesnakes, Cage's party had proceeded down Panorama Trail to Illilouette Fall, then gutted out the uphill leg, which slowed their progress. Beyond that point, they set a good pace en route to Nevada Fall and a much-anticipated break. The six arrived at the falls shortly after Rice's crew had left. Everyone stripped down to their shorts and swam out to the same big slab in the river, where they performed their own distinctive ritual: an air-guitar rendition of the Jimi Hendrix classic "Purple Haze."

Refreshed, they returned to shore, got dressed, packed up, and headed out through Little Yosemite Valley as the thunderstorm brewed.

Buchner and Ellner didn't arrive at Nevada Fall until nearly two o'clock, and stopped only briefly amid the steady rumble of thunder. Ahead lay darkening skies. Buchner desperately wanted to make up for lost time. Ellner followed his friend up the trail but wondered if it was wise to keep going. In fact he didn't like anything about how the day was shaping up.

The phalanx of menacing clouds forged down Tenaya Canyon, taking direct aim at Half Dome.

4

THE CLIMBERS

Go climb a rock!—Yosemite Mountaineering School

O N LATE FRIDAY AFTERNOON, July 26, 1985, while scaling the northwest face of Half Dome, rock climbers Ken Bokelund and Rob Foster were halfway to the summit. Bokelund was nineteen years old, Foster eighteen. The previous summer, both had completed their first Yosemite climb, the south face of Washington Column. Throughout that modest, one-day ascent, the face of Half Dome had stared at them from directly across the Valley, never leaving their sight. Its peerless image seared their minds and beckoned their souls. When they left Yosemite the next day, they were already planning their next climb—of Half Dome's face, one of the most famous big-wall climbs in the world.

And now, a year later, here they were.

In the preceding days, the weather had been unstable, with clouds building up and thunderheads forming. As Bokelund and Foster scaled Half Dome on Friday, a fierce thunderstorm broke out in late afternoon. This storm was particularly intense; frenzied rain pounded them. The two climbers wore rain pants and jackets, and hard yellow helmets to protect their heads from fatal head trauma in the event of a slip or fall. To escape the sprays and sheets of water blasting down off the rock, making it almost impossible to see, Bokelund and Foster sought refuge at a rock structure called the Chimney. They wedged themselves into the flue between this spire and the mountain's face, their feet butted against the spire and backs against the face. Runoff funneling down through the surrounding crevices drenched them while the thunderstorm roared overhead. Lightning flashes and thunder cracks soon became almost simultaneous.

Bokelund and Foster were, in their own words, "scared shitless."

They heard the air around them crackle and then, almost immediately, a bright flash from above momentarily blinded them. A lightning bolt had just thrashed the summit. Its electrical current streaked down the water on the granite surface and shocked the two climbers leaning against it. Within minutes, another strike hit the mountain, delivering another jolt to their bodies. Foster felt as if the electrical charge were driving his tongue out of his mouth. For the next several minutes, the two men bore repeated electric shocks. Fortunately, the voltage was not high enough to injure them seriously.

Foster screamed, We've got to get off this mountain!

◄○►

THE SPORT OF ROCK CLIMBING first became fashionable in the French Alps and the Italian Dolomites. Its popularity had skyrocketed over the years, especially in Yosemite, where granite monoliths challenged the world's best climbers like no others. For starters, some of the most continuous vertical surfaces anywhere on the planet were found there. Climbing them required supreme skill, strength, and endurance. Unlike European granite, Yosemite's rock was extremely smooth, as a result of glacial polishing and the processes of exfoliation (sheeting) and erosion, all of which shaved off corners and angles and left the rock slick and curved. Jamming hands and toes into vertical cracks—natural avenues to the top—was the standard mode of ascent. Some of the climbing was friction climbing that entailed the smallest of fingerholds. Clinging to these holds often had less to do with technique than faith.

As sports go, rock climbing is a world unto itself, a vertical wilderness of sheer rock. A climber packs not only everything a backpacker carries—food, cooking gear, sleeping bags, and all the rest—but also huge coils of rope, carabiners, hammers, pitons, wedges, blocks or camming devices, headlamps, webbing, and a bag of chalk to keep fingers dry and gritty. And water—lots of it. The standard rule is two liters per day per climber; three if the weather is hot. Each liter weighs 2.2 pounds. So a four-day climb means each climber must lug a minimum of nearly eighteen pounds of water.

Overnight climbers prefer to sleep on ledges and always tie themselves in. When there's no ledge, they snooze on the face in a hammock-like sling, or portaledge, that is anchored at the belay or tied in.* Mice, rats, and squirrels live in the cracks on Yosemite's walls. These rodents, as well as ravens or crows, may raid precious food supplies or ravage gear such as sleeping bags; the helpless climbers can do little else but watch such thievery. There are unique procedures for relieving oneself on a mountain face and packing out excrement so it doesn't contaminate the environment.

*A belay is a means of securing the climber by using a rope and usually a belay device to prevent or minimize falls. The rope is attached to a pin or cleat anchored in the rock, to the climber, and to the belayer below. A belayer is the person on the ground or at the belay station who secures the lead climber, feeding out rope as the climber ascends or gathering up the slack as he descends.

The climber's main companions are vertical rock, empty space, and vertigo-inducing depths.

◄o►

AMONG THE PANTHEON of granite megaliths, Half Dome has long been seen as special. Early on, would-be climbers viewed this unique structure as the most difficult climbing challenge in Yosemite, if not the world. George Anderson was the first to hoist himself to the top with rope and spikes, in 1875. He subsequently established a trail for others that was more of a hike than a technical climb. Almost sixty years passed before anyone climbed Half Dome via another route.

John Salathe, a Swiss blacksmith in Yosemite, accomplished that feat in 1946 when he and a companion scaled the southwest face. Much like Anderson, Salathe applied his occupational skills to forge a climbing breakthrough. He had climbed on many of the best routes up Yosemite's rock walls but found that the soft metal pitons available at that time were inadequate; they bent and mushroomed when driven into granite cracks.* By cannibalizing the axle of a Model T Ford, Salathe fashioned pitons out of hard steel, which he and his partner Anton "Ax" Nelson used to ascend the Dome's southwest face. His innovation became the standard for Yosemite climbers who followed, and for climbers across the globe.

Salathe proved there was more than one way to ascend Half Dome, but the southwest face wasn't anywhere near as challenging as the northwest face, the nearly vertical wall staring down at visitors on the Valley floor. Up to then, few believed it was possible to scale the eighty-degree slant that characterized much of the

---

*A piton is a metal spike with an eye on one end that climbers place in the rock to secure their rope. The rope is attached to the piton placed by the lead climber. If the leader falls from ten feet above the nearest piton below her, she would fall a total of twenty feet before drawing the rope tight, assuming the piton holds.

cliff's twenty-two hundred feet. A few of the world's best climbers in the mid-1900s thought otherwise.

In 1954, three climbers attempted the ascent but were thwarted just two hundred feet up. The following year Royal Robbins, Jerry Gallwas, Warren Harding, and Don Wilson also tried but made it up just 450 feet. Nonetheless, they surveyed a possible route to the top. Two major obstacles were a smooth section more than a hundred feet high and about halfway up, and the overhang at the summit known as the Visor.

More than a year after the Robbins team's failed attempt, Robbins, Gallwas, and Mike Sherrick laid new plans to conquer the northwest face. In this increasingly competitive arena and hoping to scoop any other would-be climbers, they launched their try up the face in early summer 1957. Inch by inch, they lifted up their hundred pounds of gear in a haul bag suspended below them by ropes. The climbers used a flashlight to signal their progress every night to companions on the ground—but, to avoid publicity, only during the firefall spectacle, when the attention of everyone in the Valley was riveted on Glacier Point. A fourth companion had hiked to the top and posted a sign warning people not to throw rocks over the edge—a popular and innocent activity among Half Dome summiteers, who were completely unaware there might be climbers below.

On day two, the three men confronted the 125-foot-high smooth section. To continue, they had to reach a series of chimneys and flakes three hundred feet off to the side. Robbins managed to climb fifty feet up the smooth granite. There he placed three pitons. He fixed his 150-foot climbing rope to these anchors and lowered himself back down. Then, in a display of daring and skill, he gripped the rope and launched into an explosive horizontal charge across the seemingly unassailable barrier, swung back, and charged again. At the outermost reach of his fourth pendulum swing, he grasped a narrow ledge with his fingertips and secured a hold. He now had a route to continue up. His two companions executed the same maneuver. (This part of the climb—a signature move that Robbins pioneered on several other climbing routes in Yosemite—has since been named the Robbins Traverse.)

The three climbers continued up until they were three hundred feet from the top, directly below the Visor. Securing meager foot- and handholds, they inched their way up another hundred feet, only to encounter another slick, insurmountable section. But to their surprise, they came upon a walkable ledge—virtually a climber's highway—that circumvented the barrier. At the end of what has since been dubbed Thank God Ledge, the climbers found more foot- and handholds.

The trio completed their feat by executing a series of mantle maneuvers, pulling their bodies up to a point where they could then push down with their palms, jack themselves up, and gain a foothold. After five days on the wall, Robbins, Gallwas, and Sherrick had surmounted the "unclimbable" northwest face of Half Dome. They completed the climb in twenty-three pitches. A pitch is the distance between one belay stance and the next, usually 100 to 150 feet, with the maximum distance being the length of the rope, or about 165 feet. Thus, the vertical length of their route was about twenty-two hundred feet.

The next successful ascent of the northwest face didn't take place until three years later, and it entailed only two nights in bivouac. A one-night ascent quickly followed. Then, in May 1966, Jeff Foote and Steve Roper completed the climb in a single, long day.

In 1967, Liz Robbins, wife of Royal, became the first woman to climb Half Dome; she followed the same route as her husband's first ascent of the northwest face a decade earlier. Her accomplishment signaled the revolution in women's climbing that would soon follow. Greg Lowe and Rob Kiesel made the first winter ascent in January 1972, overcoming a fierce storm with howling winds. Their hands were nearly frozen.

The route that Robbins and his mates blazed is called the North-west Face Regular Route. By 1971, that and three other routes up the northwest face—Arcturus, Northwest Face Direct, and Tis-se-yak—were active. Today rock climbers can choose from among a dozen technical climbing routes to reach Half Dome's summit.

◄O►

THE CLIMBING WORLD, in which scaling big walls had become the ultimate measure, needed a way to grade the difficulty of ascents. As early as the 1930s, a five-point grading system was devised to rate hikes and climbs in the Sierra Nevada. Technical free climbs were consigned to Class 5. But because they varied widely in the level of difficulty, Class 5 was subdivided in the 1950s into nine ratings—5.1 to 5.9. As climbers became more accomplished and skillful with each passing decade, this Yosemite Decimal System* was extended up to 5.15, the most difficult climb ever completed up to that time. Subcategories (a through d suffixes) in each numerical category were added to delineate the variations even further.

Up to 1970, the adventure in climbing was conquering virgin vertical terrain. Fierce rivalries took root on the floor of Yosemite Valley. Tested Yosemite climbers jealously guarded their turf and were contemptuous of others who didn't meet their standards. For them, it wasn't just a question of which route someone climbed; it was also a matter of technique and speed. Some of the world's greatest climbers—the so-called granite astronauts—achieved major breakthroughs on Half Dome and that larger, even more imposing mass of granite nearby, El Capitan, with its thirty-two-hundred-foot face—"the Crown Jewel of American Rock Climbing."

---

* This system is not to be confused with the decimal system in common use. Under the Yosemite Decimal System, the levels following 5.9 are 5.10 (not the same as 5.1), 5.11, and so on. The original Sierra Club grading systems also had a Class 6 for artificial and aid climbing, but it is no longer used. Artificial or aid climbs are graded on a separate A0 through A5 scale.

These breakthroughs included many first ascents on new routes. Among the climbers in that Golden Age of Climbing were Royal Robbins, Yvon Chouinard, Tom Frost, Warren Harding, David Brower, Galen Rowell, George Whitmore, and Allen Steck. Some parlayed their success into business ventures, such as sponsorship or work in commercials and movies. Robbins, for example, established a successful line of clothing; Chouinard started an outdoor equipment retail firm, Patagonia, which was initially based on climbing devices he invented.

Yosemite climbers settled in a campground in the park and made it their own. Camp Four was a much-abused place where a motley assortment of climbers hung out and slept, a number for the entire climbing season. Some lived on as little as fifty cents a day and ate mainly oatmeal. Like a gypsy camp, Camp Four had its own subculture whose members felt they owned Yosemite. Its scruffy ambience and characters aside, Camp Four gave birth to the sport of rock climbing as the world would come to know it.

◄◦►

IN THE EARLY DECADES, nearly all climbing involved the use of aids, particularly pitons and expansion bolts. When Warren Harding completed the first ascent of El Capitan—the Nose Route—back in 1958, he hammered in more than one hundred bolts. The entire climb, which involved many descents to the Valley floor and returning to the spot where he had left off, took forty-five days over a year and a half. But the sport had become so popular by the mid-1970s that piton scars and abandoned hardware and bivouac webbing were degrading the formerly pristine rock walls. So climbers sought ways to reduce the impact. Purists used as few aids as possible, heeding John Muir's exhortation to "leave no mark except your shadow." As Royal Robbins said, "It isn't getting to the top that's primary, but how you climb there." Not all climbers bought in to this newfound sensitivity, however.

Climbers invented new kinds of low-impact aids that could be wedged into rock crevices to prevent a fall and then removed, leaving no trace. These included a variety of metal chocks, stoppers, and hexes—essentially, rectangular or hexagonal pieces of metal—that are still in use today. In clean climbing, as this approach came to be called, climbers didn't hammer any new protective devices into the rock; they employed only removable items.

A natural progression in the sport of rock climbing was free climbing—climbing without any gear that you could stand on or use to pull yourself up, including rope. Free climbers used only the natural rock surfaces to ascend; they adapted themselves to the rock rather than trying to shape the rock with mechanical devices. Free climbing had its own techniques* and demanded a higher level of gymnastic flexibility and fitness (especially for the most difficult climbs), along with exceptional strength and unique muscular development. Climbers in Yosemite developed new techniques that revolutionized so-called crack climbing. Previously, climbers relied on gaston—putting their fingers in a crack and pulling outward, as if opening a sliding door—for support. Now they were jamming hands and fingers into cracks, squeezing them to create tension within, then hanging by that limb, a technique that required far less strength than gaston. The skeleton rather than muscles did the work.

Free climbing the major walls in Yosemite wasn't really where the action was up until the mid-'70s, mainly because few thought it possible. Events on June 15, 1976, dispelled that notion.

That day, two Colorado climbers, Jim Erickson and Art Higbee, launched an audacious attempt to free climb Half Dome's Northwest Face Regular Route and thereby scoop the Yosemite fraternity

---

*These techniques are perhaps best illustrated by the one-finger pull-ups that climbing legend Wolfgang Gülich made famous. No mere party trick, this incredible maneuver enabled Gülich, a shy German, to complete some of the world's most difficult climbs, a number of which have not been duplicated to this day. Actor Sylvester Stallone was so impressed by Gülich that he got him a job doing stunts in the 1993 movie *Cliffhanger*.

in its own backyard. Beginning in 1971, Erickson had attempted this climb nine times and failed. Still, he believed it could be done. Underlying his latest venture was a movie project. Cinematic technique, like climbing technique, was undergoing its own revolution of sorts. It had evolved to the point where a crew could capture an ascent on film from above, below, and the sides.

Everything began as planned. Erickson and Higbee inched their way up the face. From Ericksons's previous attempts the two climbers knew they could not free climb the Robbins Traverse. In order to circumvent the smoother section, Erickson spotted a possible option. He climbed straight up two hundred feet, and when he couldn't go any further, he traversed forty feet to the right, and then he descended forty feet, arriving at the ledge at the end of the Robbins traverse. Higbee followed suit. This free variation approach has since come to be known as the Erickson Traverse. The pair contined up to Big Sandy Ledge, where they spent the night.

In the morning, staring down on them from above were the Zig Zags, a four-hundred-foot course of narrow cracks that offered the smallest of toe- and fingerholds. Indeed, cracks in the third Zig Zag were so tight, only fingertips could squeeze in. Previous climbers always relied on aids here. Erickson and Higbee each fell several times trying to surmount this stretch. But eventually, Higbee, taking to heart his belief that a climber "has to push himself through the doubt," found one more crack to wedge his hands into, one more potato-chip flake to crimp with his fingertips, and the strength to pull himself up onto Thank God Ledge. Erickson followed. Success seemed to be within grasp. After thirty-four hours on the face, after twenty-two pitches, after twenty-one hundred feet of successful climbing, only one hundred feet remained. This last leg would take thirty minutes at most.

However, Erickson and Higbee were shocked to encounter yet another granite slab blocking their ascent, not very high but smooth and slick. They scoured the rock again and again looking for something to grasp but came up empty. Finally, an exhausted and feverishly hot Erickson used aids to scale this one last obstacle, thereby ending the free climb. Although the two men called their effort a "magnificent failure," the climbing community called it a "magnificent achievement." They had showed the climbing world what was truly possible. From then on, free climbing took center stage.*

Erickson returned to Yosemite later that summer. First he went to Half Dome's summit and affixed a top-rope that hung down over the northwest face. Then he repeated his and Higbee's climb. When he reached that last troublesome slab, Erickson free climbed it with the top-rope for his protection, thus completing the task he and Higbee had set out to achieve. Technically, however, the top-rope compromised the ascent as a pure free climb. Recognition for that feat would go to Leonard Coyne in 1981.

◄○►

SMOOTH GRANITE, OVERHANGS, unstable granite flakes, bivouacs on the narrowest of ledges—all of these and much more test the tenacity, skill, strength, and endurance of climbers. The commitment is such that, beyond a certain point, the only escape is up. Mountaineers live for—and sometimes die for—this challenge.

Each year there are more than a hundred climbing accidents in Yosemite. Nearly all of the 51 climbing deaths between 1970 and 1990—an average of 2.5 per year—were due to trauma injuries; hypothermia caused 4 of them. In the intervening years, the fatality rate has slipped to two per year. Yosemite's search and rescue division typically performs fifteen to twenty-five rescues of rock climbers annually.

In addition to the obvious risk of falling, there are numerous weather hazards, including thunderstorms that seemingly erupt out of nowhere. Torrents of rain may fall. Often the rain is near freezing and intermingled with hail. Sheets of runoff soak climbers, reducing

---

*The film documenting Erickson's and Higbee's feat, *Free Climb*, won many awards.

visibility and rendering the granite slick. If a storm rides in on a cold front, packing chill winds, potentially fatal hypothermia can overtake unprepared climbers.* Sometimes the wind is so fierce, it whips climbers from their moorings or sends their tent and supplies flying into the void.

Another serious danger is lightning, which imperils anyone exposed on a rock face. A direct lightning strike is unlikely, but lightning branches may lash the granite, shooting deadly electrical charges in any direction.** Stifling heat and insufficient water can also be dangerous. Some climbers become so dehydrated, they can't continue. Absent more water or a rescue, they die a slow death.

Anyone climbing Half Dome is particularly prone to weather attacks, because a system can slide into lower Yosemite without causing a disturbance, then unleash raw fury when it hits the Dome. Two climbers got trapped on its south face in October 1968 when a storm brought snow and freezing conditions. Hypothermia and a shortage of supplies threatened their lives. Expert climbers flown to the summit by helicopter rappelled down the face and rescued the pair.

-◄o►-

DESPITE THE DANGERS and discomforts, climbing is for many an all-consuming passion. They interrupt, end, or never start their careers, focusing exclusively on completing the next climb. Climber Todd Skinner said free climbing means "going right to the edge" of your capabilities. For many climbers, this closeness to death—the risk of dying—produces an adrenaline rush that

---

*On October 21, 2004, a fierce, early-season snowstorm hit Yosemite and snared two Japanese climbers who were about two-thirds of the way up El Capitan. They were unprepared for such brutal conditions and died from exposure. Another climber was rescued.

**On June 25, 2000, four climbers were struck by lightning while climbing on Yosemite's Cathedral Peak. Three of the climbers lost consciousness and all of them suffered burns. One went into respiratory arrest. A rescue team reached the stricken party and, by ground evacuation, carried out the most seriously injured climber, who survived.

most other life experiences simply can't. It is what keeps many of them married to the sport. Probably no other sport creates such a feeling of oneness with Mother Nature. Attached to a mountain-side by fingertips and toes, the climber necessarily becomes part of the rock—or else. One climber says that while scaling a granite face, she felt close to God, so intense was her relationship with the natural world.

Climbers speak of "floating" or "performing a ballet" over the rock, each placement of foot and each reach into a crack creating unity with the mountain. The sport is one of total engagement with the here-and-now, which frees the mind from everything else. Climbers' concentration is complete and focused. Their only thought is executing the next move.

Rock climbing has been called the King of Sports, not only because of the skills, courage, and mental conditioning it demands but also because it takes place in the grandest of places. There is no stadium, court, diamond, gym, field, or track that can rival nature's arena.

Ken Bokelund, who was on the face of Half Dome the day Rice, Esteban, and company battled nature at the summit, and who went on to become a highly accomplished climber, said: "Climbing for me has always been the strength of the body over the weakness of the mind. If you train so that you are very strong physically and you have mastered the techniques, then all that's left is believing. Freeing your mind of fear is the key. This is very difficult to do, but when you can achieve it, then you are in true harmony with the rock. Fear is just one more thing to worry about and is very distracting. It can make you fall.

"What sometimes happens when fear enters the climber's mind is sewing-machine leg—a leg that starts shaking out of control. It happens to all climbers at one time or another and obviously is very dangerous when one is clinging to the side of a rock. But when you know you are strong enough to complete any maneu-ver, once that level of physical confidence is achieved, then you are able to put fear out of your mind. Climbing becomes a very simple pleasure. It's just you and the rock. It's a total clarity of being, a time when nothing matters, you're moving without any thought, you're in a place where time stands still. Even when you're on a wall for days, when you get down, everything seems exactly the same, as though time never passed."

—◄○►—

BOKELUND AND ROB FOSTER, his climbing buddy, first hooked up at Burlingame High School in Burlingame, California, just south of San Francisco. Bokelund was five foot eight and weighed 140 pounds, undersized for most sports but just about perfect for rock climbing. A mountaineering school introduced him to the sport when he was in elementary school. In short order, he became a very good climber.

Before Foster got involved in rock climbing, he was generally unmotivated. He hung out with a group of other anti-establishment types in high school who cut classes, didn't do homework, smoked pot, and earned poor grades. Then Foster discovered climbing through Boy Scout camp. It changed his life. Like Bokelund, he was slim: 150 pounds on a five-foot, ten-inch, frame. He began eating well, exercising to build muscle, and climbing instead of bumming around. His schoolwork improved.

Rock climbing brought Bokelund and Foster together. With only a modest amount of climbing gear, the two started clambering up trees, buildings, rocks, stone bridges—whatever was available. Then they put their budding skills to the test at Castle Rock above the town of Saratoga in the South Bay, a big training rock for climbers. Each took a few falls and got banged up. Foster's mother insisted they get climbing instruction, so the pair enrolled in a two-day course at Lovers Leap near Lake Tahoe, where they learned technique and safety skills. After that, as Bokelund put it, their commitment to rock climbing soared "off the Richter scale."

They saved money and bought more equipment, and built a ply-wood climbing wall in Bokelund's backyard.

After graduating from high school in 1983, all Bokelund lived for was climbing. His lifestyle for many years was spartan; he earned just enough money at various jobs to pay for shelter and food. Unemployment checks sometimes filled the gaps. He played guitar for enjoyment.

Foster, a year behind Bokelund in high school, was also addicted to climbing. When few climbing challenges remained in the Bay Area, he and Bokelund set their sights on Yosemite. They developed climbing muscles—in their forearms, triceps, and lats—and worked religiously on technique. The pair was ready to tackle a big wall.

In summer 1984, they successfully scaled the south face of Washington Column, one of Yosemite's easier wall climbs. The next summer they planned to climb the face of Half Dome.

Their intent was to complete the ascent of the Northwest Face Regular Route in three days, beginning on Thursday, July 25. The two teens possessed the zeal of youth but not much in the way of sophisticated gear or clothing. With little money to fuel their passion, they scrimped and scrounged to get by. For the Half Dome ascent, they decided to go light, carrying only the bare necessities. All of the climbing gear weighed about thirty pounds. They chose not to bring their sleeping bags, which were too bulky and heavy. And they couldn't afford new, lighter ones. So each packed a canvas sack to sleep in, along with rain gear, wool pants, a synthetic shirt, and sleeping pad. They didn't pack gloves, although later they would be grateful to discover a stray pair in the bottom of a pack. Their single haul pack was an old army duffel bag. It contained their sleeping sacks and other items plus ropes, food, and climbing paraphernalia. By packing lean, they could lug eighteen liters of waters, which weighed about forty pounds—half the total weight of their stuffed haul bag.

Bokelund and Foster planned to employ several climbing techniques. Portions of the ascent would entail clean climbing—that is, using pitons and bolts already hammered in the granite, and their own removable protection. For sections rated above 5.10, they would do aid climbing—ascending their ropes using nylon ladders (called etriers), slings, and daisy chains. Otherwise, the pair would free climb—use only their hands and feet on the natural rock features while hitched to rope in case of a fall. They arrived in Yosemite on Wednesday, July 24.

Just reaching the base of the northwest face poses a physical challenge for climbers who are carting loads of gear. There are two approaches.

One involves hiking to Sub Dome, as do those headed up Half Dome via the cables, and then skirting the hump and traversing the base of the cliff to its bottom. This stretch alone takes more than six hours. Some climbers, especially guides with clients, rent mules to haul their gear—including cushy sleeping bags, portaledges, wine, good food, and other comforts—to the staging area.

The second approach entails a three-hour scramble through the slabs, a rocky jumble at the bottom of the face where the footing is treacherous and the route so confusing that climbers may not arrive at their intended destination. A spring at the base supplies drinking water.

That first day, Bokelund and Foster hiked the eight-plus miles to the base of Sub Dome and then descended the circuitous route to the bottom of the face, where they camped for the night. They began their climb at sunrise on Thursday.

Their first day on the rock went well. The only others ahead of them were a guide with his female client, about half a day up. Clouds materialized, but no storm. Light showers doused the mountain that night. Although it was midsummer, moisture, wind, and low mountain temperatures made for chilly nights on Half Dome's face. Bokelund and Foster slept tied in on a sloping ledge, snuggled in their canvas sacks and wearing wool pants and synthetic shirts for additional warmth. Each wore one of the two gloves from the stray pair that fortunately showed up; each tucked the other hand inside his clothing.

On day two, after thirteen pitches, they reached the halfway point by midafternoon. They had successfully executed the Robbins Traverse and were on schedule. However, a storm was building. By 3 P.M., the sky had darkened. Then it unleashed a deluge. For the next hour, rain hammered the two climbers, soaking them to the bone despite their rain gear. Not wanting to get caught on the exposed rock directly above, they sought protection at the Chimney, where they could wait out the storm. When lightning zapped the summit, though, both absorbed several electrical shocks. An extremely frightened Foster wanted to rappel down and get off the face, while Bokelund urged calmness. In the back of his mind was the potential loss of their meager but cherished equipment, all two hundred dollars' worth, if they retreated down the mountain without it.

But as savage lightning bolts flailed Yosemite's granite, repeatedly shocking the two men, Bokelund had second thoughts. Maybe it wasn't so wise to hunker down after all; maybe they should retreat. On the other hand, a descent would require thirteen rappels down the thirteen pitches that had taken them half a day to complete, not the least of which was Robbins Traverse. Rappelling down that stretch wouldn't be quick or easy, much less safe. Indeed, rappelling under any conditions is dangerous. Most climbing fatalities occur on descents rather than ascents, when climbers don't rappel properly or rappel off the end of their rope or slip off a steep trail while hiking down from the summit. Bokelund and Foster stayed put. They were trapped.

Patches of sky soon appeared among the rain clouds. The end of the storm was in sight. When the rain stopped and sun broke out, Bokelund and Foster committed themselves to completing the climb as the best of two bad choices. Water still poured down the mountain through chutes and crevices. To decide who should lead the climb at that point, they played the game ro-sham-bo, or rock-paper-scissors. Foster lost. Up he went, out onto wet granite and the bare section. Meanwhile the guide and female climber far ahead had boogied up the face as fast as they could to reach the summit, leaving only Bokelund and Foster on the wall by late Friday. That night it rained some more. Bokelund and Foster, hunkered down on a ledge to sleep as best they could, were wetter and colder than they had ever been.

On Saturday, July 27, with Foster still leading the way, they scrambled up the granite. Only six pitches separated them from the top. Frantic to reach the summit, they wedged their fingers and toes in crevices, and balanced on tiny ledges and whatever rock protrusions were available. Storm clouds began building again—this time, later in the afternoon. Again, the situation became risky. Although the climbers were farther up the face, they were even more vulnerable closer to the summit. Fear drove them—they were desperate to evade another lightning barrage. Bokelund and Foster willed their bodies to work harder, to overcome exhaustion. Their physical conditioning was pushed to the limit.

At 4 P.M., menacing storm clouds were moving toward the Dome. Flashes of lightning and rumbling thunder carried a very clear message. The pair traversed Thank God Ledge, pulled themselves up the remaining smooth face on ropes, and, by means of hasty mantle maneuvers, surmounted the last section of rock around 5 P.M. But there was no time for celebration. They felt terror rather than glee. Foster spotted a small rock enclosure in the Visor and wanted to take cover there until the storm passed.

It was the same enclosure awaiting Esteban and Rice, who at that moment were gunning for the summit.

Nothin' doin', said Bokelund. We need to get the hell off this mountain!

In a frenzy, they stuffed the gear in their packs and raced off. Bokelund and Foster scurried down the granite slope so quickly, half slipping and sliding, that they burned their hands on the metal cables. At the base of Half Dome, they ran across the saddle, up to the top of Sub Dome, and then down the granite stairs. Farther along, two backpackers—Esteban and Rice—were coming up the trail.

Bokelund and Foster warned the two older hikers not to go up there, it was way too dangerous. They then scampered down the trail with one goal in mind: to put as much distance as possible between them and the ferocious storm brewing over Half Dome.

5

THE STORM

*When the glorious pearl and alabaster clouds of these
noonday storms are being built, I never give attention to anything else. No mountain or mountain-
range, however divinely clothed with light, has a
more enduring charm than those fleeting mountains
of the sky. . . .*—John Muir

Storms were brewing across the Sierra Nevada, threatening any
sightseer or wanderer who was ignorant or dismissive of their
power. Mounting thunderheads accompanied the hikers pressing
on toward Half Dome, each intent on reaching the summit.

Hoog's contingent departed Nevada Fall and hiked as a tight unit. Pippey and Jordan left shortly afterward and quickly passed them on the trail. Also skirting by them were Esteban, Rice, and Brian Jordan. Frith and Weiner lagged; the forty-five-pound pack they took turns hefting was bogging them down. Buchner and Ellner were nowhere in sight.

Cage's party was farther back. Their later start and slightly longer hike from Glacier Point meant they would arrive on the summit around 6:30 P.M. if they stayed the course.

The mounting storm soon would require that the hikers respond in some fashion. However, none really knew the capacities, behaviors, and dangers of thunderstorms. On that particular day, they would base their decisions more on misinformation, happenstance, and emotion than knowledge.

◄○►

THUNDERSTORMS HOLD massive quantities of energy, one of the most powerful of which is lightning—a random, chaotic, and treacherous phenomenon. Every thunderstorm demands respect. One may occupy a confined cloud mass and appear quite tame. A distant observer might see telltale gray streaks directly below the cloud, indicating rain. Perhaps a streak of lightning flashes within the cloud, followed by a peal of thunder. This confined type of storm represents, in John Muir's words, a "Sierra mid-summer thunderstorm reduced to its lowest terms." Yet it can form abruptly and then suddenly unleash a deadly lightning bolt that strikes objects directly below or several miles away where the sky is blue.

A mountain thunderstorm spanning thousands of acres can be a violent, tumultuous affair. Driving, flooding rains accompany sheets of hail and terrifying lightning bolts that lash out from anywhere at any time, savagely blasting whatever stands in the way. Explosive cracks of thunder shatter the atmosphere as though it were made of fine china, prompting sheer terror in anyone caught in the inferno. As lightning strikes here, there, and everywhere, the thunderbolts bring ear-piercing booms so intermingled with sheets of blinding light that it can be difficult to pair each flash with each roar. This is Mother Nature in one of her most over-whelming displays of power.

Watching a thunderstorm from a safe haven can be glorious beyond words. It is a symphony of mesmerizing sounds, sights, and smells.

◄○►

IN CONTRAST TO weather systems that originate over the Pacific Ocean, Sierra Nevada thunderstorms develop inland. The mois-ture comes from the Pacific, but initially it is stored in the air rather than in clouds. The air flows across California's Central Val-ley, rises, and accumulates in thermals, or ascending currents of air. As the thermals drift toward the mountains, warm air from the foothills propels them upward. At higher elevations, infusions of warmer air from canyons and valleys send the thermals spiral-ing farther aloft, where they meet colder air. This mixing destabi-lizes the atmosphere; countless crystals and droplets combine to form a puffy, white cumulus cloud—frequently the first harbinger of a thunderstorm.

If other cumulus clouds develop in the vicinity, they often combine into a single, large cloud or sometimes clusters of clouds. This mass may hover over one mountain peak in an otherwise clear sky but can move in any direction.

Because air surrounding the cloud is cooler, the warmer air within keeps funneling upward, creating the cloud's vertical shape. In the troposphere (the lowest, densest part of the atmosphere), this ascending parcel encounters lower air pressure, which causes the cloud to expand and cool as its interior air mass becomes sat-urated with moisture. Ice ultimately forms within the cloud. When this mass becomes too heavy to keep rising, precipitation falls as rain, hail, or snow—sometimes all three. When the mass reaches the tropopause (the boundary layer between the troposphere and stratosphere above), where the temperature is constant, it stops rising and the cloud top flattens into a fearsome anvil shape. This is a cumulonimbus cloud, or thunderhead.

Cumulonimbus clouds are vast, dark, moisture-laden, and formidable. They may tower twenty to forty thousand feet into the atmosphere—even, in the case of a super thunder cell, sixty thousand feet. Ragged formations called scuds hang down menacingly from tops that push up against an invisible ceiling. Within the thunderhead, violent updrafts and downdrafts generate enormous power and energy, resulting in fierce winds and torrents of rain. Sometimes the updrafts break through the flattened cloud top and punch into the stratosphere. This so-called overshooting of the top usually portends the most severe of thunderstorms.

Often accompanying such fury is a frenzied but usually short-lived barrage of hail. Hail is formed by water droplets freezing as they climb within a cloud, dropping back down and picking up more water, then rising again. The frozen droplets may repeat this cycle hundreds of times, adding layer upon layer and increasing in size until, too heavy to remain aloft, they fall to earth. Hail can be as small as a pea or, in midwestern states, as big as a baseball or even a volleyball. Hail in the Sierra Nevada seldom exceeds half an inch in diameter.

At any given moment, nearly two thousand thunderstorms are happening somewhere on earth. More than forty thousand occur every day, sixteen million each year. They keep the planet's heat stores in equilibrium: The vast quantities of moisture in the air that result when sunlight reaches and heats the earth, causing evaporation, are returned to the earth by thunderstorms. The moisture evaporates into the air again, and the cycle begins anew.

A thunderstorm may develop quickly, although not without advance notice. Especially in the afternoon, cumulus clouds can darken and thicken fast and then rapidly evolve into more menacing cumulonimbus clouds. The one-cloud storm, or single-cell thunderstorm, doesn't linger for long. Larger thunderstorms have multiple cells—clusters of storms that combine and feed off each other and that widen and prolong the turbulence. This process sometimes occurs in a predictable pattern, as it does over Florida, where thunderheads form on many afternoons.

Thunderstorms have three stages: developing, mature, and dissipating.

The developing stage, amid high convection turbulence and air movement, is very dangerous, especially for people who are caught unprepared (as frequently happens) or don't take precautions quickly. Lightning can strike ten miles ahead of the storm where skies are still blue—hence the phrase *a bolt out of the blue*. Because every bolt originates in a storm cloud, one can exit from a concealed cloud—a cloud behind a mountain ridge, for instance—and literally streak sideways to hit something miles away. It seemingly strikes from out of nowhere.

The heaviest precipitation, winds, and lightning take place in the mature stage, which can last from a few minutes to several hours. Surprisingly, fewer people are killed or injured during the raging chaos of this stage than during the developing phase, maybe because fewer people are outdoors and exposed.

In the dissipating stage, rain and lightning activity decreases as the storm winds down. But even as thunderheads move away from the immediate region, lightning bolts may continue to strike it. The safety rule is to wait at least thirty minutes after a storm has passed before venturing out.

During the summer in mountainous regions, thunderstorms typically develop between 2 and 6 P.M., the hottest time of day. That's also when the descending angle of the sun's rays prompts a temperature drop higher up in the atmosphere, which in turn creates atmospheric instability. The storm's precipitation snuffs out the warm updrafts of air—its fuel—and the thunderstorm ends. Once again, nature has achieved the homeostatic balance it seeks.

The wise mountaineer follows this rule: *Up high by noon, down low by two.*

◄o►

A STORM CAN GENERATE lightning, its most menacing element, only when hail and ice form in a cloud. When turbulence causes these icy particles to collide, the electrical charges within the cloud divide. Positive charges usually travel to the top and negative charges to the base, thereby creating a giant storage battery. Because the earth below a thunderhead also becomes positively charged, there is a potential for cloud-to-ground electrical transmission. It's the attraction of these opposing charges—also within a cloud and between clouds—that produces lightning. Again, nature equalizes opposing forces and achieves stability.

Various forms of lightning play out. The flash from a discharge within a cloud or between clouds, which often resembles a bursting bomb or fireworks, is called sheet lightning. A single jagged bolt from cloud to ground is streak lightning, and a bolt with multiple branches or "leaders" is forked lightning.

Strong, horizontal winds can cause streak lightning to appear as parallel luminous or blurred bands with multiple flashes, a phenomenon known as ribbon lightning. When parts of a lightning streak are longer lit or brighter than other parts, it is bead lightning, or rocket or chain lightning. Ball lightning is just that—a sphere that seems to float in the air and then disappear in a loud explosion. Typically the size of a baseball, ball lightning can be as much as a foot in diameter. People have seen such lightning balls bounce off walls within a structure or tumble down mountainsides.

When the buildup of opposite charges is insufficient for lightning to form, a coronal discharge or circular bluish glow—or even a mass of sparks—may appear over a high, sometimes pointed object. This phenomenon, first noted at the top of ships' masts, is called St. Elmo's fire, for the patron saint of sailors.

About one in four lightning bolts strikes the ground. These spectacular exchanges between cloud and ground occur when tremendous negative charges of static electricity build in the bottom of a cloud, and positive charges accumulate on the ground.

Their strong attraction to each other creates an electrified or ion-
ized atmosphere that can make the air buzz and crackle, and a person's hair bristle. When the potential for a discharge overwhelms
the insulating air's ability to keep them apart, the negative charges
shoot down toward the positive charges in an invisible, jagged,
zigzag pattern called a stepped leader.

An object on the ground—usually one that is elevated, such as
a tree, building, or rock—may launch a discharge, or lightning
streamers, to connect with the leaders, thus triggering a lightning
bolt, which neutralizes the opposing charges. This process can recur
tens or even hundreds of times in a storm. An observer usually sees
the discharge shooting upward—manifested by upward branching
—to meet the downward-moving stepped leader.

In mountainous areas, where clouds are close to earth, the lightning bolt may be shorter than three hundred feet. In flat country
with high clouds, a cloud-to-earth flash may be as long as four miles
and, in some extreme instances, twenty miles long. The intensely
bright lightning core is extremely narrow—as little as half an inch,
according to some authorities. The core appears to be wider because
it is surrounded by a glow discharge, or corona envelope, that may
be ten to twenty feet wide. The speed of the lightning discharge
varies between a hundred and a thousand miles per second for the
downward leader track and up to eighty-seven thousand miles per
second for the more powerful return stroke. More than one discharge can happen in the same lightning bolt, a process that causes
lighting to flicker until the charges have dissipated.

Sometimes the polarity within a cloud is inverted: Negative
particles ascend and positive ones descend. In inverted polarity,
positive charges in the bottom of the cloud first rush to the ground
and create a lightning channel. Electrons then flow from the
ground up through the channel back to the cloud. Such reversed,
"positive cloud-to-ground" lightning strikes usually carry more
charge, last tens of milliseconds longer, and are less branched than
the more common negative to-ground lightning. Why or how this

reversal of charge occurs is unknown. Indeed, there is much about lightning that remains a mystery.

One hundred lightning bolts strike hit the earth every second, or more than 8.6 million a day. Annually, twenty million lightning bolts strike the ground in the United States.

A lightning bolt can contain an electrical potential of one hundred million volts and reach a temperature of fifty-five thousand degrees Fahrenheit, which is five times hotter than the sun. The average flash is brighter than ten million, hundred-watt lightbulbs. A single strike can generate more energy than all U.S. power plants combined at that instant. Theoretically, a thunderstorm could meet the nation's electricity needs for four days.

Lightning has an impact on more than just the atmosphere: Its electrons can travel beyond the upper atmosphere and affect the radiation belt in the ionosphere for several hundred thousand square miles. A lightning strike in Texas, for example, might influence the radiation belt over South Dakota.

It all happens in a brilliant, single one-thousandth of a second.

◄○►

WHEN INTENSE HEAT generated by lightning causes the surrounding air to expand explosively, the resulting shock wave, also referred to as a sonic boom, is thunder. Sound travels at about eleven hundred feet per second, so it takes five seconds for the sound of thunder to reach someone a mile away. In contrast, light travels at 186,300 miles per second; anyone near or far who has a clear view can see a lightning flash instantaneously. Counting the seconds between a lightning flash and thunderclap is an easy way to gauge how far away the lightning is. Importantly, the distance between one lightning strike and the next in a sequence of strikes can be six to eight miles. If someone hears thunder forty seconds or less after the flash, the lightning is eight miles or less away—in other words, within striking distance of that person. Whenever you can hear thunder, the next lightning bolt can strike you.

When a lightning strike will occur is completely unpredictable. Moreover, there is no safe interval between one bolt and the next; the second may follow almost immediately. *Where* a lightning bolt will hit is more predictable, although still a crapshoot. Lightning usually assails the closest and most accessible object, not necessarily the highest point, as many people believe. It's more a matter of which objects *respond* to electrical charges in the cloud. The downward-moving stepped leader from the cloud draws a reaction or discharge from the closest point, which often is the highest object around, such as a tall tree, rock outcropping, or mountain summit. And contrary to popular belief, metal does not attract lightning. It does, however, concentrate and conduct electricity far more efficiently than most other materials.

After a lightning bolt hits something directly, the electrical charges may then shoot off in multiple directions, conducted by receptive matter such as water or damp ground, rock, or trees.

◄○►

LIGHTNING CAN DEVASTATE a human being. Except for floods, it kills more people in the United States annually than any other weather event. In each of the last thirty years, on average, lightning killed sixty-seven people and injured about three hundred in this country. However, these are only documented cases. The true number of fatalities may be closer to a hundred and the number of injuries well in excess of five hundred—there is no requirement that lightning injuries be reported, and many victims don't seek treatment.

Based on reported data, the odds that people living in America will be struck by lightning are about one in seven hundred thousand. Including the additional estimated deaths and injuries puts the odds at 1 in 240,000. The odds that you will be struck in your lifetime are one in three thousand, while your chance of being affected by someone who has been struck is one in three hundred. Those who live where there are numerous thunderstorms and who spend a lot of time outdoors are at much higher risk.

From 1990 through 2003, the most lightning deaths each year occurred in Florida—twice as many as in any other state—followed by Texas, Colorado, Ohio, and North Carolina. Eighty percent of all lightning fatalities are male. A man playing golf in Florida is at high risk. Tampa Bay has been dubbed the nation's lightning capital.

There are four ways lightning can injure: by striking directly, by striking an object that someone is in contact with, by using the human body as a pathway, and by ground current, also known as step voltage. In each case, injuries may result from the electrical discharge itself or from mechanical trauma—in other words, if the victim is "thrown" by a muscle contraction or suffers a fall. The shock wave from a lightning strike can hurl a person many feet. Those who are thrown on the ground or against a tree, boulder, or other hard obstacle may sustain contusions, internal organ damage, bleeding, fractures, or concussions.

Lightning hits people indirectly much more often than it does directly. A person standing under or near a tree usually is injured or killed by an indirect strike, sometimes referred to as splashing or a side flash. Someone in an enclosure, such as a cave or crevice, or under an overhanging rock, or in a chimney on a rock wall, might be at greater risk: If lightning strikes in the vicinity, the charge can travel on the ground or rock—especially when it's wet—and streak within the enclosed space. Because rock is solid and therefore highly resistant to penetration and the flow of current, lightning shoots across its surface. A person in contact with that surface draws the whipping electrical charge because the human body is far less resistant than the rock.

Some lightning injuries and deaths occur indoors. Lightning can enter homes and buildings directly, through externally exposed wires or pipes, or through the ground. Once inside, electrical, telephone, plumbing, and radio/television systems, and any metal wires or bars in the walls or floor, can conduct the charge. If these things aren't grounded—that is, able to conduct the charge into earth, where it dissipates—the lightning may jump through the air as it seeks a better or different path. A person nearby could become the new conductor. Lightning has claimed the lives of people who were washing dishes, taking a shower or bath, talking on the phone, or standing near an appliance.

Critical to any electrical shock, whether from lightning or a home outlet, is the degree to which it passes through or over a human body. A body's condition can either enhance or minimize that passage. Dry, clean skin tends to resist electricity, while wet skin—say, from rain or sweat—offers little or no resistance and easily becomes a conductor. Even ten to fifty volts, which normally causes only a mild tingling, can generate a strong shock if you have damp, sweaty, salty hands. Increase the voltage to beyond 50 volts and touching a live wire will give you a good jolt—and possibly kill you if you're immersed in water, such as a bathtub. A shock from 220-volt wiring, which is standard in American homes, can cause severe injury or even death. Shocks from industrial accidents (responsible for about eight hundred deaths a year in the United States) typically involve a range of twenty thousand up to sixty-three thousand volts.

But that pales in comparison with one lightning bolt, which typically packs an electrical potential of fifteen million volts.

◄○►

PERHAPS SURPRISINGLY, only about 10 percent of those struck by lightning die. The most dangerous and potentially fatal injuries involve the cardiovascular and neurological systems. The only cause of immediate death from lightning is cardiac arrest or the complications thereof, partly because electrical energy tends to travel through the least resistant parts of the body, especially blood vessels, which lead to the heart. Normally, only immediate and effective cardiovascular pulmonary resuscitation, followed as soon as possible by emergency medical treatment, can save cardiac-arrest victims or help them counter the serious consequences of cerebral hypoxia, a lack of oxygen in the brain. If lightning victims' hearts don't stop, the chances that they will die from any other cause directly attributable to the lightning injury are low—but only if medical care is readily available.

Fortunately for lightning victims, most strikes aren't fatal. Despite the enormous voltage, the current passes over the surface of their body, a process called external flashover. Minimal current enters it. Additionally, the extremely short duration of a lightning shock, measured in milliseconds, results in a very brief flow of current internally or externally. The result: little, if any, skin breakdown. Burns or tissue destruction may be insignificant.

Even though lightning injuries may not be lethal, however, they can be severely traumatic and damaging to the victim and also very stressful for the family. Because such injuries are primarily neurological, they may entail sleep disturbances, memory and attention deficits, dizziness, chronic fatigue, irritability, depression, severe headaches, anxiety attacks, acute pain syndromes, peripheral nerve damage, and fear of storms. A person's "software" gets scrambled. Some victims develop an intense pain syndrome from injury to the nervous system, a condition that is almost impossible to cure. These symptoms may make it impossible for the victim to hold a job, which poses dire financial consequences for the family.

When lightning strikes near the head, it can enter orifices such as the eyes, ears, and mouth. That may explain the myriad eye and ear maladies related to lightning injury. If lightning does flow internally, it can short-circuit the body's electrical systems, leading to temporary tinnitus, blindness, confusion, amnesia, cardiac arrhythmias, and vascular instability. Other indirect consequences may include severe brain damage and seizures caused by hypoxia during cardiac arrest.

Some people have been zapped by lightning more than once. Roy "Dooms" Sullivan, a former ranger in Shenandoah National Park in Virginia, holds the somewhat dubious record. Between 1942 and 1977, he allegedly survived seven lightning strikes—at a campsite, while fishing, in his front yard, backyard, in a fire tower, inside a ranger station, and while driving a Jeep. Sullivan committed suicide in 1983 because someone he loved rejected him.

Far behind this record holder are several people who have been struck "only" three times.

◄◦►

ALTHOUGH LIGHTNING and mountains go hand in hand, the numbers of deaths in mountainous national parks have been surprisingly few. (Data on lightning injuries in the parks are largely unavailable.) Still, even under routine circumstances by park standards, lightning has brought grief to a number of individuals and families.

Most visitors to Yellowstone National Park are aware of the frequent thunderstorms there. Yet lightning deaths since Yellowstone opened in 1872 have totaled only five. One occurred on Yellowstone Lake beneath a blue sky when a bolt from a cloud hidden behind a mountain ridge struck a boater directly in his head. The other four were a canoeist on Lewis Lake, a sheepherder standing next to a lake, a hiker on a mountain ridge who fell two hundred feet after he was struck, and a twenty-one-year-old man who had left his broken-down truck and taken refuge under a large tree during a rainstorm.

Sharing a border with Yellowstone is Grand Teton National Park, with mountain peaks towering above thirteen thousand feet that entice hikers and climbers. Grand Teton, designated a park in 1929, has recorded fatalities since 1950. Lightning has caused just one death there. (Another one occurred just outside the park's boundary on 11,101-foot Table Mountain.) The fatality happened in July 2003 among a party of thirteen climbers. Nearing Grand Teton summit, the climbers began a hasty retreat when a thunderstorm erupted. Six reached a ledge called Friction Pitch, and one, a twenty-five-year-old mother of two tots, settled down alongside a large puddle of water. Suddenly a buzz filled the air; then a colossal lightning bolt lashed the mountain. A climber on the ledge was toppled and plummeted fifty feet before a safety rope arrested his fall; he dangled out in space upside down. Seated next to the woman at puddle's edge was her husband. The lightning knocked him momentarily unconscious. When he awoke, his wife wasn't breathing, her lips and throat were black, and her clothing was shredded. The puddle was gone; lightning had completely vaporized it. Despite intensive CPR, the woman couldn't be revived. In all, seven hikers suffered injuries, five seriously. The clouds parted about three hours later, and two private companies carried out a dangerous two-helicopter rescue operation. In gusting winds one helo picked up the dead and injured one by one from Friction Pitch and whisked them down to a second helo holding at Lower Saddle, where they were flown to the meadows below and then transported to a hospital.*

Rocky Mountain National Park, with its high mountains, numerous trails above ten thousand feet, and frequent thunderstorms, has been the scene of ten lightning deaths. The park boasts the nation's highest continuous paved road—Trail Ridge Road—much of which is above the tree line. The road crosses the Continental Divide at Milner Pass at 12,183 feet. All but two of the fatalities happened above eleven thousand feet, including three alongside Trail Ridge Road. Another three involved climbers on or near mountain peaks. The two exceptions were a motorcyclist and a hiker, both of whom got stuck at about seventy-five hundred feet in elevation.

You might think that lightning is a killer on 14,494-foot Mount Whitney in Sequoia National Park. In fact, there have been only two deaths. The first occurred in 1904 when eight federal fish commissioners were researching golden trout in the region. A thunderstorm broke out, and all but one in the group sought shelter under a rock shelf near the summit. A direct lightning strike killed the exposed man standing on the rock; two of his compan-

---

*The two helicopter pilots, Laurence Perry and Rick Harmon, were both honored with the Pilot of the Year Award for 2003 by Helicopter Association International.

ions were knocked unconscious but survived. The second fatality happened on a July afternoon in 1990 when a thunderstorm battered the summit. All thirteen people there felt the ground zinging; their hair stood on end. They took shelter in the Smithsonian Hut located on the summit, a historic structure with rock walls, a cement floor, and a corrugated iron roof. While inside, the hikers heard the rock walls and concrete humming, followed by several booms and a bright flash. Then, according to eyewitnesses, a white and yellow ball of lightning one foot in diameter bounced off each of the four walls before exploding in a loud crack. One person was knocked unconscious, another suffered third-degree burns, and the rest incurred minor burns and numbness. The unconscious victim, a twenty-six-year-old man, stopped breathing and had no heartbeat; intensive CPR by those in the hut failed to revive him. A helicopter evacuated him to a hospital, where he was pronounced dead.

His family and three people who were injured filed suit against the National Park Service, contending it should have posted a warning about the danger of occupying the hut in a storm. The court upheld their claim.*

Sequoia National Park was the site of another lightning fatality. It took place on Moro Rock, a 6,725-foot granite dome that juts out from the forested surroundings like a giant thumb. Much as on Half Dome, a quarter-mile trail follows Moro Rock's contour and leads hikers up a 325-foot elevation gain to the summit, which offers a sweeping view of the Great Western Divide to the east. Some sections of the human-made, five-foot-wide trail are concrete, and large granite slabs have been placed elsewhere as steps. An iron railing traces the outer side of the trail, while a rock wall borders the other side.

On August 20, 1975, about twenty-five people—half of them children between seven and fifteen years old—were on the Moro Rock summit trail. The day was clear—only three cottony cumu-

---

*The disposition of this lawsuit will be covered in chapter 10, Aftermath.

lus clouds occupied the distant sky. But the clouds consolidated, enlarged, and started moving swiftly toward Moro Rock. Soon a sea of black loomed over the dome. It started to sprinkle. Several hikers felt electricity in the air; hands tingled and hair bristled. The sprinkles morphed into a deluge of rain, then a barrage of hail, prompting most of the hikers to retreat hastily to their cars.

One party halfway up the trail included Lawrence Brady and his wife, mother, and two sons (ages seven and nine), along with the wife's brother and mother. To escape the driving hail, they hugged the rock wall while heading back down. Brady's shoulder was leaning against the granite when a ferocious lightning bolt struck, illuminating Moro Rock in a spectacular flash. Electrical charges streaked about the dome, blasting stone into fragments wherever the trail's iron pipe touched it and sending rock splinters and dust into the air.

Brady exclaimed, "My God, we've been hit by lightning!"

His wife checked first on their two screaming sons, then him. By then, the thirty-one-year-old man was lying facedown on his mother-in-law's lap, unconscious. The electrical charge must have struck his shoulder before it shot across his body, giving him just enough time to utter something. When his wife turned him over, she saw his pupils beginning to dilate and his tongue in a gag reflex. She hit him hard in the chest a couple of times, then cleared his airway and mouth with her fingers and began mouth-to-mouth resuscitation. A trained nurse arrived to help with CPR. After several more minutes, two park officials appeared and took charge. They administered oxygen.

Meanwhile, two other rangers came racing up the trail to check on another victim, Edward Schieler, a thirty-eight-year-old man who had been struck directly in the head while snapping photos on the summit. The lightning whizzed down his entire body, shredded all his clothes, exposed even his genitals, and blew off his left hiking boot. Only the cuff of his pants clung to the shod foot. The blast threw him beyond the railing, where his convulsing body teetered near the edge, about to topple over to certain death. Fortunately, his uninjured cousin was able to lift him back. He and another man grasped Schieler's arms and legs and began carting him down the trail. When the two rangers met them, the victim's eyes were slightly dilated, his pulse was weak and fast, and his coloration slightly bluish. He was incoherent and his body shook violently, but he was still breathing. Blood oozed from his ear and nose, and burn wounds and cuts covered his entire front side. A hole the size of a quarter perforated the bottom of his left foot. On the stretcher, he twisted and turned. His arms lashed out reflexively, and at one point he grabbed the railing. He vomited twice, which forced the rangers to stop and turn him on his side so he wouldn't choke. They doubted he would survive.

In the case of Brady, rangers continued administering oxygen and CPR to the man where he lay, despite the still-raging storm. At one point, his pupils constricted back to normal, his lips and ears became pink, and his tongue relaxed. But soon, his pupils began dilating again and his skin returned to a bluish tint. He had "doll's eyes"—completely blank. Further efforts to revive him were futile. More than an hour after the lightning first struck, the rangers concluded that he was gone. They asked the family to go to the nearby visitor center so the two young boys would be spared the sight of their father, then hoisted him down to the parking lot. An ambulance took him to a hospital, where he was pronounced dead.

Schieler also was taken to a hospital. Doctors there determined he had a severe skull fracture, probable brain damage, and injuries to his arteries and organs. He remained in critical condition for several days and was hospitalized for three weeks. According to his physician, Schieler's exceptionally strong heart kept him alive. But he sustained a total loss of hearing in one ear and a 90 percent loss in the other. A hernia protruded into his bowel; the resulting blockage caused severe hemorrhoids that eventually had to be surgically removed. Ever since the episode, he has suffered bouts of acute depression and fits of imbalance that have prevented enjoy-

ment of most physical activities. Kidney and prostate problems
also developed years later. He was unable to work again, and his
family endured financial hardship.

Mr. Schieler and Mrs. Brady each filed suit against the National
Park Service. They argued that a sign should have been posted
warning hikers about the danger of hiking on Moro Rock in thunderstorms. The courts did not uphold this lawsuit.*

—◄o►—

UP TO 1985, only three lightning deaths had definitely occurred in
Yosemite, with a fourth possibility. The first happened in May
1921, when lightning struck a worker at Hetch Hetchy Reservoir, and the second in July 1936, when a middle-age man was
killed at the Tuolumne Meadows garbage dump.

The third took place on August 27, 1972. Randall Boone and
Edward Williams were on the first leg of a two-week camping
adventure when they departed Yosemite Valley at midmorning en
route to Half Dome. These best of friends, both in their late teens,
had graduated the previous year from Serramonte High School in
Daly City, just south of San Francisco.

Only one downy-white cumulus cloud drifted in the west as
they ascended the trail past Vernal and Nevada falls. The sky
directly above was still blue when Boone and Williams started up
Sub Dome. But by that time, the single cloud—behind Half
Dome, out of view—had joined other cumulus clouds to form a
giant thunderhead that eclipsed lower Yosemite Valley and was
moving rapidly.

Atop Half Dome, they encountered a gray, leaden cloud mass,
its furls folding over one another like ocean waves. As Boone and
Williams savored the sweeping vistas at 3:30 P.M., the dense cloud
suddenly unleashed a torrent. The pair weren't prepared for rain,
so they frantically sought cover in and around the rock forms

---

* The disposition of this lawsuit will be covered in chapter 10, Aftermath.

sprinkled about the smooth granite surface. Near the edge, they peered down into a crevice and spotted refuge—a chamber tucked within a jumble of rocks. A solid stone ceiling kept it dry.

Nearby, a hollow, two-foot-high iron pipe jutted up. Someone had drilled a hole in the granite and planted the pipe there for an unknown reason.

Boone and Williams slid into the shelter. It was the driest place on Half Dome, aside from a tent. Within minutes, two other damp hikers squeezed in. The four men huddled together while the storm played out its drama. Through openings in the rock, they saw lightning slice occasionally through the thick, wet air.

Boone reached for his camera in the hope of snagging a photo. That's the last thing he remembers. Lightning hammered the Dome and shot through the cave, slamming his head against the stone wall and knocking him out.

When he regained consciousness, Boone saw Williams slumped over, not breathing. The other two occupants, who also had been knocked unconscious briefly, were alert by then, too. No one knew CPR. Boone frantically attempted to breathe air into his best friend's mouth, and when that didn't revive Williams, the three men hastily carried him a couple of hundred yards over to where other campers were. One tried unsuccessfully to find a pulse. Boone again tried mouth-to-mouth resuscitation but finally gave up. Williams was dead.

Park officials attributed Williams's death to the iron pipe. Lightning had struck the pipe, they theorized, zoomed into the chamber via wet granite, entered the back of Williams's head where it rested against the rock, and exited from his foot. Rangers ultimately sawed off the iron pipe, leaving a protrusion less than two inches long.

Yosemite's records on a fourth fatality possibly due to lightning are not definitive. The case is instructive nonetheless. In June, Timothy Clark, 22 years old, had been hiking in Yosemite's high country when he got caught in a lightning storm. Desperate, he abandoned all of his gear, descended the mountain and hiked five miles back to Merced Lake High Sierra Camp, where he told persons he got struck by lightning. Observers noted during the next couple of days that he behaved strangely and was somewhat disoriented about his location. After another two days had passed, Clark set out on the four-mile hike back to Yosemite Valley. He left the trail at one point, walked onto a grassy ledge, and apparently fell to the switchback below. Hikers later stumbed upon his body and notified a trail crew working at Merced Lake. Authorities later confirmed that Clark had died as a result of the fall. But if he had indeed been struck by lightning as he claimed, then it may have been the true culprit by causing erratic behavior that led to the mishap.

◄O►

ON SATURDAY, JULY 27, 1985, as the Rice, Hoog, and Cage parties, along with other hikers, tramped toward Half Dome, another tragedy was unfolding just to the south.

Kings Canyon National Park, which borders Sequoia National Park, is only forty miles from Yosemite as the crow flies. It took John Muir several weeks to travel there from Yosemite Valley with a pack mule named Brownie. His purpose was to locate groves of giant sequoia trees, an effort that eventually led to their protection from timber mills. Today the drive from Yosemite Valley to the lower reaches of Kings Canyon takes three or four hours.

James Wunrow, twenty-seven, who worked on a park survey crew in Kings Canyon, left early that Saturday morning for a day hike by himself. He didn't tell anyone where he was going; nor did anyone see him leave, including the ranger who at 7 A.M. opened the Roads End Permit Station at Cedar Grove, located at the eastern end of the canyon. Wunrow must have started up Bubbs Creek Trail before the ranger arrived, aiming for the high country.

In 1984, while trimming trees for the Forest Service in Superior National Forest in Minnesota, Wunrow had touched a live power line and received a severe shock. Ever since, he had been prone to intense headaches. His co-workers and supervisors in Kings Canyon found Wunrow to be extremely introverted and often depressed, even disoriented at times. Wunrow wasn't a skilled or knowledgeable outdoorsman. He took only day hikes, always alone, and stayed on maintained trails.

The weather pattern that week had been consistent—warm, clear mornings followed by a buildup of midafternoon storm clouds, then an hour or two of heavy rain and some lightning. On that particular Saturday, however, thunderheads began building earlier, around midday. By one o'clock, a severe thunderstorm had moved east from Kern Canyon into the Bubbs Creek drainage. At one thirty, Wunrow was hiking back when, about four miles from the Cedar Grove trailhead, a violent thunderstorm swept in, producing high winds, drenching rains, fierce hail, and frequent lightning bursts. He was on a moderately forested hillside at sixty-three hundred feet in elevation, about three hundred feet below the ridgeline and up from the gully where Bubbs Creek flows. Wearing only a T-shirt, jeans, and baseball cap, Wunrow donned a long-sleeved wool shirt that he had wisely brought along. He hurriedly searched for shelter and spotted a rock formation just off the trail. On the side of the formation away from the trail was an opening formed by two boulders and covered by a large stone slab—a small, cave-like structure about five feet wide, four feet deep, and two and a half feet high. He crawled in and lay down to escape the downpour.

Around ten the next morning, a woman backpacking up the trail saw Wunrow's boots and part of his day pack sticking out from the rock shelter. Only someone ascending the trail could have seen them. But she assumed that the person inside was napping, so she continued on. The same thing happened an hour later when another backpacker came up the trail. He didn't stop, either.

Backpackers Steven King and Marvin Talbert set out on the Bubbs Creek Trail later that afternoon. Three miles up, they met a ranger coming down who, citing a bear nuisance, advised the two men to stow their food properly. It was around five o'clock when they approached the rock structure and saw Wunrow's boots. At first, like the two earlier hikers, King and Talbert assumed someone was resting inside. But on second glance, the feet seemed to be at an odd angle, so they decided to investigate.

Wunrow lay on his left side in a semi-fetal position, steel-rim eyeglasses askew on his face, his right arm at his side, and his left arm resting on the ground.

Hey, buddy. You okay?

No response.

They noticed that Wunrow's fingernails were purple, a condition that King, a police officer, recognized as being caused by a lack of blood circulation. He looked closer and concluded that Wunrow was dead. King's training had taught him that any death could be a homicide, so he didn't touch the body. On the left side of Wunrow's head was a wound—it looked liked a bite of some sort—and there was a small rip in the back of his shirt. These signs and the ranger's earlier warning triggered a question in King's mind: Had a bear killed this man?

King and Talbert marked the spot with handkerchiefs and returned immediately to Cedar Grove, where they called the ranger dispatch office. The park dispatcher, in turn, contacted rangers Debbie Bird and Richard Fishbaugh, who packed overnight gear and headed up the trail. They arrived at the fatality scene around 10 P.M.

Illuminating the body with their flashlights, Bird and Fishbaugh didn't see any evidence of an animal attack. In any case, fatal attacks by black bears were very rare. The rangers considered hypothermia, although Wunrow's wool shirt should have provided adequate warmth. Then they detected a singed hair on the victim's scalp, which raised the specter of lightning. But the evidence wasn't conclusive. They could only speculate that Wunrow had died of hypothermia or from a natural cause such as heart attack, or had been struck by lightning. They radioed in their report and pitched camp.

The next morning, a helicopter brought Fresno County coroner Robert Hensel to the scene. He examined the body and noted a small puncture with dried blood in the victim's scalp, behind his right ear. Hensel thought it might be a gunshot wound, but then quickly determined it was superficial and probably caused by an ear loop on Wunrow's wire-frame glasses. However, on the left side of the head were numerous burned and singed hairs, and almost imperceptible wounds that looked like tiny hemorrhages. Body hairs on the right wrist, lower back, and just above both knees also were singed. Midway down and in the center of the back was scarred tissue, as if someone had bored small holes in the skin and created little craters with black, cauterized edges. Hensel concluded that lightning caused the wounds—that the electrical charge had entered Wunrow's head, traveled through his body, and sparked a fatal cardiac arrest.

Exactly how Wunrow had been struck wasn't at all clear. There weren't any signs of a lightning strike in the vicinity, nor any high trees or jutting rock formations nearby to attract a bolt. But surely lightning had hit somewhere, perhaps on the ridge, and streaked across the moist ground into the rock enclosure where Wunrow lay. The damp conditions, including his wet clothes and skin, obviously placed him at greater risk. His death, a chance occurrence, illustrates the fickle nature of lightning.

The savage storm that had erupted in Kings Canyon and claimed Wunrow's life was part of a larger, intense weather system rumbling north toward Yosemite.

—◦—

BILL PIPPEY AND BRUCE JORDAN were setting a furious pace, hoping to outrace the burgeoning storm. Close behind, Tom Rice and Adrian Esteban made a quick stop at their secret spring. Brian Jordan soon joined them. Meanwhile, Mike Hoog's party leapfrogged ahead. The hikers weren't unfriendly with each other, but neither did they mingle or banter back and forth in good spirits, as hikers often do. Those with Hoog still viewed Rice's band as rowdy and crude. Back at Nevada Fall, someone—maybe Pippey—had jokingly referred to Hoog's party as a "bunch of weenies."

Leaving Nevada Fall, Weiner felt encouraged that the remaining distance wouldn't be as steep. Still, he and Frith plodded. The pair fell behind again, in part because they stopped every ten to fifteen minutes to trade off carrying the forty-five-pound backpack but also because Weiner was fast becoming exhausted, especially his leg muscles, which were cramping up due to dehydration. They gulped down the last of their water. Esteban had told them about the secret spring, but Weiner and Frith couldn't locate it. Other hikers they asked didn't know its whereabouts, either. Though Weiner wanted to take a longer rest, Frith, gung-ho as ever, urged that they push on and catch up with the others.

Pippey and Bruce Jordan were shooting to reach the top first. For Pippey, it was more than a competitive thing; he was proud to be in good physical shape. So, despite the intimidating weather, the two hikers plowed ahead, never stopping. They ignored the danger warning at the base of Sub Dome and never once pondered the potential hazards as they scrambled up the cables on Half Dome.

But a hundred feet up, Pippey's stomach suddenly became bloated.

Pippey: "One minute, I'm fine. The next, I can barely keep my bowels from exploding."

In a voice loud enough for Jordan to hear, he uttered, Yes, God, I understand.

Clearly, Pippey thought, a very powerful force was trying to discourage him from going up there. He and Jordan retreated down the cables so Pippey could relieve himself.

◄○►

ESTEBAN AND RICE, with Brian Jordan not far behind, were putting on steam to reach the summit ahead of the storm. Two wild-eyed young climbers—Ken Bokelund and Rob Foster—scampering down the trail advised Esteban and Rice, Don't go up there—it's too dangerous, then continued on down toward the Valley, obviously in a rush to get off the mountain.

The warning sparked rather than doused Esteban's and Rice's motivation to pick up the pace.

Esteban: "If there was one trait that set Rice apart from everyone else, it was his strong will. When he committed himself to something, it was all or nothing."

Esteban, of course, was Rice's alter ego—just as tough mentally, just as unswerving in grit and determination. Neither was likely to cower when he faced a physical challenge or risky situation on his own. Together, such a response was unthinkable.

Buchner and Ellner still poked along somewhere far behind. A fearful Ellner wanted no part of a lightning storm. His snail's pace and constant complaining angered Buchner, who didn't like being held back. When the two were about halfway between Nevada Fall and Sub Dome, lightning flashed ahead and thunder growled. A shaken Ellner slowed even more. The next lightning burst prompted him to turn around abruptly and pound back down the trail.

Buchner dropped his pack and ran after him, arguing, It's crazy to go back down now!

He persuaded Ellner to hike toward Half Dome. If necessary, Buchner said, they would camp at the base.

◄○►

HOOG'S GROUP METHODICALLY clawed away at the miles between them and Half Dome. In addition to all of his camping gear and supplies, Hoog hauled a three-gallon water container weighing more than twenty-five pounds. The five hikers arrived at the camping area beneath Sub Dome soon after the retreating Pippey and Jordan. Although dark clouds were moving in, the blue sky directly above still glistened.

Without hesitation, Hoog led his group up Sub Dome but didn't get far before he encountered a gentleman descending the granite stairs. The older hiker, who was fiftyish and carried a staff, said a storm was about to hit and strongly advised Hoog and his companions not to continue up.

Heed the sign, he said, referring to the public warning that Pippey and Bruce Jordan had ignored.

Hoog badly wanted to spend the night on Half Dome. Initially, he dismissed the man's cautionary words and was about to press on. On second thought, however, the advice seemed wise. Hoog stared at the stairs for several long seconds, deliberating. Then he and his four cohorts turned around and retraced their steps. The gentleman had already disappeared from view.

The third party back was Cage's, which held a steady pace. All members of his troupe were experienced backpackers, so they didn't think much about the oncoming storm, a familiar phenomenon in the Sierra Nevada. They would continue hiking through the forest, and if the weather got nasty, the group would simply stop, wait, and decide what to do next.

Esteban and Rice charged up the trail. Just below Sub Dome, they encountered Hoog's group in retreat. Dan Crozier repeated the gentleman hiker's precaution.

Rice brushed by Crozier, muttering, Someone's gotta do it.

He and Esteban pushed on.

Adrian Esteban
on outdoor outing,
pre-1985.

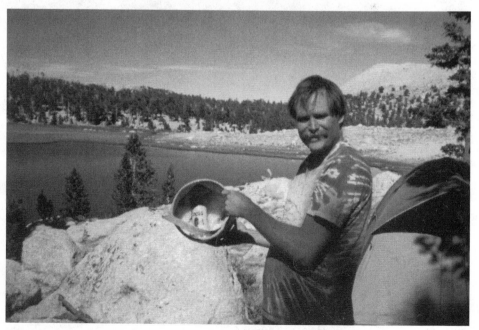

Bill Pippey on Mt. Whitney trip, pre-1985.

Adrian Esteban makes the leap at Paradise.

Ken Bokelund
climbing
Half Dome.

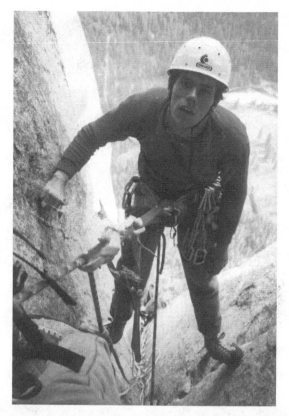

Rob Foster
on the face of
Half Dome.

View from inside the cave.

View looking out past the King's Chair.

Rick Pedroncelli, Linda Crozier, Mike Hoog, and Jennie Hayes waiting out the storm.

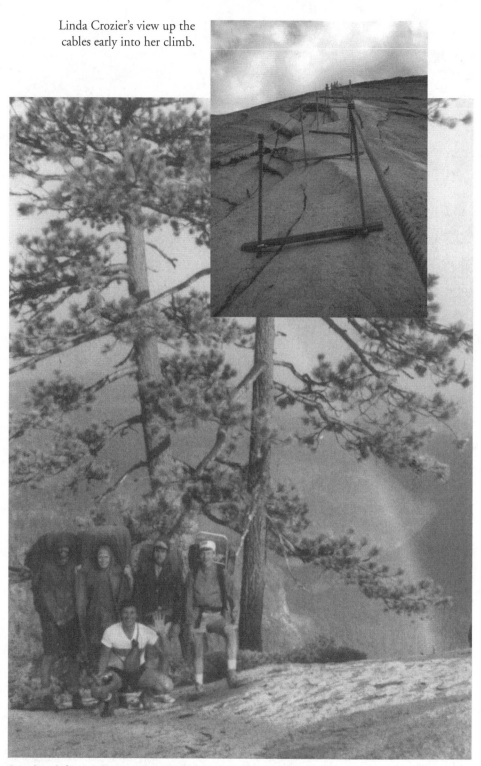

Linda Crozier's view up the cables early into her climb.

Standing left to right: Zip Cotter, Steve White, Clu Cotter, Monroe Bridges. Brian Cage in foreground.

Ranger Colin
Campbell on his
horse, John Paul.

Half Dome on the evening of July 27, 1985, after lightning had struck.
(photo by Ken Bokelund)

Medi-Flight pilot, Al Major.

Medi-Flight helicopter on Half Dome's
summit during rescue operation.

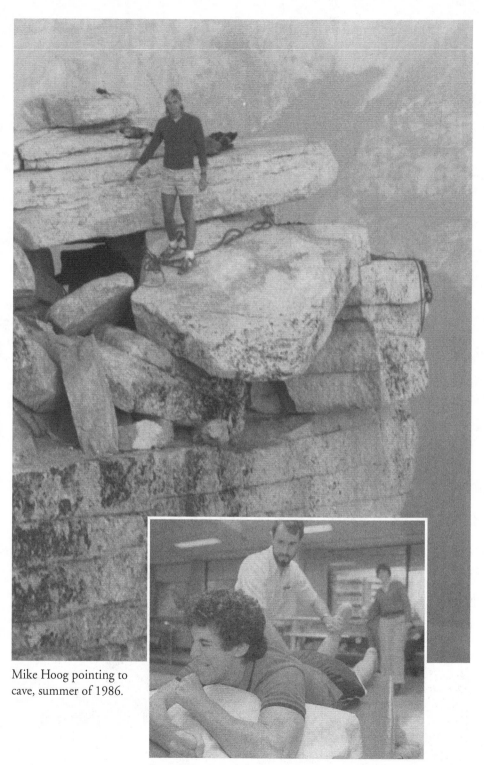

Mike Hoog pointing to cave, summer of 1986.

Bruce Weiner undergoing physical therapy weeks after the episode.

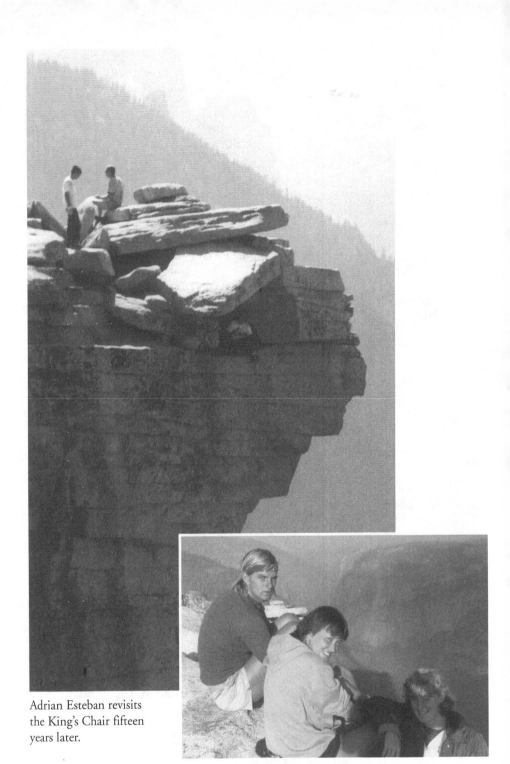

Adrian Esteban revisits the King's Chair fifteen years later.

Mike Hoog, Linda Crozier, and Jennie Hayes revisit Half Dome the following summer

6

FIRST STRIKE

*Zigzag lances of lightning followed each other in quick
succession, and the thunder was so gloriously loud and
massive it seemed as if surely an entire mountain was
being shattered at every stroke.*—John Muir

Well ahead of their companions, Esteban and Rice reached
the bottom of the cables at 5:40 P.M. and appraised the
impending storm. Heavy dark clouds in multihued layers already
blanketed the sky and sagged into the mountain cavities. Lightning continued playing over the ridges and spires, and thunder
rumbled like battleship guns nearby.

They stared up at the top of Half Dome six hundred feet away, shrouded in mist. Nobody else was in sight. Their take-no-prisoners pace had put them ahead of the pack when Bill Pippey forfeited the lead due to a bilious stomach.

Rice and Esteban now had to weigh their next move. A strong climber could ascend in less than fifteen minutes; they had done it themselves many times. Their thirty-five-pound backpacks would be a hindrance, but the threat of lightning would spur them on. At the top, they'd reach the cave's shelter in less than five minutes.

Roughly twenty minutes in all, then. Risk it or not?

While a lightning bolt might possibly strike the granite slope near them or even hit the cables they would be clinging to, a strike higher up, on or near the summit, was far more likely. The trouble was, even if lightning struck at the top, a potent charge could streak anywhere on wet surfaces. Anyplace on the mountain would be dangerous if Half Dome were coated with water.*

As Esteban measured the sky, he felt drizzle on his upturned face and blinked. Hard rain, he sensed, wasn't far off.

Neither of them spoke as they peered up the cables. Rice was the undisputed leader, and Esteban, ever the good soldier, would accept his decision. If Rice expressed doubts or caution, Esteban would mull them, but he didn't really expect dialogue. When the pair faced challenges, they seldom resorted to reasoned deliberation and judgment. Instead, they trusted their guts and seized opportunities for adventure. From that standpoint, this storm was no different from past hazards. Together they would improvise to meet all threats. The two exchanged a glance and Esteban knew the decision had been made.

Fuck it, Rice muttered. This is our mountain—let's just do it!

Okay, Esteban replied.

---

*In June 1963, a lightning bolt struck rain-dampened granite near the top of the cables, streaked across the rock, and hit the cables and approximately fifteen hikers gripping them. They screamed as the electrical charge clutched their hands and whipped across their arms and chests. No one was killed, but several incurred severe burns.

He realized nothing would deter Rice now. Nor, despite some apprehension, did he really want to deter him. The two were connected by karma, were brothers in arms. Esteban wouldn't let his brother down. The others would have to look out for themselves while they waited out the storm.

It's you and me, Esteban said, believing that only he and Rice would be heading into the vortex.

Shirtless despite the growing coolness, Rice moved rapidly toward the cables, Esteban immediately behind him. As if cued by their movements, a mosaic of jagged lightning streaked the sky followed by rolling claps.

Before the thunder had faded, Esteban's sixth sense kicked in with a sensation of foreboding. He took a few more steps, then stopped and called to Rice.

Whatever happens, he said, I want you to know I love you, man.

Rice turned with a quizzical expression. After a moment's hesitation, he gripped Esteban's outstretched hand and said he loved him, too. Then he attacked the slope.

Their legs drove hard against the granite and their arms strained at the metal cables. Atmospheric energy seemed to draw them magnetically as they ramped upward in a fury. Esteban imagined the scene as a vast battlefield, explosions drawing nearer, the thunder a precursor to combat. Despite his repressed fear, or perhaps because of it, Esteban felt more alive at that moment than at any time in his life. His senses seemed heightened far beyond their normal range. Perhaps, he thought, this is the kind of rush other extreme thrill-seekers experience when they surf a twenty-foot wave, bungee jump off a high bridge, skydive, rock climb a big wall, or ski off a cliff. Never before had he and Rice felt this level of intensity.

He became aware of Rice talking, of words spilling out quickly. Rice offered dire calculations about what could happen to them if lightning zapped the cables. Maybe he was just trying to ratchet up the thrill level. Or maybe he was indulging his engineer's mind.

In any case, they both jerked their hands off the steel cables each time deadly brilliance lit the skies.

As if it mattered.

With lightning, there was no margin for last-second adjustments.

◄o►

THE STRAGGLERS IN THEIR GROUP were spread out some distance behind. Closest to Rice and Esteban, and at that moment approaching the top of Sub Dome, was Brian Jordan. He'd split from the others early on, content to hike at his own pace. Proud of the stamina he was displaying and eager to impress the older men and make his mark as a budding outdoorsman, he followed in Rice and Esteban's footsteps without a second thought.

Farther back were Frith and Weiner. The warning sign at the base of Sub Dome stared at them as they approached the stairs. A concerned Weiner wondered aloud if they should stop and wait out the storm. Frith assured him that refuge—the cave—awaited them at the summit. Once there we'll be safe, he said, repeating Rice and Esteban's mantra.

Weiner's legs were still cramping. He doubted he could make it up those stairs. If he delayed much longer, however, his muscles might tighten further and completely rule out a final ascent, even after the storm passed. Soon it would start raining. Where could they find shelter in a drenching downpour? As the newcomer in the group, Weiner didn't want to hold anyone else back, especially Frith, whose heart and soul were committed to summiting Half Dome on this day.

We're close, Frith urged. We'll be able to dry off and rest in the cave.

Believing he had little choice at this point but to continue, and mustering every last bit of his physical strength, Weiner forced his aching legs to move step by step up the punishing staircase.

Once atop Sub Dome, they caught a glimpse of Rice and Esteban nearing Half Dome's summit just as clouds unleashed pouring rain. There it is! Frith said excitedly. One last push and we've made it! The two donned ponchos, dropped down to the base of the cables, and started up the granite slope.

The possibility of mortal danger occurred to neither of them.

◄o►

RICE AND ESTEBAN surmounted the final incline and hit the summit running. Though they had ignored the signs warning of danger, they still were acutely aware of their vulnerability. Lightning would strike the Dome—it was only a matter of when. In effect, the pair had engaged nature in a round of Russian roulette. But the rain-drenched air remained mercifully free from that terrifying flash as they dashed across the summit toward shelter.

They dropped their packs at the cave entrance and scrambled in. We made it! they yelled jubilantly and high-fived each other, then reclined on the rocky floor, energy and emotions spent.

It was 6 P.M.

Minutes later, Esteban heard someone yell his name. He clambered back out and was astonished to see Brian Jordan standing on the summit and peering around, a worried look on his face. Esteban beckoned to him, motioning urgently. As the boy hustled over, Esteban saw Frith and Weiner appear at the summit's edge. Esteban and Rice's presumption that they alone would challenge the storm by summiting Half Dome was flawed.

Come on! Esteban yelled.

It's absolutely bitching! Frith gushed when he reached the cave entrance. It's everything you said it was!

Rice, who had stripped his drenched clothes in the cave, emerged nude to greet the new arrivals. Laughing, he broke into a dance of celebration, feet jigging on the rough granite, rain pelting his body. Caught up in his euphoria, the others slapped hands and shuffled their feet; that is, except for Weiner, who was near collapse.

Bring on the lightning show! somebody yelled as they settled down in the enclosure.

The newcomers cast off their backpacks and sought space in the tight quarters. After pushing so hard up the mountain, they were relieved to be in the cave's shelter; in their minds the thick granite walls and ceiling provided an invincible fortress against the raging storm. Later, when the storm ended and the others rejoined them, they would celebrate their accomplishment in full.

Brian Jordan was flush with pleasure. The youngster had demonstrated he could aim high and hit his goal. If he could climb Half Dome in the face of a storm, he could accomplish just about anything. He sat squeezed between two backpacks, savoring the glow of his triumph and pleased to be there with the veterans Esteban and Rice.

Bruce Weiner had amazed even himself. He'd completed his first hike—to the top of a famous mountain, no less. Though practically numb from pain and fatigue, he felt supremely proud. The easterner had proven he could measure up when it counted. Best of all, he'd done it in the company of Bob Frith.

If Frith was tired, he didn't show it. He exuded his customary jovial spirit. Being there on the top of Half Dome, he told everyone, was the high point of his twenty-four years. Now that he'd discovered the wonders of mountains, he intended to make these marvelous treks many times. Nowhere but in California could he experience something like this. He and Weiner would share many future adventures. Life was very good indeed.

In his quiet manner, Esteban also enjoyed a sense of profound fulfillment. He believed he was right where he belonged, having journeyed once again to his personal mecca. While he couldn't find the precise words to describe this feeling, he was one with the elements in this spot, no question about it. Others might find their mystical connections elsewhere, but for Esteban, those connections were here, with Rice. Sharing the sanctity of the moment with newcomers only deepened his appreciation.

Rice, too, had reason to be pleased. He'd seized the moment and led the way up the granite monolith. He'd inspired the others to confront their fears and challenge the storm. More than ever before, Rice's bond with this mountain seemed firmly cemented. The Dome was sacred, a primal link to nature. What he found here transcended the material realm and imbued him with a higher purpose: to remain physically and morally fit.

The rain turned colder. Hailstones began clattering on the rocks. The five men dug into their packs for dry clothes—long pants, sweatshirts, sweaters. The small cave obliged them to huddle, which generated a soothing body heat. Some broke out trail mix and granola bars. Rice, now clothed in shorts and a sweatshirt, reached into his pack for a small head of broccoli to munch on.

Anyone got beer? Esteban asked.

Only Pippey, somebody answered, which drew laughter and speculation about how long it would take their usually hard-hiking companion and the other Jordan twin to join them.

Esteban slid over near the cave's entrance and lit his camping stove. He brought water to a boil, then carefully carried a tin cup of tea with him out to the ledge. The hail had ceased and the rain slackened.

Come check out the greatest scene in the world! he called back to Frith as he settled down on the King's Chair.

Frith crawled over the boulder and came face-to-face with the twenty-two-hundred-foot drop to the rocky slabs. He swallowed nervously and cautiously lowered himself down beside Esteban. With his legs dangling over the edge and nothing but emptiness before him, Frith confessed he'd never experienced anything like this before.

This is unreal, he said, searching for the right words. It was worth everything to get here.

Esteban nodded pleasurably.

We're on top of the world, man, he said. The gods are smiling on us.

The time was 6:25 P.M.

◄○►

EARLIER, BILL PIPPEY, having voided his stomach and intestines, finally was ready to move on. With Bruce Jordan he retraced his steps up Sub Dome and started up the cables in the chill rain, dense, ominous clouds overhead. The two men were only twenty feet up the cables when an enormous bolt lashed the rounded surface of North Dome directly across the Valley. Like a laser light show, the jagged streak shuddered in place for almost a full second.

Jordan halted and said he was scared and wanted to stop. Pippey studied him. Under normal circumstances, he might have cheered the youngster on. But now, dehydrated and severely weakened from diarrhea, he was in a different frame of mind. And this was hardly a normal situation.

Got no quarrel with that, he said agreeably.

Actually, he thought, it's damn sensible.

They headed back down to the base camp, where they quickly pitched their tent. At about six fifteen, they hunkered down to wait out the storm. Pippey fished beer from his pack. While consuming it, they had little concern about the tremendous light show flashing all around them outside, feeling secure in their shelter. The pyrotechnics peaked at six thirty with a ferocious explosion that lit up their nylon tent as if a billion flashbulbs had detonated.

◄○►

FARTHER DOWN, Brian Cage and his group reached tree line during the storm's crescendo. The edge of the forest provided a good view of Half Dome. In disbelief, they spotted men moving above the cables, seemingly among the storm clouds.

Shaking their heads, Cage's group put on all available rain gear and gathered under the arms of a big Jeffrey pine. There they clustered against the trunk, fairly warm and dry and in good spirits, although not as protected as they might have assumed.* They broke out crackers and salami, passed around a bottle of Yukon

---

*Tall trees, like other high spires, are natural targets for lightning. During this storm, a female hiker took refuge under a tree. A stringer from a lightning bolt struck the tree and the electrical charge shot down the wet trunk and along the exposed roots under her feet, delivering a jarring shock to her and searing each of her fingernails.

Jack, and settled back to wait. There was still plenty of daylight to get to the summit if the storm let up. If it didn't, they would camp somewhere near their present position.

From beneath the Jeffrey pine, they watched the lightning grow ever more intense as flash after flash illuminated the sky. It seemed to pinpoint Half Dome. Suddenly an enormous, radiant blast shattered the air, followed immediately by a piercing *boom*—the loudest thunder crack Cage had ever heard. Another flash arrived moments later. He watched as the bolt shot across the summit of Half Dome, then made a 180-degree turn to strike at the lip of the overhang there. Though he had grown up in Oregon and seen his share of electrical storms, Cage was awestruck. Never had he seen lightning take such a radical path. Nor had he ever heard anything to match the brain-splitting *craack-boom* that resonated off the granite walls.

He later described his group's reaction:

Frankly, it scared the crap out of us.

―◦―

MIKE HOOG'S GROUP made shelter in an open area by spreading a plastic sheet on the ground and covering it with a large tarp overhead. The hikers lay under the tarp in their sleeping bags and ate trail mix, salami, cheese, and crackers. Although they were close to Half Dome, they had decided to complete their hike the next day. Meanwhile, the storm raged. Linda Crozier felt as if the clouds were closing in around them, which made everything murky and ominous. The pounding thunder was louder than ever, a relentless assault on her ears. Lightning, it seemed, was striking everywhere at once.

In fact, though, at the eye of this hell broken loose stood Half Dome.

―◦―

THE OPENINGS IN THE CAVE afforded eerie, fleeting images cast in ghostly hues. Lightning tracers glowed—the veins of an irate god?—as thunderclaps battered the granite formations again and again. Inside the enclosure sat Rice, Weiner, and Brian Jordan. For the moment, Rice had little to say. The youthful Jordan was sand-wiched between two pack frames. Weiner was bent forward, adjusting his bootlaces.

Outside, Esteban and Frith sat in the King's Chair.

Did you hear that? Esteban asked suddenly.

What? Frith looked at him. Hear what?

That funny buzzing—it seemed to fill the air.

You must be high, Frith told him. I didn't hear anything.

Esteban laughed. Whatever, he said. True, he was high. But not on drugs. No drug could produce the kind of elation he was feeling.

He sobered slightly as the buzzing sounded again. This time, Frith heard it. Their hair bristled. The air seemed to crackle, like sizzling bacon, but neither man grasped its portent. Frith relaxed and began to say again how unbelievably bitching all this was, just awesome, the greatest experience of his life.

Distracted, Esteban turned to crawl up over the boulder back into the cave. With his left hand on the rock for balance, he pushed off on his left leg, his right poised in midair. At that instant, the cave exploded with a cataclysmic roar as lightning ripped across its surfaces.

Esteban was slammed against a wall, his left hand pinned there as if by an electromagnet. He thought he saw his arm inflating and warping and twisting like something grossly overcooking in a microwave oven. He felt as though he was imploding, being fed into a vacuum. He screamed but didn't hear his voice. Everything grew dark. He was somewhere above his body, peering down at himself and those in the cave. He was being transported far away.

No! he bellowed.

Suddenly, somehow, he was back in his body. But it was numb and couldn't move.

I'm dead, he thought.

Electricity had entered through a single knuckle and shot down his body, departing simultaneously, as buckshot might, from the cheeks of his buttocks, left thigh, and left heel. Esteban had no way of knowing then how lucky he'd been. At the instant of the strike, his limited contact with the granite had confined the charge to the left side of his body.

Weiner also had been lucky. Bending to adjust his laces, he was touching the wall only with his buttocks and thighs. As the lightning whipped about the enclosure, residual moisture on his clothing and skin served as a conductor and restricted the charge to the surface of these two body parts.

When the cave exploded, Weiner felt that the detonation was in his head and he was being sucked into a vacuum, his body being wrenched in a thousand directions simultaneously. For one long instant he couldn't feel, see, or hear anything. Everything was black; he didn't know where he was. When he regained his senses, he heard himself screaming. He had no feeling from the waist down. His first thought was that Esteban's portable stove had blown up. But then he heard Esteban moaning:

Oh, my God, we've been struck by lightning. I'm dead, I'm dead, I'm dead.

Weiner looked at Brian Jordan next to him. Eyes vacant, Jordan deadpanned, We've got to get out of here. His chin then dropped to his chest.

In hoarse tones, Weiner tried to convince Esteban he was still alive. The message didn't register right away. In Esteban's blurred consciousness, everything was taking place in extremely slow motion. A strong odor like burning sulfur filled his nostrils. Objects and sounds drifted in and out of focus. At length, as though he were fiddling with the image and volume controls on a TV monitor, the picture began to clear. He discovered he could move his arms.

Turning his head to scan the cave, he saw Rice slouched sideways against the granite wall in a fetal position, his body jerking and twitching. His bare legs were badly charred, the blond hairs blackened. Lightning had shot into Rice's back where it rested against the rock wall and out through his thighs and legs. His glassy eyes were expressionless.

Esteban looked over at the youngster, Jordan, who was slumped forward, his still form reeking of burned flesh and hair. The two packs flanking him bore basketball-sized holes, as though there'd been a grenade attack. Conducted by the metal frames, the lightning had passed instantly from them onto Jordan's right shoulder and out his left pectoral.

The sixteen-year-old appeared lifeless. This realization unleashed a crushing sense of tragedy in Esteban—almost as if he'd suffered a second lightning bolt. Injuries, no matter how severe, were one thing. But death meant finality, hope extinguished. Nature had an answer for those who dare challenge her preeminence. With sickening clarity, Esteban now saw that the risks had been miscalculated, limits exceeded—and it was too late for corrections.

He pulled himself forward painfully, dragging his still-paralyzed legs behind. Twisting to glance out at the King's Chair, he was horrified by what he saw: Frith contorting on the stone perch, vomit and froth gurgling from his mouth, eyes rolled back and showing their whites. His forehead bore a dramatic, cauterized-looking gash no more than an inch long, as if someone had plunged a white-hot dagger into his skull. In this case, though, the thrust probably had come from within. Frith's lower body had absorbed the violent charge, which apparently rocketed up through him and out his brow. Or had lightning traveled through the air and pierced him directly in the head? It didn't matter now. He was making dreadful noises. His thrashing body threatened to catapult itself off the narrow ledge.

Esteban maneuvered his upper body over the boulder. Grabbing frantically at Frith's pants, he managed to snag the waistband. He pulled him back from the lip, but Frith's body continued to convulse toward the edge, as though seeking the void beyond. Esteban strained to hold on. With a monumental effort, he tugged Frith back again. He tried to pull him over the boulder and into the chamber, but Frith's writhing, 190-pound bulk was too much for him.

Fighting off panic, Esteban yelled over to Weiner, You've got to help me, man! He's gonna fall off the ledge!

Seeing his friend's peril energized Weiner. His legs still numbed, he struggled to where Esteban was, leaned over the boulder, and managed to grip the sweater on Frith's left arm while Esteban grasped the right. Together they pulled Frith back so he lay more securely. They tried to raise him off the ledge and over the boulder, but with their legs useless, they couldn't exert enough leverage.

Momentarily releasing his hold on the sweater, Weiner gripped Frith's hand with all his strength, hoping that he might return the grip.

Wake up! Weiner yelled frantically at Frith.

A chilling awareness that another bolt could strike at any moment seized Esteban.

Convinced he could do no more, his brain shrieking at him to seek safety, Esteban let go of Frith's right arm and allowed him to slump on the ledge, desperately hoping he would stay there. Esteban started to drag himself past Weiner, who had renewed his grip on the sweater. As he did so, a violent convulsion arched Frith and propelled his legs over the edge. Weiner desperately held on.

Frith slid farther, his weight yanking Weiner closer to certain death.

Weiner had no choice but to let go.

In horror, he and Esteban watched as Frith disappeared over the precipice to the rocks twenty-two hundred feet below.

Weiner screamed *No! No! No!* then clamped his eyes shut and began to sob.

◄○►

DRAINED OF EMOTION by what had happened, Esteban felt remarkably dispassionate as he looked over at Rice, whose left leg was twisted beneath a dislodged rock. Rice retched and gagged on regurgitated broccoli, unintelligible noises issuing from his mouth. Dragging himself over to where Rice was, Esteban propped his friend up slightly, cleared his mouth of food, shook him gently in a vain attempt to restore consciousness, and wondered what else he should do. Severe burns scorched Rice's legs, which even then were smoking. His wounds were bloodless, cauterized by the searing electricity, and blanched, like acid burns. To Esteban they resembled the insides of charred, split-open frankfurters. He lifted Rice's shoulders to turn him and was alarmed to see a fire-blackened hole in the back of his shirt. Through the hole he saw a skinless depression about six inches in diameter. Esteban slowly let Rice down again, thinking maybe there was spinal damage. Rice's eyes were open but unfocused. Minute seizures—aftershocks—still wracked his body. Esteban stared into his friend's eyes. Was it just his imagination, or had he seen a flicker of expression? Was Rice trying to communicate?

An ominous, atmospheric crackling sounded outside. The hairs on Esteban's arms stood upright. His newfound calm vanished in a torrent of fear. He screamed to Weiner, to all of them, conscious or not:

We've got to get the fuck out of here!

Weiner heard the terror in Esteban's voice and tried to stand but fell back again, the muscles in his legs severely knotted. Knowing he couldn't get very far, he hoped and prayed that lightning would not strike the same place twice.*

Esteban, convinced that he was in mortal peril, could think only of escape. He turned away from Rice, gripped Weiner's shoulder in passing, and pulled himself toward the cave's entrance. His legs were inept, but with his powerful arms and upper body he thrust himself up onto the summit and then powered his battered frame across the granite, his elbows clawing the unyielding rock

---

*A naive hope, actually, because lightning follows no such rule. A case in point is the Empire State Building, which has been hit by lightning dozens of times in a year and several times during a single storm.

like a belly-crawling soldier. His sights were on a crevice called the outhouse that was about 150 feet away in a depression obscured by rocks. Campers used it as a toilet, but that was the least of Esteban's concerns at the moment.

His senses, leavened by fear, told him another bolt was coming. Crawling frantically, rolling down a decline, scrambling even faster, he finally reached the depression. Another blast shattered the heavens just as he scrunched himself into the crevice. The granite around him shuddered. His body absorbed a charge from the moist rocks, but this one seemed no more potent than from a household outlet.

He had been spared.

Giddy with relief, Esteban blended tears with shrill laughter. He was alive!

And for an instant, that was all that mattered.

7

SECOND STRIKE

The Half-Dome possesses one feature in particular that I always found remarkable and charming,— the strange manner in which it catches and holds the last light of the day. Often for a full hour after the valley has sunk into shadow, this high Alp, over-looking by two thousand feet the intervening heights, receives the western glow, and like a great heliograph reflects the peaceful messages of the evening over all the quiet valley.—J. Smeaton Chase, author of *Yosemite's Trails*, 1911

Although Weiner was shaken to the core by the catastrophe that had befallen him and his companions, and despite his weakened legs, he survived the first electrical blast with no apparent major injuries. Amazingly his body was slowly coming back to where it was before the lightning blast. Whether Rice would come out of it alive, however, was not yet clear; he was still unconscious, his head sagging to the side.

Fearing the worst, Weiner thought that he wasn't going to make it.

Weiner possibly could have mustered enough strength to scramble out of the cave, as Esteban had. But getting down those cables with legs still immobilized—more from fatigue and cramps than from the lightning—was unthinkable. And he wanted no part of being out there on the bare summit, a human lightning rod, during another killer strike. So, desperately praying that lightning wouldn't strike the cave a second time, he stayed put.

Buzzing and crackling suddenly filled the air. Weiner didn't have time to budge before another blinding explosion blasted the granite and ripped through the enclosure. Unlike the first strike, when the electrical arc streaked across his bottom half, this one engulfed most of his body.

Weiner immediately found himself floating in inky nothingness. In the next instant, he was halfway outside his body, watching it convulse once, then slowly sink into a relaxed state. He was drifting away. He sensed that if the connection between his body and fleeting spirit were broken, it would mean death.

Then he started flowing smoothly and effortlessly back into his body. He was in the cave again, lying on the cold stone floor, his entire physical being seemingly frozen. He became aware of a cool breeze blowing across his bare skin, suggesting that indeed he was still alive. He also felt a deep, pervasive, excruciating pain in his chest, as if that cavity had been blown wide open.

All Weiner wanted was for it all to end. A seductive, soothing thought fleetingly entered his consciousness: If I crawled to the King's Chair, I could throw myself over the edge and join Bob Frith in blissful death, forever free of pain.

For several minutes, he lay motionless. His fogged mind slowly cleared. He knew now that, in the wake of the second strike, he was seriously injured, that perhaps these were his final breaths. Charred remnants of his shirt, which had been burned open by the electrical blast, stuck to his exposed skin. Though the outside of his chest seemed to be intact, his ribs felt broken, tormenting him each time he sucked in air. And searing pain shot through his legs whenever he moved even slightly. The hiking boot on his left leg had been completely blown off.

Soon after the second blast, Rice gradually regained consciousness—almost as if the jolt had recharged his brain. He moaned, then screamed in agony from the weight of Weiner's body on his stricken leg. Rice's other leg was bent grotesquely under a rock. Weiner rolled off him. He removed his belt and, using it for leverage, he and Rice in turn pulled each other to an upright position, both experiencing excruciating pain in doing so.

Next to them was Brian Jordan, his face bluish, his body slumped over and as still as the surrounding granite.

By now the rain had slowed to a drizzle, the mass of storm clouds was marching eastward, the thunder and lightning were now just lingering remnants of their former rage. Weiner peered through the cave opening and saw the clearing sky.

He began yelling for help.

◄○►

IN HIS CONFUSED STATE, Weiner thought the second strike had happened mere seconds after Esteban had left the cave and that he had probably been struck dead. In fact, Esteban's frantic roll down the slope to the outhouse crevice surely saved him. As he lay there, Esteban thought only of his own miraculous survival and thanked God over and over for sparing him.

But the reality of what had just happened—the Jordan kid killed, Bob Frith spilling over the precipice to certain death—doused his momentary relief. Tragically, Esteban's long-standing premonition that someone he knew would fall from Half Dome had come to pass.

His thoughts turned to Weiner and Rice in the cave. He heard screams coming from that direction but was too frightened to leave the crevice.

Minutes passed. The unfolding clouds in the tumultuous skies above Half Dome, like the last wild leaps and thrashes of spawning salmon, were releasing their final charge before weakening and then dying. Soon, patches of evening sky showed between the fast-moving billows, their tops now illuminated by the emerging evening sun. Only faint rumblings of thunder persisted from afar.

In this part of the Sierra Nevada, the storm was over.

Esteban's feet were numb, but he had feeling in his lower body. Finally, believing that the danger had sufficiently subsided, he left the crevice and began crawling back up the slope toward the cave.

Nearing the summit, Esteban saw someone coming over the ridge at the top of the cables. He waved his arms and shouted to attract the hiker's attention.

It was Mike Hoog.

◄◦►

THROUGHOUT THE DOWNPOUR, Hoog and his four companions had stayed mostly dry under their tarp below Sub Dome, where they planned to camp for the night. Hoog wanted a sunset photograph from the summit now that the sky was clearing. He asked if anyone cared to join him, but no one made a move. So he took off by himself, hustling up the stone stairs of Sub Dome and then up the incline to the top of Half Dome. Black clouds still hovered above, casting sinister shadows on the mountain. To the west, a light blue sky was dappled with wispy clouds. A distinct line separated the darkness of the departing storm and brightening skies.

On the summit, Hoog saw someone frantically waving and shouting at him. It was Esteban, whom he recognized as a member of the rude, boisterous group at Nevada Fall. That earlier encounter made Hoog suspicious now. Was this guy high on drugs? Were he and his pals playing a joke, hoping to scare Hoog or, as a dark inner voice warned, push him over the edge?

He approached cautiously. When Esteban told him his buddies were injured, Hoog followed Esteban to the cave but avoided getting too close to the brink, his senses on heightened alert. Bending down and peering into the enclosure, he first saw a frenzied Weiner, screaming for help and begging that someone remove him from the cave. Close by was a second man, Rice, his body inert, his face pallid, his eyes glassy. Smoke wafted from the legs of both men. Farther in, there was a boy slouched to one side; a breeze tussled his light brown hair, the only thing on him that moved.

Odors of burned hair and flesh hung in the air.

Hoog was a trained emergency medical technician, or EMT, but this was the first time he would treat injuries in the field. The seriousness of it all and his place in these unfolding events dawned on him: Lives might be at stake.

He was scared.

The first emergency response in such cases is to ensure the scene is safe, that whatever caused the mishap has passed. Only then, after appropriate triage (providing priority assistance to patients, if there's more than one, either immediately or as other resources become available), should an EMT proceed with medical care. Triage often entails a color scheme to denote the order for giving attention. Black typically represents someone beyond help, in most cases dead; red denotes someone who is in critical condition but might be saved; yellow means serious but not critical; and green signifies that a person is injured but capable of getting by on his or her own. The EMT does a quick assessment and then treats the red victim first, followed by the yellow.

Other than the nearby cliff, Hoog didn't detect any lurking dangers now that the storm appeared to be over. He inhaled deeply and steeled himself against his own nervousness so it wouldn't prevent him from doing what he had to do.

Esteban told him about Frith falling over the edge and how Brian Jordan hadn't stirred since the lightning strike. Trying his best not to freak out, Hoog lowered himself into the cave and squirmed past Weiner and Rice and over to Jordan. With two fingers, he felt for a pulse in one of the two large arteries—the carotids, which deliver blood to the head—in the young man's neck. No pulse. That indicated a stopped heart and probable death. Hoog concluded there was nothing he could do.

Then he turned to Weiner. First he checked to see if Weiner had any feelings in his legs. If he didn't, that could mean a spinal injury, possibly caused by a violent impact against rock or a severe muscular contraction. Weiner would then have to be immobilized and stabilized right there; improperly moving a patient with a broken neck can prove fatal. Fortunately, Weiner confirmed that he could feel and move his feet. In a quick inspection, Hoog detected no other immediate life-threatening circumstances. He focused on Rice.

Although Rice's leg muscles were very tight and swollen, he, too, had feeling in his legs and toes. He also could move his upper body, so a serious back injury seemed unlikely. But his pallor suggested the likely onset of shock.

Esteban, who now had full use of his legs, approached the cave to assist.

When Rice saw him, he started yelling: Adrian, get your fuckin' ass in here and get me out. Don't leave me behind to die like you did!

A shaken Esteban crawled to Rice and slapped and then shook him, shouting: Goddamn it, I was going to die! I had to go. It wasn't my fault! Esteban couldn't cope with this accusation, and his body began trembling. He had to get out of there.

Outside the cave, he stomped around, violently upset. Esteban pleaded to himself: How could he accuse me of leaving him to die?

What more could I have done? If I had stayed, I probably would have been killed by the second bolt. Then no one would know that anyone was in the cave, no one would be helping him now. I had to leave—I had no choice. Can't he see that?

Still highly agitated, Esteban lowered himself back into the enclosure to help Hoog, who was grappling with choices, among them whether he should move the two men.

He knew he shouldn't if there were any possibility of spinal or neck injuries. On the other hand, the cave was cramped, with insufficient space for both of them to lie comfortably on their backs and be treated. Hoog concluded that the chance of spinal injury was remote; he would remove both victims from the cave.

First he pushed the rock off Rice's leg. Then he and Esteban shifted the four backpacks and other odds and ends out of the way. The pair lifted Weiner, one supporting his upper body by holding him under his armpits, the other grasping his legs. With much careful and strenuous maneuvering, they managed to get him out and up onto the open granite, and gently laid him down. Hoog took off his own jacket and covered Weiner with it.

In similar fashion, Hoog and Esteban retrieved Rice and placed him near Weiner. Both men lay there, groaning and twisting in anguish. To Hoog, it looked like either or both could slip into shock, a potentially fatal development.

Shock is a downward spiral of bodily functions triggered by the inability of the circulatory system to send an adequate supply of blood to tissues. Infections, burns, heart attack, spinal cord damage, and rapid blood loss from an injury or wound can cause it. With impaired blood flow, valuable resources are shunted toward the more vital brain and internal organs. Surface blood vessels constrict, leaving the skin pale and clammy. Heart rate increases, breathing becomes more rapid, and digestion slows and ultimately halts. Body temperature is erratic, with hypothermia a threat. If blood pressure drops, mental functioning deteriorates. First the victim experiences a sense of impending doom, then apathy and weakness, then disorientation and incoherence. The final result is coma. If the regression in bodily functions isn't diagnosed, halted, and reversed early, the patient is likely to die. Even in hospitals, the mortality rate for acute shock is 50 percent.

Hoog, who knew that a potential shock victim must be kept warm, returned to the cave to gather warm garments from the men's backpacks. He reexamined Brian Jordan and, despite his extreme queasiness, searched his body for a pulse. He couldn't feel one anywhere. The boy was indeed dead, becoming one of the 10 percent of lightning victims who perish.

◄O►

WHILE HOOG was doing what he could for the victims, Rick Pedroncelli, having decided to follow him to the top after all, was making his way up. Once there, he spotted Hoog and others off in the distance, near the edge. When he got closer, he saw his friend attending to one of two individuals lying prone. A third, Esteban, was sitting and looked dazed.

When Pedroncelli approached, Esteban leaped up and said: We need to get help!

Initially, Pedroncelli was quite reluctant to get involved, for reasons that had to do with another death—that of his mother. She had died unexpectedly when he was only twelve years old. The event left him with deep-seated feelings of insecurity and made him less willing to take chances. Still, it was evident something terrible had happened, that Hoog needed help.

After Pedroncelli got a quick update on the situation, he asked if he could do anything. Hoog told him to retrieve the men's sleeping bags and air mattresses from inside the cave. Pedroncelli slipped down through the opening and crawled to the backpacks near the body of Brian Jordan. Shaking uncontrollably, he hastily snatched a couple of bags and mattresses, and retreated outside as fast as he could. He and Hoog positioned Rice and Weiner on the mattresses, and covered them with the bags.

By this time, both Weiner and Rice were fully delirious, squirming and moaning under the sleeping bags, obviously in acute pain. Esteban appeared to be stable but extremely distressed and understandably panicked about his companions. Pedroncelli didn't see any way for these two men to get the medical assistance they clearly needed. Here they were on top of a mountain with nightfall approaching, far away from the Valley and possible assistance. He felt powerless.

Hoog said: We have to get Linda up here.

—◄o►—

LINDA CROZIER, eager to finally see the view from the top that her good friend Hoog had long touted, had already decided to climb to the summit to join him and Pedroncelli. Wearing only running shorts, a T-shirt, and a sweatshirt tied around her waist, she struck out for the Dome, the time now being around 7:30 P.M.

At the base of the cables, alone, she gazed up the rock incline wrapped in shadows and total silence. The scene, in her words, was "very moody."

She began the climb feeling more than a little intimidated by the steep, black, wet slope and the absence of other hikers to lend psychological support. Pulling on the cables with sufficient arm strength to keep moving upward taxed her to the limit. She stopped halfway to take a photo looking up the cables, and as she pointed her camera, Pedroncelli suddenly appeared in the viewfinder where the cables ended. He was beckoning her with his arms and calling out. Sensing something was wrong, Crozier put away the camera and yanked even harder on the cables, making her legs respond in kind.

As she drew nearer, Pedroncelli shouted: Hurry! Lightning killed two guys and three others are badly hurt!

On top, heading over to Hoog and the others, Crozier rehearsed in her mind the basics of cardiopulmonary resuscitation. Then she saw Weiner and Rice lying on the stone surface. Hoog told her about the dead boy in the cave and about the hiker who had vanished over the cliff. The irony of it all didn't escape Crozier: These were the very men whose behavior she had found so distasteful back at Nevada Fall. Her brother Dan had conveyed to their two leaders, Rice and Esteban, the older hiker's warning about not scaling the summit with a storm brewing. But whatever negative feelings she may have had regarding this crew evaporated amid the tragedy that now engulfed them.

Her first reaction—why, she doesn't know—was to peer down over the edge. There, in the rocky jumble far below, was something white—probably Frith's body. She was also thinking about what Hoog had said about the dead boy in the cave. Up to this time she had never seen a dead person before, and she felt squeamish about confronting that possibility now. With this chilling consideration kicking around in her head, she accepted Hoog's conclusion, cleared her head of distractions, and returned to where the injured lay. Hoog gave her a quick rundown of the treatment he had provided so far. Crozier, who had more experience than Hoog in emergency medical care, took charge at that point.

A teacher in Crozier's EMT training had emphasized the importance of problem-solving skills in addition to knowledge of standard medical applications. Absent medical equipment in an outdoor emergency, you must be able to improvise and use all available resources. Although the curriculum included electrical injuries, the instructor had touched only briefly on those caused by lightning.

Without any medical gear or medicine on Half Dome, Crozier's medical training would be supremely tested. Yet it was her more intangible qualifications—knowing how to deal coolly with various athletic injuries as a trainer, for example, and how to take decisive action in life-threatening situations as a whitewater guide—that would be brought to the forefront this night.

She moved right away to the third phase of emergency care—assessment—which entailed checking the life-essential functions, or ABCs: airway, breathing, and circulation. In EMT terminology, this is a primary survey. If either victim had an ABC problem, such as a blocked airway, it would have to be dealt with immediately.

A quick inspection showed that neither man had any major breathing obstructions or bleeding. Given Rice's unmoving and quiet state, he appeared to be the most critically injured at this juncture, so Crozier examined him first. She noted extensive burn lesions, cauterized by the lightning's searing heat, and knew that such traumatic wounds could produce shock. She felt for pulses at his wrists and elbows but found none, which signaled low blood pressure and the probable onset of shock. Reaching up into his shorts, she checked the femoral artery in his groin and was relieved to feel a pulse. So, at least for now, Rice had some circulation to vital organs. Crozier would tap this particular pulse in follow-up checks as a baseline reference, and use it to assess the rate, rhythm, and strength of his overall cardiac system. If the pulse diminished, it would mean Rice was slipping deeper into shock.

Crozier detected a pulse on Weiner's wrist, but it was weak. Judging from his intense writhing, his pain seemed all-encompassing. His murmurings suggested that he believed he was going to die.

Esteban suffered only a few dime-sized blisters on his left elbow, hip, and knee where the lightning had exited. By this time, he had regained all feeling in his entire body and was fully coherent.

Two new hikers appeared on the summit. They said they, too, were EMTs and offered to assist. One, Renee Miller, was in her early twenties; the other was a man who only gave his first name, Brutus. They were camped below the summit and, like the others, had climbed up to enjoy the sunset. Crozier, thankful for their presence, enlisted Miller's help in assessing the victims. She asked Hoog and Brutus to examine Brian Jordan yet again.

Inside the cave, the two men found that Jordan's face had turned a cyanotic blue, the result of insufficient blood oxygen. They also noted a wound in his upper right shoulder where the lightning most likely had entered. On the left side of his chest, just above the nipple, were signs of electrical burns—probably the exit wounds. The electrical charge appeared to have flashed across and possibly through Jordan's chest near his heart, shocking it and causing ventricular fibrillation, a chaotic twitching of cardiac muscle that completely disrupts the pumping of blood. Only immediate CPR and an electrical jump start from a defibrillator (a device that restores normal heartbeat), followed as soon as possible by emergency medical treatment, might have saved him.

Crozier wanted a head-to-toe examination of both Weiner and Rice to ensure there were no injuries to the neck, spine, or back, no broken bones, and no other wounds or injuries requiring prompt attention. This is a secondary survey, in EMT parlance. While she examined Rice, Renee Miller did the same for Weiner. The two women worked in tandem and compared findings, each advising the other what to look for as they scanned the men's bodies.

Now more awake, Rice complained of severe pain in his legs and feet. Crozier spotted a wound in his left ankle—the lightning probably exited there—that resembled a bullet hole. His legs looked as though a potato peeler had scraped sections of skin off of them and left white blotches of burned flesh. He also had burn wounds on his arms; he could barely move the left one.

Miller discovered that Weiner's wounds were almost identical.

As Rice's and Weiner's wounds made clear, lightning not only had scorched the outside of their bodies, vaporizing any residual moisture from the rain and thereby causing severe burns, but also seemingly had penetrated their backs—hence, the gaping, leathery lesions there—and blasted out through the feet.

This had triggered a cascade of calamitous and potentially fatal physiological events. The burns caused swelling in the legs, which in turn shut off circulation to lower extremities, just as a tourniquiet would. That explained the pair's whitish blue feet. Though Rice and Weiner still had some feeling in the legs, the swelling, if untreated, threatened to starve tissue of the oxygenated blood it needs to stay alive. Because dying muscle tissue releases toxins that can cause kidney failure or damage other bodily systems, the legs would have to be amputated if it reached that point.

On an impulse, Hoog abruptly left to see if any more hikers were coming up the cables who could turn tail and summon more help. Meanwhile, Pedroncelli thought of another strategy—sending an SOS by Morse code with his flashlight to campers in the Valley.* He went to the edge, in line of sight of the campgrounds far below, and began flashing SOS, which he remembered from war movies. The evening sky was still light, however, and Pedroncelli doubted that anyone down there could see the flashes. So, after several attempts, he stopped.

At this point, other than the small contingent on top of Half Dome—those few who were giving and receiving aid—no other people in all of Yosemite had any inkling of the calamity.

-◄o►-

ROCK CLIMBERS KEN BOKELUND and Rob Foster made it to the Valley floor by 7:30 P.M., physically and emotionally spent but grateful they had survived their brush with lightning uninjured. Rainwater immersed the parking lot at Camp Curry. Bokelund gazed up at Half Dome as the last rays of sun bathed the famous rock face they had just scaled. A shimmering golden glow radiated from it, framed by turbulent, multihued clouds. It was the most striking image Bokelund had ever seen. He snapped a photo.

The climbing duo tossed their gear into the car and headed out, not once thinking of the two hikers they had warned about

---

*Morse code, widely practiced for decades, is now rarely taught, except in pilot training and in the military. The emergence of cell phones has rendered this form of emergency communication even more passé. We can confidently conclude that with this new technology, the 1985 Half Dome episode would have proceeded quite differently.

going up there and unaware of the life-and-death drama that was playing out on the summit at that very instant.

◄o►

BRIAN CAGE'S PARTY of six remained under the giant Jeffrey pine at the base of Half Dome, waiting for the storm to pass. After the rain stopped and as the clouds began to disperse, early-evening sunlight filtered through. Splashes of blue punctuated the western sky, and to the north, just beyond Half Dome, a rainbow arced across the heavens. The six agreed there was still time to reach the summit. They removed their ponchos, hoisted their backpacks, and headed up the trail toward Sub Dome.

As they plodded along, Steve White remarked how good he felt after the extended rest. Zip Cotter, who was taking long, slow strides, responded in his usual laconic manner that all he wanted was to get to the top. They had already hiked nine miles from Glacier Point that day lugging forty-pound backpacks. Though dog-tired, the hikers were intent on finishing the climb; they could rest on Half Dome.

They reached the base of the cables at 7:50 P.M., dropped their backpacks, and rummaged through them for gloves to better grip the cables. Given the fading light and slick surfaces, the climb was going to be tricky this evening.

Just as they were about to start up, a man with long blond hair—Mike Hoog—appeared at the upper cables and shouted down to them: Go get help! Two guys got hit by lightning!

Then he disappeared, before they could get more information. They weren't sure if he was serious, and if he was, what kind of help did he want? Not knowing what to make of all this, the hikers decided to scurry up there and find out.

Clu Cotter led the way up, closely followed by Steve White. The other four—Cage, Zip Cotter, Paul Kolbenschlag, and Monroe Bridges—lagged behind. Clu Cotter, a Half Dome first-timer, was taken aback by the steepness of the grade and the far distance between stepping boards. Fearful of heights as well, he didn't look down. When he and White reached the top, they saw people bent over individuals in sleeping bags at the point overlooking Yosemite Valley.

White's first thought was: God, it really happened!

He and Clu Cotter waited for their four companions to catch up. As all six men reached the scene, Weiner and Rice were howling and squirming in pain.

Cage: "I specifically remember one calling to the other by name and screaming, 'My God, my God, we're going to die, we're going to die!' And frankly, my buddies and I were thinking that one or both might very well die."

The new arrivals shed their backpacks and offered to help. Those loaded packs would prove to be a lifesaver, because they were stuffed with valuable supplies—sleeping bags, food, stoves, clothing, and, especially important, water. Linda Crozier immediately put Brian Cage's party to work, requesting that they move Weiner and Rice to a more level spot. With three on a side, the six men gently lifted each victim where he lay on a mattress, carried him a short distance, and set him down. When they finished, Weiner and Rice were at right angles to each other, their heads about six feet apart.

Crozier then asked Cage and White to try to find a pulse anywhere on the victims' feet. Cage pulled the boots off Rice and was astonished to discover that the bottoms of his socks on both feet were missing, as though they had vaporized inside the boots. The bottoms of his feet seemed okay—cold and pink-white, not burned in any way—though the edges of the remaining sock material were charred. Cage and White couldn't locate a pulse in either Weiner's or Rice's feet. Cage leafed through a pamphlet from his first-aid kit for information on how to treat lightning injuries and found nothing there on the subject.

Kolbenschlag and Zip Cotter walked a short distance away to another part of the Dome, unnerved by the obvious pain and anguish of the two injured men. Kolbenschlag was so physically beat, he could do little more than collapse on the granite. He was in poor shape for the hike and had barely made it to the summit.

As the dampness and frigid stone stole warmth from their already compromised bodies, Weiner and Rice both complained of feeling chilled. Crozier didn't observe any deterioration in their vital signs, but she was still very aware of the threat of severe shock and the extreme danger it would pose. Getting and keeping them warm was crucial. At her request, Clu Cotter, White, Bridges, and Cage pulled sleeping bags from their backpacks. Bridges went into the cave to retrieve more bags. When he shone his flashlight in the dark enclosure, the sight of Brian Jordan's body made him recoil.

Bridges emerged with two more sleeping bags, deeply traumatized by the image of the boy whose brief life had been abruptly extinguished. Crozier placed one bag under and two more on top of Weiner and Rice; each was now enveloped by four bags.

It was 8:30 P.M. The victims' weak and rapid pulses indicated to Crozier that their blood pressure was dangerously low. In her assessment, one or both might perish if they spent the entire night there. She and the others could continue to treat for shock, maintain the ABCs, periodically monitor the pair's condition, and try to make them comfortable, but both needed advanced medical treatment.

One option crossed her mind: Could a team of hikers somehow transport Weiner and Rice down to the Valley floor? Not likely. Even if they had enough agility and strength to do so, how could this maneuver take place without causing further injury?

Meanwhile, the clock was ticking. In little more than thirty minutes, darkness would fall.

Crozier fought back against the panic rising within her. Weiner's and Rice's fates were squarely in her hands—she and she alone had to make the right decisions. She desperately wanted someone to lift this burden from her shoulders, to have the park rangers take over.

But no relief was in sight.

◄○►

HOOG WAS A long-distance runner, and whenever life became stressful, he turned to running as an outlet. Confident that Linda Crozier could manage with the others' aid, he announced that he would go and get help. With that he left, intent upon sprinting to the ranger station in Little Yosemite Valley over four miles away. Pedroncelli, sensing he was no longer needed, followed Hoog down the cables.

Crozier accepted that no other help was forthcoming anytime soon. In her mind, she needed more control over the situation, more continuity in the care of the two victims. So she organized teams. She, White, and Clu Cotter would attend to Rice, and Miller and Brutus to Weiner; Bridges would remain at Esteban's side. If any of the injured took a turn for the worse, Crozier reasoned, those who were closely attending him would be more apt to spot it. To supply nourishment for the group, Cage boiled water and cooked food on his camp stove.

Given the extreme pain in Rice's right leg, Crozier feared it might be fractured or broken as a result of the severe muscle contractions that often accompany electrical injuries. His right foot was angled. She gently pulled the foot to straighten it out and then instructed White how to hold it in traction. Squatting, he grasped the foot with both hands at the ankle and lightly drew it toward himself by leaning his weight back, thus producing tension in the leg. This relieved Rice's pain somewhat.

White asked Rice why he and his buddies had risked coming up there in the storm.

Rice proved as unyielding as ever. What he felt and was thinking he would keep to himself. That had always been Rice's way, and apparently even this tragic incident would not dislodge him from his long-rooted stance. His clipped, muted response: We wanted to dance in the lightning.

Off to the side, Bridges sat with Esteban, who by now had become morose and stoic. He, too, was not talking, not responding to Bridges's questions about what happened, and why. He'd withdrawn, tormented by the disastrous turn of events precipitated by their dash up the mountain. With brutal awareness, he now realized how wrong he and Rice had been in thinking that together they could meet any challenge; that overcoming fear was the way to reap life's rewards. The suddenness, unpredictability, and ferocity of lightning were unlike anything they could have ever conjured up or overcome. He sat there, plagued by the harsh penalties wrought by their misjudgments. Two people had been killed. How would he ever get over that?

His outer face was indeed a stoic mask, but inside was the deepest pain anyone could ever feel.

There was nothing he could do now about what happened, except pray that neither Rice nor Weiner died as well.

◄○►

BILL PIPPEY AND BRUCE JORDAN had wisely stayed below Sub Dome after the sixteen-year-old said he was afraid of the lightning storm. Karl Buchner and Steve Ellner also stayed below due to Ellner's fears. Now they all hooked up and prepared to join their companions on the summit. They repacked their backpacks and began the ascent.

While climbing the stairs, they encountered a frenzied Hoog dashing down. He blurted out that hikers had been hit by lightning up on top, that he was going for help.

Ellner said: That's it, I'm not going any farther. I'm out of here.

He headed back down. Pippey initially thought Hoog meant the strike had occurred some time ago, but Buchner told him no, it must have just happened. Pippey refused to believe that the incident involved anyone in his group. As he later stated, "I simply blocked that notion out of my mind."

On the cables they met Pedroncelli coming down. Stammering, he reported that two guys got killed and one was a young kid, that two others were badly hurt. Pedroncelli also said he thought the group was from San Jose but wasn't sure.

Those words stunned Buchner, Pippey, and Jordan. Buchner acutely felt Bruce Jordan's presence right behind him; it was probably his brother who had been killed. In silence, the three continued their climb, the full weight of the unfolding tragedy now hanging over them like a landslide about to give way from above.

Dan Crozier, Linda Crozier's brother, remembers that Hoog had a ghostly look on his face when he reached the camping area below Sub Dome and explained what had happened and where he was going. Like Hoog, Dan Crozier was in excellent physical shape and said he'd go with him. By this time, Pedroncelli had arrived; he remained with Jenny Hayes as Hoog and Crozier bounded down the terrain in dimming light with little regard for the trail.

As soon as Buchner, Pippey, and Bruce Jordan arrived at the summit and Rice saw them coming his way, he shouted: The kid's dead, man, the kid's dead! Frith fell over the edge!

Buchner absorbed the full impact of the news, then said: I can't handle this.

He retreated back down the cables.

When Buchner joined Ellner at base camp, he couldn't speak. His eyes, according to Ellner, were glazed over and blank, zombie-like. Ellner waited for Buchner to say something, anything. Then, as though a third person was speaking through him, Buchner told Ellner about the two deaths and how Weiner and Rice were all messed up.

Referring to Esteban, Ellner asked: How's Adrian?

He seemed to be okay, Buchner replied.

Ellner: "At that point, I was just glad he was alive and that I was, too."

He and Buchner chose to stay put for the night, out in the open without setting up their tent, but neither slept much. Each attempted to digest the horrifying news about their comrades whose care, whose very lives were in the hands of strangers.

On the summit, meanwhile, Pippey rushed up to Esteban and asked: Is it true? Is it true? Oh my God, oh my God, oh my God.

Pippey was responsible for Brian Jordan coming on the trip. Now he was dead and so was Frith, and it looked like Weiner and Rice were going to die, too. The enormity of it all crushed Pippey. He stood planted in place, crying uncontrollably.

Bruce Jordan, as if he hadn't heard the news, just stared blankly at the ground. Although the reality had dented his consciousness, a world without his twin brother hadn't fully penetrated yet.

◄o►

IT WAS 8:45 P.M. Darkness was settling over Yosemite Valley. On Half Dome, efforts to keep Weiner and Rice alive and as comfortable as possible continued unabated. Those caring for the stricken hikers also attended to each other.

All the activity was taking place just feet from the precipice. Pippey and Bruce Jordan were the most shaken by what had happened, and their mental states were the most unpredictable. White noticed that Jordan stood off in the shadows by himself, his blond hair, white shirt, and ashen face illuminated by remnants of the evening light, all of which made him look ghostly. He had shown no emotion so far. Given the psychological impact of what had transpired, there was a danger that yet another hiker might plummet over the edge, either intentionally or accidentally.

Crozier went over to Pippey, who was still sobbing, and grabbed him by the shoulders, shook him, yelled at him to get control of himself. It was important, she said, that he look out for Bruce Jordan. She told Pippey to take him to the middle of the Dome, a safe distance from the edge, and sit with him, comfort him, and keep him away from the first-aid area. She stressed that the pair were not to hike back down in the dark.

His shoulders still shaking, Pippey put an arm around Jordan. Together they ambled over to the broad granite saddle between two elevations on the summit.

Kolbenschlag, who knew Morse code from his pilot training, came up with the same idea Pedroncelli had earlier that evening. He stationed himself near the edge with a direct view of the camp-grounds below and began sending an SOS with his flashlight. Fatigued from the climb and stress, he reclined in a sandy spot with his upper body braced against a rock and flashed a signal every ten minutes or so, closing his eyes and resting between trans-missions. Zip Cotter, who had retrieved two cups of hot choco-late, spelled Kolbenschlag, and together they sent SOS's intermittently over the next hour. It still wasn't dark enough, how-ever, for anyone down in the Valley to readily notice a faint emer-gency signal from Half Dome.

While dozing at one point, Kolbenschlag was startled by some-thing on his hand. He reflexively flung his arm up and out, and glimpsed a furry object—a chipmunk or similar creature—hurtling off the mountaintop with a pathetic squeal. When he came to his senses, Kolbenschlag felt awful about what he'd just done.

—◄o►—

LINDA CROZIER continued to check Weiner's and Rice's pulses periodically to monitor their condition and stay alert for any sudden change. Every twenty minutes, she and Renee Miller also did a serial exam of the two men: Does this hurt? Do you have feeling here? Are you warm enough? Because the lightning strike had knocked Rice unconscious and because he was com-plaining of neck pain, Crozier feared that perhaps he had suf-fered a head or neck injury after all. She had Clu Cotter take over in keeping Rice's leg elevated, and told White to hold Rice's head immobile.

The leg wasn't broken, Crozier concluded; rather, his pain—like the severe ache in Weiner's legs—was due to burn-related internal problems aggravated by repeated cramping and swelling. The inflammation was stealing fluids from the rest of their bod-ies and made them crave water. But Crozier wouldn't give them anything to drink because she worried their stomachs couldn't absorb gulps of fluid. If they threw up, they might inhale vomit and suffocate, which sometimes happens to shock victims. Instead, to slake their thirst and prevent dehydration, she offered them T-shirts partially soaked in water to suck on.

Weiner cried out that he had to pee. Crozier asked Brutus to get a plastic bag so they could collect the urine for later examination by doctors. But when they helped Weiner into position, he couldn't relieve himself. Although his bladder was full and his need to urinate overwhelming, the lightning probably traumatized his sphincter muscle, causing it to spasm and block his urinary tract. A more remote possibility was the blockage of his kidneys with burned blood cells, a condition that can trigger kidney failure. Weiner screamed in agony. Alarmed that his organs might be damaged, he became frenzied.

Rice yelled at him: Get fuckin' control of yourself! You're going to be all right!

The words had a calming effect on Weiner.

It was crucial that neither of them fall asleep, slip into semi-consciousness, or, worse, lapse into a life-threatening coma. By staying awake, they could respond to questions and communicate how and what they were feeling—a barometer of their worsening or improving condition. If either sank deeper into shock, Crozier would have to try a different medical tack. She called over to Esteban and asked him to come closer and make sure Weiner and Rice remained conscious.

This snapped Esteban out of his own mental distress. He crouched near each victim and turned first to one, then the other, saying over and over: I love you, man. You're going to be okay. You're going to make it.

By now, Pippey was more composed, too. He offered to help Crozier. She inquired about Bruce Jordan, whom Pippey said had fallen asleep in his sleeping bag. Crozier asked Pippey to heat water for coffee, tea, or hot chocolate for anyone who wanted refreshment. It was important to keep him busy, she knew—to make him feel like he was contributing.

Nine o'clock. Only a faint glow silhouetted the western mountain ridges. As darkness took command, Kolbenschlag's and Cotter's more visible SOS signals by flashlight began to elicit responses from the Valley floor. Soon there were tens of lights blinking back from the campgrounds. But did anyone down there really know Morse code? Might campers be thinking this was merely a gambit, a playful exchange of light beams? Actually, in his exhausted state, Kolbenschlag had been flashing the wrong signal. In Morse code, SOS is dot-dot-dot, dash-dash-dash, dot-dot-dot. He had been transmitting dash-dash-dash, dot-dot-dot, dash-dash-dash, or OSO.

Pippey wandered over to where Kolbenschlag and Zip Cotter were and observed their signaling efforts. Like Pedroncelli, Pippey knew from movies what the proper SOS was. He detected the error and told Kolbenschlag, who promptly started flashing the correct signal. Soon one light brighter than the others began flashing in return. It was what Kolbenschlag was looking for—SOK, the code for "I acknowledge your call, will get help."

When Zip Cotter shouted to the others that the SOS had been seen and rangers would be told, loud cheering erupted. Someone in the Valley now knew of their plight.

◄o►

THE SENDER OF THE SOK contacted a park ranger, who quickly forwarded it to Jim Reilly, the supervising ranger that evening. He in turn dispatched John Dill, a park search and rescue technician, to investigate.

Dill drove to a parking lot near Mirror Lake, where there is a good view of Half Dome's summit. He had no idea what this emergency was all about, but using a bullhorn amplified by a battery hook-up, he could gather clues by shouting questions to those on top. This was a standard communication mode for Yosemite's search and rescue division when rock climbers got into trouble on a mountain face. Communicating this way with someone on the top of Half Dome was a first, however.

At 9:25 P.M., through his bullhorn, Dill instructed the signaler (Kolbenschlag) to blink the light once for "yes," twice for "no" as he posed questions. Cotter was the relay man: He yelled the questions to Linda Crozier, fifty feet away, who shouted back answers for Kolbenschlag to translate into one or two blinks of the flashlight.

Is this emergency for real?

Yes.

Is anyone dead?

Yes.

How many?

Two blinks.

Is anyone injured?

Yes.

How many?

Three blinks.

Are the injuries the result of a fall?

No.

Is anyone bleeding?

No.

Are there broken bones?

No.

If you don't receive help, will someone die?

Everyone on the summit could hear the exchange among Dill, Cotter, and Crozier, and everyone zeroed in on Crozier when Dill shouted up this last question.

Crozier: "I knew that if I said no and someone died that night, I would blame myself for it, that I didn't do all I could have. Until I had to respond to this question, I hadn't needed to think this way. When I shouted yes, it was as if we all accepted that, yes, it could happen."

Kolbenschlag flashed one blink to Dill. Moments passed without a response.

Then Dill repeated: If we can't get to you tonight, will someone die?

Cotter again relayed the question to Crozier. Why had Dill asked it twice? Did it mean they weren't going to send help?

With all eyes on Crozier, she hollered more resolutely this time: Yes!

There was an extended pause down below. Dill then shouted up that he would get back to them.

When Cotter relayed Dill's final statement, a collective sign of relief could almost be heard from those on top. Help was in sight —park rangers and medics would arrive soon.

The nightmare was about to end.

—◀◦▶—

THE OPTIMISM on the summit soon gave way to the immediate realities. Weiner's and Rice's legs had become increasingly numb. Crozier couldn't detect circulation in their feet, which were turning white. This indicated that capillaries in the feet weren't transporting blood, a bad sign. So she and Miller vigorously massaged the pair's legs and feet hoping to boost circulation.

Weiner seemed to be in worse shape at the moment, both physically and psychologically. He reported more pain throughout his body and was more incoherent than Rice. He still had to pee urgently but couldn't, and that caused agony. At one point, he gasped that he was having trouble breathing. Crozier, listening to his chest, heard a slight gurgling in his lungs—a possible indication of pulmonary edema, or fluid in the lungs, which could drown him. Treatment for pulmonary edema is oxygen delivered through nasal prongs or a facemask; sometimes a breathing tube is inserted into the windpipe or the patient is hooked up to a ventilator. But, of course, Crozier had no such equipment.

Rice became more demanding and hostile, which is typical behavior in trauma cases. He demanded water. Crozier relented but gave him and Weiner only about two tablespoons' worth. Rice craved more.

Fuckin' bitch! he yelled.

After almost three hours of lying in the same position on his back, one foot elevated and held in traction, his head immobilized, Rice was extremely uncomfortable. He wanted to move, wanted more to drink, but Crozier refused. His verbal abuse turned more vociferous—he called her one nasty name after another. She placidly accepted his tirades, realizing they stemmed from agony and frustration, and were a good sign that he was coherent and stable and gaining strength.

Esteban told Rice: Listen to Linda and do what she says. You'll be okay. I love you, you're the greatest.

Esteban also reassured Weiner, who at one point muttered he wanted to die. He appeared to be fading.

Crozier later recalled that Esteban proved to be a bulwark in this crisis. "He was like the Rock of Gibraltar, absolutely the greatest. Except for Pippey and Bruce Jordan, he was the only one there whom Rice and Weiner knew. He stayed by them, talking to them, telling them they were going to be all right and to thank God they were alive. He was able to calm them down and sustain their spirits."

—◦—

AT 10:20 P.M. there was still no more word from Dill or anyone else in Yosemite Valley. Why hadn't authorities followed up by now? The joy that everyone had felt forty-five minutes earlier had evaporated. As interminable minutes dragged by, Linda Crozier's confidence ebbed. More doubts crept into her mind about the sole responsibility she had assumed for decisions, whether she was making the right ones, whether others should continue to defer to her judgment, whether she could keep this up.

She thought: How did I ever get into this position, being responsible for two men, either of whom could die at any moment? Outwardly, despite her inner turmoil, she projected a sense of cool-headedness, self-assurance, and resolve.

To help the others stay alert, she rotated their assignments while they still cared for the same victim. They also checked with each other and provided mutual support and encouragement: How are you doing? Are you okay? Do you need anything?

As time passed, the temperature fell and a cold breeze swept across the bare granite. Still under cloud cover, the dome's cast was dark, almost pitch black. Crozier, skimpily clad, was becoming increasingly chilled. Sitting, she stuck her bare legs, riddled with goosebumps, under the edge of the sleeping bags covering Rice. Others also clustered next to Rice or Weiner. Warm clothing was parceled out. Anyone who wanted a hot drink could tap Cage's and Pippey's ready supply of boiling water.

Slivers from a partial moon finally peeked through scattered clouds, diffusing the thin light that now reflected off granite and that illuminated, in eerily gray hues, the Dome and everyone huddled there. Zip Cotter described the scene as "surreal, what I imagined being on the surface of the moon would be like."

Group morale was of concern to White. What would happen if there weren't a rescue that night? He told jokes in an effort to perk everyone up and bolster their spirits. He didn't want anyone to become disheartened or lose their focus if they had to spend the entire night on Half Dome. It was White whom Crozier leaned on most for support. He kept asking her how she was, telling her she was doing a great job and not to take Rice's insults to heart.

White had a strong opinion about the tragedy—that sheer stupidity and craziness had kindled it. But he kept his thoughts to himself.

White: "While I felt deeply sorry about what happened to these guys and tried to do everything I possibly could for them, I also became very angry about what they did. In the face of extreme danger, they acted like there was none, almost in defiance of the storm and lightning. Just unbelievably reckless. It was all so unnecessary, a waste."

Every now and then, a semidelirious Weiner called out: I can't feel my legs! I can't breathe! I'm going to die!

Again Rice yelled at him to get a grip, that he'd be all right, and again the words soothed Weiner. Rice's inner strength was helping Weiner—and himself—survive the crisis.

It was now 10:45 P.M. Physical as well as mental fatigue overcame Esteban. Crozier urged him to try to sleep while Bridges sat nearby, nudging Esteban periodically so he wouldn't drift into a coma. But Esteban couldn't sleep. Numbed, he just closed his eyes and wrestled with distressing thoughts about the day's events.

Rice suddenly exclaimed he was going to throw up. Crozier went into emergency mode, enlisting White and Cage to help her swiftly turn Rice on his side so he wouldn't choke on vomit. The three grasped his sleeping bag and carefully rolled him over, avoiding any movement that might jar his neck or back.

Then Rice coolly announced: Just kidding. I wanted to see if you know what you're doing.

White and Crozier looked at each other, incredulous. But as she regained her composure, Crozier reckoned that Rice, in his own twisted manner, was probably just trying to loosen everyone up, show he could roll with the punches, counterattack, take control again. The incident, however irritating to his caregivers, once more revealed his unflagging and indomitable spirit.

Eleven o'clock came and went without additional communication or sign of help from below.

Was a rescue under way or not?

And what had happened to Mike Hoog?

Stillness descended upon the Dome. When they weren't conferring about the status of Weiner or Rice, everyone was silent, and the silence aggravated their anxiety and stupor. The hikers were drained. They were cold and weary and somber, and just wanted to curl up inside a sleeping bag, though if Weiner or Rice made the slightest noise, someone rushed to attend to him. How much longer could the two injured men hold on without a bodily collapse of some sort?

As Linda Crozier's morale began to sink, too, her fears increased. The thought of what might happen to Weiner or Rice under her care was almost unbearable.

She quickly suppressed another surge of panic. The voice in her head said: Get a hold of yourself, Linda. You can't be the one who gives up hope—the others are depending on you. If you despair, the whole group will lose confidence. And that would be disastrous.

Esteban: "One of the most heartwarming emotions I felt and that sustained my will on this terrible night was watching these unknown persons comfort and care for me and my fallen buddies in our most dire hour of need. I remember people giving me their food, water, clothing, blankets, attention, caring, and human warmth throughout that night, which seemed to last forever."

Rice became more clearheaded as the night deepened, though he still complained vehemently about everything. Crozier made a pact with him: If help doesn't arrive by midnight, we'll move you into a more comfortable position. At this point, she had concluded privately that Rice probably would survive until morning if there were no rescue before then. He was stubborn and belligerent, intent on getting his way—a good omen.

However, the deterioration in his legs meant that without some kind of enhanced treatment, he would probably lose one or both of them to amputation.

The outlook for Weiner was bleaker. He lapsed into longer and longer periods of quiet punctuated by whimpering and sobbing, and into and out of consciousness. His injuries seemed more critical, his pain and unease more intense. Moreover, Weiner didn't have Rice's dogged determination. His fragile mental state might make him less inclined to resist death.

It was now 11:45 P.M., more than five hours since the lightning strikes.

Where were the rangers?

8

RESCUE

*The age-long stability of nature—my God, you can
depend on it! There's eternity in these rocks.*
—Carl Sharsmith, Yosemite ranger, 1930–94

Ranger Colin Campbell felt uneasy that no one was on duty
in Little Yosemite Valley; the assigned ranger had left earlier
that Saturday morning due to illness. Many hikers and campers
frequented this area—especially now, at the end of July—which
meant that any number of issues involving campers, bears, injuries,
and the like could demand the ranger's attention. Campbell told

his supervisor, Dan Horner, that he thought he should cover the station, at least for the night. Horner agreed. So Campbell saddled up his horse, John Paul, gathered some toiletries and a rain slicker, and departed for Little Yosemite Valley in late afternoon. He expected to return the next day.

Campbell, an assistant horse patrol supervisor, was thirty-five years old, married, and the father of a two-year-old daughter. More than six feet tall and husky at 195 pounds, he had held several National Park Service jobs, all in Yosemite. He'd received his bachelor of science degree in natural resource management from California Polytechnic College in San Luis Obispo in 1980 and, the prior year, had begun working for the National Park Service manning an entrance station at Yosemite for the summer. The next season he worked in campgrounds, mainly handling campsite reservations. Then he patrolled the park in a vehicle as a ranger. After two years in that position, he settled into the horse patrol division. This was the post Campbell occupied in 1985, his first year as a full-time ranger.

At 4 P.M. on July 27, as John Paul plodded up the John Muir Trail, a storm was building over Tenaya Canyon. It's going to be a real douser, Campbell thought. And, his experienced eye told him, unusually menacing. Moreover, it was sweeping right smack toward this part of Yosemite. Ordinarily, he gave hikers and backpackers freedom and space to enjoy the backcountry as long as they obeyed the law. Campbell kept a sharp eye out for potential problems, but he usually played it low-key and attempted to stay in the background. This time, though, his instincts made him uneasy. Something about this storm seemed different. So, with John Paul's hooves clacking on the granite, Campbell told people he passed not to take any undue risks, not to get caught out in the open, to be particularly careful in case of lightning.

When he reached Little Yosemite Valley, Campbell first stopped at the ranger station there, which consisted mainly of two wall tents. He then made rounds throughout the area to make sure everything was all right. Back at the station, he settled down for the evening. Scott Jackson, a trail maintenance employee who lived here in one of the tents during summer, soon returned from a day of hiking and joined him.

Lightning and thunder started blasting the heavens as they sat. When heavy rain began falling around 6 P.M., Campbell and Jackson took cover in the tents. Sheets of rain hammered the canvas for the next forty-five minutes, accompanied by barrages of lightning that left a distinctive scent, like burned gunpowder, in the drenched air. Ferocious cracks of thunder sent shock waves more powerful than Campbell had ever felt reverberating in the very ground under their feet.

By seven o'clock, the storm had passed. Campbell fired up a propane gas stove, opened a can of SpaghettiO's from the station's food stash, and spooned it into a pot to heat. He and Jackson then plunked down in a couple of chairs and ate their meager dinner.

Mike Hoog and Dan Crozier reached Little Yosemite Valley a little before 9:30 P.M. It took them a few minutes to locate the ranger station in the dark. When they did, Campbell was in front of a tent brushing his teeth, while Jackson was seated by the campfire. Hoog gushed out the details: Five guys hit by lightning, two dead, one fell over the edge, three guys injured, two seriously, they could die, need medical help fast!

Campbell now knew that his decision to man Little Yosemite Valley had been a good one—and that it was going to be a long night.

On his walkie-talkie, he reported the information to the ranger at the dispatch station down in the Valley. He and Jackson then hastily loaded a couple of packs with gear kept there at the Little Yosemite Valley station: oxygen canisters, a breakdown litter, ropes and anchors, climbing hardware, flashlights, and a "blitz pack" of emergency medical supplies. Campbell's walkie-talkie would keep them in close contact with the Valley. Because John Paul wasn't equipped with a pack saddle, Campbell decided to leave him tethered at the station and go on foot, a decision he would later regret.

Without further delay, each man hefted his forty-pound pack and, in pitch darkness, they departed up the trail for Half Dome.

◄o►

AT THE VERY TIME Hoog was spilling the news to Campbell, John Dill was shouting questions via his loudspeaker up to Paul Kolbenschlag on the summit of Half Dome. Just after Dill repeated the question, Will anyone die if help doesn't arrive? his walkie-talkie came on. It was the park dispatcher relaying Campbell's report. Now Dill knew what had caused the emergency.

Dill yelled up to Kolbenschlag that he would get back to them, leaving those on top clueless about what would happen next. He himself didn't know.

As in most of the country's national parks, hundreds of emergencies occur in Yosemite every year—crises involving injuries, fires, climbers in trouble, lost hikers, lawbreakers, and more. When something potentially serious happens, the news is first reported to the central dispatch station. The ranger on duty there then forwards it to the shift supervisor. Usually the supervisor assigns each case to an "incident commander," who then assumes operational responsibility for that emergency.*

The standard response to an emergency, if at all possible, is to move a ranger or team of rangers—a "hasty team"—quickly to the scene to assess the situation and report back to the shift supervisor. Regardless of whether a site report comes in, the supervisor and incident commander assign resources and brainstorm on

---

*In 1985, the National Park Service had five divisions in Yosemite: protection, resource management, maintenance, interpretation/education, and administration. Only personnel in the protection and interpretation/education divisions were referred to as rangers. Protection rangers were generally responsible for fee collections, law enforcement, emergencies, and search and rescue operations, while interpretation/education rangers handled public information activities.

strategies—including contingency or backup plans—to deal with the emergency. *Reach, treat, and evacuate* is the approach in most cases, *reach* being a ground action typically.

The shift supervisor this night was James Reilly. Rangers wouldn't be able to reach the top of Half Dome anytime soon, so he would have to make decisions without valuable information from the scene. Given the extreme nature of this particular incident and potential rescue attempt, Reilly chose to keep matters in his own hands rather than assign the case to an incident commander, at least until things became clearer.

Campbell and Jackson would be first on the scene, but they would need at least two hours from Little Yosemite Valley, placing them on the summit sometime around midnight. For support after their arrival, Reilly dispatched a team of rangers—Dan Horner, Mike Mayer, and Paul Ducasse, each a park medic capable of providing advanced medical care, such as starting IVs, administering medications, immobilizing limbs, and using MAST (Military Anti-Shock Trousers)—inflatable pressure pants to increase blood pressure and ward off shock. They would go on horses.

Reilly also sent a crew of seven, headed by top-notch rescue climber Dimitri Barton, in case anyone had to be removed from Half Dome. That would require team skills, such as lowering a victim by rope down very steep sections of rock. If victims couldn't be evacuated this night, Barton's team would establish a support camp in Little Yosemite Valley. Medical and other supplies could be brought there from the Valley for transport to the summit by runners.

By the time Horner, Mayer, and Ducasse rode off on their mounts, it was already 11 P.M. Barton's team soon followed on foot.

The wild-card strategy was an air rescue, a long shot at best. The park helicopter wasn't designed for night flying, plus it took a skilled and experienced pilot to carry out such a complex assignment after dark. The only real option was to summon a helicopter from a commercial service in San Joaquin Valley to the west. But even then, given the hazards of night flying at low altitudes—

power lines, trees, and other objects to avoid, not to mention possibly strong winds over Half Dome—such a mission would be dangerous and very costly. Without sufficient moonlight, it wouldn't even be considered.

Reilly was particularly conservative when he made decisions of this magnitude. He placed the highest value on the well-being of rescuers and was aware of a rash of helicopter crashes in recent years. As the clock neared 11 P.M., with clouds still filling the sky, he hadn't called for a helicopter rescue. The hikers on Half Dome wouldn't receive help anytime soon. Complicating matters was another emergency report that came in right after Reilly got word of the Half Dome incident. This one, too, was a matter of life and death.

◄O►

THE SECOND REPORT arrived at the dispatch office at 9:45 P.M. Hikers lost in the park had used a CB radio to communicate their desperate situation to a son in Yosemite Valley, who then told a ranger.

The ranger was able to piece together this much: that four females—two adults and two thirteen-year-olds—were lost in the vicinity of Tenaya Canyon; that the adults were sisters, ages forty-five and thirty-eight; and that both suffered from epilepsy and needed medicine daily. The group had intended to hike from Olmsted Point near Tenaya Lake in the high country down to Yosemite Valley via the little-used and poorly maintained Snow Creek Trail. Because this was to be only a day hike, the women weren't carrying extra clothing or food—or epilepsy medicine. The son had planned to pick them up in Yosemite Valley at hike's end.

The foursome had left Olmsted Point at 1:30 P.M. and expected to reach the Valley around 8. This left little more than an hour of daylight after the hike—a very small margin of safety. Moreover, had they scanned the skies, they likely would have noticed the cumulus clouds building above Clouds Rest.

Staying on Snow Creek Trail can be difficult where it traverses bare granite. Indeed, midway down, the women lost the trail. They spotted a "duck"—a trail marker made of stacked rocks—and then more ducks, which they tried to follow. These occasional markers led them farther down into a canyon, which seemed like the right direction. But after some distance, they found themselves over-looking an impassable cliff.

Anxious about the dark clouds massing overhead and the looming storm, the women frantically retraced their steps in the hope of locating Snow Creek Trail. A duck here and there sug-gested they were back on course, though mainly they just headed downhill as swiftly as possible on the assumption their destination was ahead. The rain that began in early evening quickly drenched and chilled them. When they hit level ground, the hikers weren't anywhere near Yosemite Valley. They were in Tenaya Canyon, about three miles east of Happy Isles.

Exiting Tenaya Canyon is extremely difficult. Its steep, pol-ished-granite walls rise thousands of feet, and dense vegetation car-pets the floor. Rangers refer to it as the "Bermuda Triangle of Yosemite," given the many hikers who have gotten lost there.*

Amid the fierce thunderstorm, wandering in the canyon maze, the women spotted and took refuge in a rock enclosure (not unlike Rice, Esteban, and their fellow hikers on Half Dome, and James Wunrow in nearby Kings Canyon National Park, all of whom took shelter in rock enclosures on this same day, with tragic conse-quences). They stayed huddled together in the enclosure even after

---

*One high-profile case dates to 1966, when Charles Frizzell, a thirty-one-year-old sci-entist at the Bay Area's Livermore Radiation Laboratory, seemingly vanished in Yosemite. Frizzell was last seen on June 4 hiking down from Olmsted Point. In those Cold War years, government authorities feared he had been killed or kidnapped, or that he had defected to China. Park rangers searched Tenaya Canyon in vain for more than a week. Some of Frizzell's co-workers joined the hunt, a contingent that later evolved into the Bay Area Mountain Rescue Unit. The mystery wasn't solved until spring 1971, when a hiker found Frizzell's credit card and a skull in Tenaya Canyon. Later that summer, another hiker stumbled upon some bones on a narrow, tree-lined ledge. Ranger Butch Farabee returned to the site with him and discovered more than a hundred human bones, pre-sumably Frizzell's, and shreds of a backpack several feet up in a nearby oak tree. Farabee suspects that Frizzell put his pack up there as a signal for help; that perhaps he had fallen to the ledge and broken bones below his waist. At the request of Frizzell's widow, Farabee buried the remains in Tenaya Canyon.

the storm had long since passed. About 8:30 P.M. they were able to contact the son with their CB radio. By this time, the forty-five-year-old woman had had an epileptic seizure. Without medicine within ten to fifteen hours, she or her sister might die. To make matters worse, both had suffered ankle sprains.

Reilly got the report on the lost hikers shortly after the Half Dome report. He assigned only two rangers, Ron Mackie and Scott Emmerich, to the Tenaya Canyon rescue because he was short-handed due to the Half Dome mission. Mackie, a supervisory park ranger, knew the area well. Emmerich was a park medic.

At 11:30 P.M., each hefting forty pounds of gear, Mackie and Emmerich embarked on a strenuous and treacherous hike to reach the four women. Their route was Aircraft Crash Canyon, so named because of numerous airplane crashes there in the early 1940s when U.S. Air Force pilots flew practice and sightseeing missions over Yosemite. (To this day, a large engine from one of the downed aircraft remains in the canyon.) In Mackie's experience, most hikers lost in Tenaya Canyon ended up in the inner gorge, in an area informally called Lost Valley. He and Emmerich headed for that location.

When the women took refuge in the rock enclosure, they wisely left their lit flashlights perched on a high rock. A ranger "spotter" on a distant point overlooking the canyon saw the light beams and guided the two rangers via radio as they descended. After hiking in the dark and cold all night, Mackie and Emmerich reached the most dangerous part of their journey, a drop down a steep and slippery granite incline. Rather than risk a fall, the two waited an hour for dawn before continuing.

Meanwhile, the four shivering and terrified hikers lay cuddled together trying to fend off the frigid temperatures. In addition to their other medical problems, one of the teens had a sharp pain in her side—a symptom, the two adults worried, of appendicitis. The night passed. None slept a single minute, their chilled bodies approaching hypothermia. Only the shared warmth from their snuggled bodies saved them.

The women left their shelter at dawn and began walking as best they could. Mackie and Emmerich, who by now had reached the canyon floor, spotted them at around 7 A.M. Emmerich administered medicine to the more seriously impaired woman, the one who had suffered a seizure, while Mackie prepared hot food and drink on his camping stove. The severe pain in the teen's side had abated and ultimately would prove to be benign.

Back in Yosemite Valley, a rescue helicopter from Lemoore Naval Air Station near Fresno had been summoned, and when it arrived, it flew to Tenaya Canyon to evacuate the party. The chopper transported the hikers and Emmerich to the Valley, then returned to retrieve Mackie. Thus ended a successful mission.

◄◦►

BY THE TIME JACKSON and Campbell left Little Yosemite Valley, it was nearly 10 P.M. Jackson, who had turned twenty-three the previous month, was in superb physical condition. A long-distance runner like Hoog, he had spent the summer weeks hiking and running the park's trails. Campbell, on the other hand, as a horse patrol supervisor spent more time getting about on horseback than on foot. And he had arrived at Little Yosemite Valley this day wearing cowboy boots rather than hiking boots, not anticipating a trek through rough terrain in the dark. Even more worrisome, how would he scale Half Dome's slippery granite in slick leather soles?

Hoog and Dan Crozier followed on the heels of Jackson and Campbell to rejoin their hiking companions at the base of Half Dome. All told, the pair would log more than sixteen miles of hiking, mostly uphill, over fourteen hours. To that, Hoog added a jaunt up and down the cables on Half Dome. As they retraced their steps, the rush of the evening's excitement overcame their fatigue.

Right from the start, Jackson outpaced Campbell, who was silently cursing himself for not having worn hiking boots. Or better, he wished he had ridden John Paul. Jackson reached Sub

Dome at 11:15 P.M. and kept on going. Campbell got there ten minutes later. By now his feet were sore and blistered. He needed hiking shoes. Approaching a tent, Campbell flashed his light, roused the sleeping occupant inside, and inquired about the man's shoe size. The startled camper surely thought this was some kind of sick joke, but then he saw the ranger uniform and concluded it wasn't.

Size twelve, he responded.

It was Campbell's size exactly—a "lucky break," he later recalled.

Campbell said he needed hiking boots. The camper offered what he had: his high-top sneakers. Campbell pulled off his boots, stashed them near the tent opening, donned the sneakers, and vanished.

It was 11:30 P.M.

◄○►

MEANWHILE, RANGERS Horner, Mayer, and Ducasse rode their horses up the John Muir Trail. The terrain blocked out moonlight in many places, making it almost impossible to see anything in the shadows. Horner, the park's horse patrol supervisor and an experienced horseman, assured his companions that their mounts knew the trail and could be relied upon to stay on it.

Mayer and Ducasse were quite leery about trusting animals to negotiate the narrow track at night, with its numerous granite steps, rocks, drainage abutments, and occasional steep drop-offs. They themselves couldn't even sense in the dense blackness whether they were going uphill or down. Flashlights were out of the question because the light might disrupt the horses' vision, creating an even greater hazard. So the riders had no choice but to place all faith in the animals' ability to grip stone with their hooves and keep a hand in front of their faces to ward off any unseen branches. All the time Horner listened to his walkie-talkie for updates on the rescue and if there would be an attempted air evacuation.

◄○►

SHORTLY AFTER 11 P.M., moonlight broke through partially clearing skies, spurring Reilly to move ahead with plans for a helicopter rescue. Although he still lacked a firsthand evaluation of the emergency scene, Reilly approved a request to dispatch Medi-Flight of Northern California, an air ambulance service from Memorial Hospital in Modesto, approximately a hundred miles west of Yosemite.

In 1985, such service was a relatively young concept, one rooted in knowledge gained from the Korean and Vietnam conflicts. In particular, army surgeons tending the 250,000 casualties of the Vietnam War saw the need for timely triage and quickly learned the importance of rapid transport and treatment of wounded soldiers. Findings showed that victims' chances of survival were best within the first hour of critical injury, the so-called golden hour. After that, the odds declined dramatically.

Also, research on heart attacks had demonstrated the value of prompt cardiopulmonary resuscitation. CPR must take place within four to six minutes of heart failure to restore cardiac function and oxygen circulation. Otherwise, the damage may be irreversible.

The emphasis on immediate treatment gave rise to a host of new emergency services. First came the expansion of emergency rooms at hospitals. Before the 1970s, many general acute-care hospitals didn't have anything like an emergency department; only a few large medical centers did, and they were mostly teaching facilities. Prehospital care was almost nonexistent, and medical treatment usually didn't begin until a patient arrived at the hospital. Typically, patients were delivered to the nearest hospital either by hearses, because they were the only vehicles available in which people could lie flat, or by an ambulance if one was at hand. At the hospital, a nurse, intern, or on-call physician would administer treatment in a room stocked only with basic medical supplies—bandages, suction, oxygen, scalpels, hemostats, splints, restraints, sutures, syringes, and a few medications. It may or may not have had any emergency equipment. If it did, this "emergency room"—now a misnomer in all but the smallest hospitals—served as the staging area for care. For serious cases, the on-call nurse would summon a staff physician, the patient's personal doctor (if known), or perhaps another general practitioner or surgeon outside the hospital.

Over time, as the importance of sophisticated emergency care gained recognition, ambulances bypassed small hospitals with limited facilities in favor of larger medical centers with better emergency services and equipment. Thus evolved dedicated emergency departments, which were common features at most hospitals by the early 1970s.* Spurring this movement was the federal Emergency Medical Services Systems Act of 1973 authorizing the secretary of the U.S. Department of Health, Education and Welfare to provide grants to states and other jurisdictions to develop and operate emergency medical services. Expanded legislation in 1976 helped promote EMS systems in rural and other medically underserved areas.

Still, high-quality emergency rooms were inaccessible to many victims within the golden hour. What these patients needed was treatment at the scene, and that meant improving ambulance services. Up to the 1970s, ambulance drivers in most areas of the country had to meet minimal standards—get their fingerprints checked, pass a special driver's test, and take a basic first-aid course. The situation called for trained professionals who could provide immediate, appropriate emergency medical care in the field, which prompted the creation of prehospital emergency medicine certification programs. Paramedics soon became essential members of ambulance teams.

Some urgent cases, however, necessitated the kind of sophisticated treatment available only at well-equipped hospitals. The solution: faster transport to those facilities by helicopter. A few

*In 1968, a group of eight physicians founded the American College of Emergency Physicians. In 1979, the American Board of Medical Specialties and the American Medical Association recognized emergency medicine as the twenty-third medical specialty. So board-certified emergency medical care has only been available for about thirty years.

advanced hospitals around the country therefore began offering air ambulance services with EMTs, nurses or paramedics, and sometimes physicians on board to provide expert care.

An auxiliary development in emergency medicine was trauma care—treating patients who have severe and multiple injuries at regional centers that offer a team of multidisciplinary experts and special trauma gear. Trauma is the leading cause of death among people younger than forty-four (auto accidents are responsible for about half of such deaths) and one of the country's most expensive health-care problems. While many trauma deaths happen immediately, many others occur past the golden hour for any number of secondary reasons. In response to this need, some hospitals gained designation as trauma centers.

On Half Dome this night, Rice's and Weiner's critical condition mandated transport to a trauma center. Not only can lightning injuries be highly destructive and lethal, but sometimes they aren't readily detectable, as with damage to vital organs or the brain, impairments to the nervous and circulatory systems, or a weakening of the immune system. Only a highly trained physician using advanced technology might correctly diagnose and treat such injuries. With each passing hour, the future well-being of Rice and Weiner hinged on Medi-Flight's ability to pluck them from Half Dome and deliver them to a trauma center.

‹o›

WHEN MEDI-FLIGHT began operating on December 1, 1978, it was only the third air ambulance program in California and one of only nine nationally. Founder Rick Donker, vice president of Memorial Hospital, had earlier developed the statewide EMT curriculum.

When an accident report came in, Medi-Flight customarily flew directly to the scene or wherever the injured person was located. There, Medi-Flight's paramedic treated and, with the help of a flight nurse, stabilized the injured party, which typically involved inserting an IV and hooking up a cardiac monitor, then strapping the patient onto a gurney. The helicopter delivered the "packaged" victim to Memorial Hospital in Modesto.

Night flights were common at Medi-Flight. It received up to three or four calls on most nights, many from the California Highway Patrol. Each response depended on the amount of moonlight available for a safe flight, landing, and evacuation.

Given its proximity to Yosemite, Medi-Flight routinely flew there, perhaps once or twice a week in the busy summer months and maybe once a month or less in winter. However, flying a helicopter into Yosemite Valley could be dicey even in daylight, particularly on summer afternoons when the heat and thinner air made it more difficult for chopper blades to generate lift. Crane Flat, which sits above the Valley floor, gave helicopters more room to maneuver; consequently many victims were taken there for airlift out of the park.

Night flights to Yosemite Valley were less common. On moonless nights, victims in critical condition were transported by ambulance to Crane Flat to await air evacuation if and when conditions permitted.

Medi-Flight became especially cautious about night flights after a tragic mission on June 23, 1982. Just after 1 A.M., a Medi-Flight crew that included a top-notch pilot, paramedic, and nurse took off from Modesto for Sonora Pass in the Sierra Nevada to retrieve an auto accident victim in critical condition. In scant moonlight, while trying to manuever the craft for landing, the pilot was disoriented by a patch of darkness. Helicopter lights don't provide adequate illumination in pitch dark, with no objects to illuminate. All the pilot sees is bright light and a black backdrop. In effect, he can't see.* Airplane pilots can navigate by instruments when flying in utter darkness or obscured conditions, but helicopter pilots don't use instruments in tight places like Yosemite Valley. For them, it all comes down to visibility. They need ambient light to see objects, landmarks, and the horizon—reference points for

---

*The improvement in night vision goggles spurred on by the first Gulf war in the early 1990s has greatly assisted helicopter pilots in their night flying.

keeping the craft properly oriented. When visibility is poor, a helicopter pilot may be unable to sense if the machine is turning, tilting, dropping, or ascending and can quickly become disoriented, lose control, and begin an "uncontrolled descent"—or even flip the craft. That's what happened in this case. When the Medi-Flight pilot hit a dark patch, he couldn't see and, hence, couldn't navigate. The craft began swerving and dropping, its tail rotor hit a tall cedar tree, and the machine crashed. All three crew members perished, including paramedic Dan Donker, Rick Donker's twenty-eight-year-old brother.

In 1982 alone, nearly twenty air ambulance personnel were killed nationwide. So when authorities in Yosemite requested a nighttime evacuation from Half Dome on July 27, 1985, Medi-Flight was understandably guarded about accepting the assignment.

The pilot on duty at the time was Al Major, thirty-five years old. Major had learned how to fly helicopters in U.S. Army Flight School at age nineteen. Immediately after graduation in April 1969, he left for Vietnam, where he was stationed at Tay Ninh northwest of Saigon on the Cambodian border. Major flew UH-1Hs (Hueys) and AH-1Gs (Cobras), first as a pilot, then as an aircraft commander, fire team leader, and ultimately air mission commander. During his nineteen-month tour, he logged close to seventeen hundred combat flying hours. Although several times he returned to base with his chopper "limping" from enemy fire, Major escaped injuries or wounds. By the time he was discharged in 1970, he had received the Bronze Star, Distinguished Flying Cross, and fifty-three Air Medal awards, each one awarded for either twenty-five hours of combat flight or fifty hours of non-combat flight. Most of Major's were the former.

Before he agreed to fly the Half Dome mission, Major contacted the FAA's Flight Service Station in Stockton for moon information. The station reported a quarter to third moon that would set behind Yosemite's ridges at 1:42 A.M. Medi-Flight's protocols called for departure within six to ten minutes after a call came in. The flight to Yosemite Valley would take approximately thirty-seven minutes, if all went well, and arrive shortly after midnight. It would be a tight window, but a rescue attempt was possible— if the moonlight held. Because he would need to refuel on this extended mission, Major also requested confirmation from Yosemite that he could access the fuel in the Lemoore Naval Air Station's cache in the Valley (its helicopter search and rescue squadron sometimes performed rescues in Yosemite).

With these matters resolved, Medi-Flight accepted the assignment. Major took off from Modesto at 11:23 P.M. in the company's TwinStar, a large, French-made helicopter geared to the demands of the air ambulance trade.

Whenever he flew, Major conversed sparingly and showed little humor. His main concern was the safety of his crew and helicopter. He strived to make each mission as routine as possible; he remained cool and detached while focusing only on immediate tasks. Major imposed a steadfast rule: When a call came in, he wasn't to receive any information about the victims. That way, his decisions would be free of emotional influence.

Accompanying Major were flight nurse Maggie Newman and paramedic Bill Bryant. Because nurses undergo more training than paramedics do, the flight nurse is in charge of medical care on air ambulance flights. But such training focuses on hospital care, so nurses typically relinquish authority in the field to the paramedic, who usually has more experience with field traumas.

As a hospital nurse, Newman once witnessed a helicopter rescue; the high drama captivated her. After that, she wanted to be part of an air ambulance team. She got her wish and soon became, as she says, a "trauma junkie," her adrenaline racing while dealing with life-and-death situations—from knife and gunshot wounds to car accidents, falls from precipitous heights, and other human calamities. Although Newman was scared to death most of the time, she tried never to show it. To achieve calm, she sometimes slept in the helicopter en route. Major didn't like that; he wanted crew members to be on the lookout for other aircraft and obstacles.

Newman occasionally donned sunglasses and a cap so Major couldn't see her sleeping.

The nurse on the ill-fated flight that crashed in 1982 had been Medi-Flight's chief flight nurse. Newman suffered panic attacks following the accident. After time off to reflect on whether this was really the right career for her, she returned to work as chief flight nurse at Medi-Flight, the position she held in July 1985.

In all of her experiences, however, she had never treated a lightning victim.

Paramedic Bryant received his EMT certification when he was only a high school senior, in a class that Rick Donker taught. Bryant had been scheduled to man the doomed 1982 flight but wanted to go to Mexico on a getaway and got Dan Donker to cover for him. Others sometimes perceived Bryant as arrogant and a "cowboy" who often ignored protocols and instructions if he thought something should be done differently. He didn't hesitate to correct doctors when he thought their actions were wrong.

Field emergencies often involve head traumas, broken necks, and excessive bleeding, each of which can cause shock. Among environmental injuries are hypothermia, frostbite, drowning, and snakebite. Logistical issues may complicate these medical problems, something that few nurses or physicians have experience handling. A patient with chest pain, for example, might be given oxygen and receive an IV and morphine—standard medical procedures. But if a victim is pinned inside a car that's upside down in a muddy ditch, what then? Bryant insisted that fellow paramedics at Medi-Flight learn how to rappel, make an accident scene safe, fight fires, extricate people, carry out search and rescue operations, and perform other important nonmedical tasks.

Ironically, Bryant had taught segments of Linda Crozier's EMT class. But as the copter lifted off in Modesto and headed toward Yosemite, he had no idea that Crozier was the very person who'd taken charge of administering emergency treatment atop Half Dome.

◄○►

AS CAMPBELL HIKED up Sub Dome, he got a report on his walkie-talkie that an air ambulance was on its way, which meant he had to reach the top of Half Dome in time to establish a landing zone (LZ). Quickening his pace, he arrived at the bottom of the cables at 11:45 P.M. as Jackson's silhouette appeared against the sky beyond the ridgeline above.

On the summit, it took Jackson a few minutes in the blackness to locate the group huddled around the two victims. His sudden appearance, seemingly from out of nowhere, surprised everyone. A greatly relieved Crozier assumed he was a ranger and immediately began reporting on the injured. But Jackson stopped her, explaining he was in park maintenance and there to help only with logistics.

When Campbell reached the summit, Jackson shouted to him. This time, the arrival of a uniformed ranger gave everyone a huge psychological boost. Crozier briefed Campbell on the victims, once again believing that, finally, she would be able to hand off the care of Weiner and Rice to someone else. Campbell quickly assessed the pair, checking mainly for any loss of vital functions and signs of trauma. He administered oxygen to Weiner, who appeared to be in worse shape. Then he told Crozier to carry on while he established a makeshift helicopter pad for a possible air evacuation.

Campbell: "I concluded right away that some good stuff happened this night in terms of how the emergency was handled. Linda was able to provide accurate information on the injured and a sense of stability about the situation. I felt I could leave her in charge and go set up the landing pad. The best care for the two victims was to get them off the mountain as quickly as possible."

Campbell radioed his report to the dispatch center in the Valley. Experience told him that an air evacuation was still a long shot, given the moonlight's small window of opportunity and the unpredictable sky. There were only two other options, neither of them good: A ground evacuation by Horner and his team, or an air evacuation at dawn. Next, Campbell radioed the Yosemite Medical

Clinic to say the victims would need to be brought there as soon as possible after the rescue. One was in very bad shape, he reported, with labored breathing and compromised vital signs.

After Campbell gave Crozier a stethoscope and blood pressure cuff, he set out with Jackson to find a suitable LZ.

Crozier took Rice's and Weiner's blood pressure. She couldn't get a reading for either of them, which indicated their conditions were very precarious. The stethoscope told her that Rice's breathing was okay but that there still was gurgling in Weiner's lungs, an early symptom of deadly pulmonary edema.

A calmer Rice again wanted to move now that help was in sight. Crozier said no. Esteban urged Rice to trust her judgment and told him he would be okay if he could just hold on a bit longer.

As seconds ticked away, the helpers entered a suspended state, as if they were holding their breath underwater while waiting to surface. It was a race between the descent of the moon and the arrival of a helicopter. With each passing minute, an evacuation this night became more unlikely.

◄○►

CLU COTTER SCANNED the western horizon, trying to estimate how long it would be before the moon disappeared. To him, it looked like there was less than two hours of moonlight left. Something had to happen soon.

He peered into the darkness. All of a sudden, a speck of light appeared far off in the distance. He fastened his gaze on the light—it was getting bigger. An aircraft was entering the Valley! He shouted the news. A resounding cheer erupted on the summit, all eyes now focused on the light coming toward them. The speck grew brighter and brighter as the helicopter's searchlight swept back and forth to illuminate the ground.

As the copter drew closer, the *whop-whop-whop* sound of rotor blades became louder, amplified by the granite walls. Surely everyone in Yosemite Valley heard the noise, but for those on the summit, the roar of the rotors seemed to lift a mountain of weight off their backs.

It was just after midnight when Major landed his aircraft in Ahwahnee Meadow, only a few hundred feet from Yosemite Village and the famed Ahwahnee Hotel, where bedded guests no doubt wondered what was happening.

Campbell and Jackson had located a mainly level site on a high part of Half Dome that was separated by a saddle from where the victims lay almost three hundred feet away. They hastily removed rocks and swept away small gravel and any other matter that the copter's downdraft might kick up.

Campbell returned to the group of rescuers to gather flashlights. Six of the hikers returned with him to the landing zone. Campbell arranged the flashlights in a circle on the ground around the LZ to outline the area where the helicopter should land. The others positioned themselves far back from the circle while Campbell got ready to guide the copter in, using his two flashlights as a mark to direct Major in his approach.

Down in the Valley, Reilly quickly briefed Major. Time was crucial. If Major landed on the summit and the moonlight vanished, he and his crew might be stuck up there overnight. Gary Colliver, a ranger and park medic, joined Major and Bryant for the ascent. Newman remained on the Valley floor; her skills would come into play when the crew and victims returned.

Major stayed tightly focused on his mission. Flying up to Half Dome and landing on top in the dark would be hazardous, but if there was some moonlight and few obstacles, he considered it an acceptable risk. The greater challenge would be taking off from the summit and dropping down into the Valley with trees all around. His concentration had to remain razor-sharp. True to his code, Major didn't want any information about the victims. In his view, "a pilot can't be influenced by such factors—they may cause him to make a bad judgment, such as trying to go too quickly."

In a roar of the engine and twirling rotors, the helicopter lifted off from Ahwahnee Meadow at 12:35 A.M. Major would have to fly forward in a spiraling, circular course, rather than climbing straight up, to make the most efficient use of the craft's horsepower at that altitude. Such a course would also provide needed visibility. Those on board couldn't see the mountain they were ascending— a "very eerie experience," in Colliver's words—as they departed the Valley and passed through a dark zone devoid of any reference points.

After about a ten-minute climb and nearly a mile of elevation gain, there it was, the summit of the Dome, a circle of flashlights off in the distance. Following Campbell's guidance, Major maneuvered his machine over the LZ for a "pinnacle approach," or one from directly above. Then he gently brought it down. When the craft got near the ground, Bryant jumped off wearing his communications headset with a cord long enough for him to remain safely away from the spinning rotors. Although Major was concerned about landing on an uncertain surface, he hovered only briefly as Bryant directed him to move the aircraft a few feet or inches this way or that for the most level spot. Major placed the landing skids lightly on the rock, barely "feeling" them settle, and shut the engine down.

Major: "This type of helicopter likes to be either solidly on the ground or sufficiently airborne, and not in between. The in-between part—that is, close to but not on the ground—can set up a sympathetic vibration or ground resonance that can destroy the aircraft, literally shake it apart, so we obviously tended to avoid that flight regime."

Bryant scuttled over to where the injured lay. After Crozier's thorough report, he concluded there was little more to be done medically on the summit.

Bryant: "There was just no time to waste. At that point, I thought it was fifty–fifty at best that we would get both patients off the rock that night. If the moon disappeared, the rescue was probably off until

daylight. The priority was to move as quickly as possible to get one—
and, if we were lucky, both—patients to the Valley."

Given the amount of floor space a patient strapped in a gurney
required, the helicopter could only take one patient at a time.

If only one of the victims could be evacuated tonight, Bryant
asked Crozier, who should it be?

Weiner, she answered.

Jackson, Brian Cage, Steve White, and Bryant lifted Weiner
onto a stretcher and moved him to the helicopter. Meanwhile,
Colliver checked Brian Jordan's body in the cave and determined
that nothing more could be done. The body would remain there
for the night.

Once Weiner was strapped in the helicopter, Colliver, with no
medical issues to attend to, climbed aboard for the flight down.
Bryant stayed behind.

Rangers in the Valley had positioned park vehicles, their red and
blue lights flashing, as a beacon for Major. One vehicle's headlights
faced Ahwahnee Meadow to illuminate the landing zone. Spotlights
shone on the highest pine trees nearby to help Major avoid them.

Major fired up the helicopter, lifted off, and flew away from
the summit. Past Half Dome's edge, he began the one-mile
descent, which he would have to execute very deliberately, especially on this first flight. The only available light came from a sliver
of moon, which reflected off the high granite, and from the vehicle beams and other lights far down on the Valley floor.

Colliver: "On the summit, the moonlight illuminated the granite and the nearby ridges, and my eyes were adjusted to the light.
However, what lay beyond Half Dome looked like a black hole.
When we dropped into this void, with no horizons or reference
features other than an occasional floating point of light on the Valley floor, it produced for me a sudden sensation of blindness, disorientation, a loss of breath, and fear for what might be out there
in the pitch darkness. It was only when we got close enough to the
Valley floor to see light reflected off the ground or nearby objects,

and could get a sense of relative motion, that I felt safe and could breathe normally again."

Unnerved by the descent, Colliver prayed that Major had a better sense of the surroundings than he did. In fact, Major considered the flight down quite normal and manageable. He had flown hundreds of more demanding and dangerous missions, his eyes had adjusted to the darkness, and he had little difficulty charting the route. Plus, as Major said later, "Yosemite officials had the landing zone lit up like a Christmas tree."

After a rightward-spiraling descent and keeping the helicopter centered over the illuminated target, Major brought his craft down in Ahwahnee Meadow at 1:07 A.M. Weiner was immediately transferred to a waiting ambulance and brought to the clinic. Although park physician Bill Bowie was in charge, Newman took over Weiner's care. She connected him to a cardiac monitor and inserted an IV and Foley catheter, or tube in his penis, to collect urine. This helped alleviate his urinary tract blockage.

Back on the summit, Crozier again reviewed Rice's and Esteban's injuries with Bryant. Only then did she and Bryant realize they knew each other from her EMT class. Bryant's knowledge, experience, and calming influence finally brought Crozier the relief she desperately needed. At last, someone else was in charge—she could give her mind and body a rest.

As the rescue activities buzzed around him, Esteban, watching in silence, felt a flood of emotions and thoughts. He was tremendously relieved that Rice and Weiner had survived the many hours on Half Dome, and were now in good hands. Still, big uncertainties remained. Would they live? And if they did, what future impact would their injuries have? Would his buddy Rice be crippled for life? Thankfully, his own fate didn't depend on an air evacuation. His wounds were primarily mental—anguish over what had transpired, psychological fragility, not to mention complete exhaustion. He had been thrashed by lightning, been deprived of sleep, and was emotionally spent from bolstering Rice's and

Weiner's spirits across several hours. Over and over he replayed the day's decisions in his mind: Why did this happen and why did we challenge the gods? What if we had done this instead of that? He couldn't stop dwelling on his leaving Frith on the ledge. What about Frith's loved ones, and those of the Jordan kid?

But one fact superseded all this and took center stage in his awareness: He was alive! Outwardly, Esteban appeared to others to be shell-shocked. Inwardly, he was screaming with joy that he'd escaped his companions' fate. He wanted to jump up and kiss the sky! At that instant, he felt more in touch with life than ever before—far more than he had while racing up the cables with Rice, which seemed like eons ago, and experiencing the rush of living on the razor's edge. Esteban wanted to freeze this moment so he would never forget what it felt like to cheat death and get another chance.

◄○►

AT 1:15 A.M., Major launched the helicopter a second time, intent on flying to and from Half Dome as fast as possible. Over the Dome and now familiar with the landing zone, he circled it, landed with little delay, and kept the copter's engine running. Bryant was attending to Rice on a nearby stretcher. Though Rice seemed reasonably stable, Bryant knew the often hidden health risks from lightning strikes. He also believed that if the rescue had to be aborted, Rice's condition would only deteriorate, and Bryant didn't look forward to spending the night with him on the rock. He was very thankful that the highly skilled Major was the pilot this night.

Before Bryant and Jackson placed Rice in the helicopter, Steve White told him to enjoy the ride because he would never get another one quite like it. This comment seemed to boost Rice's spirits. With Rice and Bryant on board, Major took off and, his route now clearly established, descended more rapidly than before. The copter set down in Ahwahnee Meadow at 1:25 A.M. Except for the Foley catheter, Newman tended Rice the same as she had Weiner.

At 1:30 A.M., only twelve minutes of moonlight remained, barely enough time for one last pickup. Esteban waited nervously, thinking how cruel it would be to have survived lightning strikes only to perish in a helicopter crash. Major didn't waste any time: He took off again, flew up to the summit, and waited as Esteban, who didn't need a stretcher, was hoisted aboard. Campbell joined him. Just as Major lifted off from Half Dome, the moon was disappearing behind the ridgeline. Campbell later said the flight down was like "dropping into a black envelope, one of the most frightening experiences in my life."

Now Major had to rely strictly on the lights on the Valley floor for direction and orientation. He completed this third and final journey without mishap. The rescue was over.

With two patients strapped in gurneys and limited space, Weiner and Rice would need to be taken in separate helicopters to the University of California, Davis Medical Center in Sacramento, which had a major trauma center. During the rescue, Yosemite authorities had summoned a second helicopter from CALSTAR, an air ambulance service at St. Rose Hospital in Hayward. Major refilled the copter's tanks from the U.S. Navy's fuel trailer and, at about 3:20 A.M., he, Bryant, Newman, and Weiner, who had been strapped into a gurney with an IV and cardiac monitor in place, departed for Memorial Hospital in Modesto. They passed the CALSTAR helicopter on its way in to retrieve Rice.

The emergency staff at Memorial Hospital examined Weiner while the helicopter refueled for the flight to Sacramento. They determined that he wasn't in any immediate danger. Major had "houred out," so he was done for the night. With a new pilot and Newman and Bryant still on board, the copter departed for UC Davis Medical Center. By that time, CALSTAR was en route to the same hospital with Rice.

Medi-Flight had done its job. Now the fates of Weiner and Rice rested with doctors in Sacramento.

9

RECOVERY

Never more, however weary, should one faint by the
way who gains the blessings of one mountain day;
whatever his fate, long life, short life, stormy or calm,
he is rich forever.—John Muir

Weiner and Rice both arrived by helicopter at the UC Davis Medical Center, Sacramento in the early-morning hours on Sunday. After Weiner gave the authorities his parents' phone number in New Hampshire, he was sedated and his world went black again. Rice, too, was sedated.

A slew of IVs delivered morphine, sedatives, vasopressors (medications that raise blood pressure), saline, and other fluids to the two men. Dr. Howard Klein, a plastic surgeon, was the attending physician.

Dr. Klein reported that massive electrical charges had shot though each of the hikers, entering at the hips and exiting at the feet. The basic injury was to microscopic blood vessels: As they clotted, tissue began to die. The sudden jolt of electrical current through the legs had also severely damaged both muscles and nerves in their lower bodies, causing leg muscles to swell. That blocked the transmission of nerve impulses and blood to their lower legs—a condition called compartment syndrome. It can produce necrosis (tissue death) of all structures in the legs and necessitate their amputation. Dr. Klein was concerned that the burn wounds would progress, which, in the case of electrical injuries, they often do.

Although he possessed feeling in his feet and could move his toes, Rice's lower body was still numbed and fraught with pain. His right leg in particular was severely damaged, his entire calf muscle split in half and exposed two or three inches deep, as if someone had split it down the middle with a knife. There was a large wound spewing pus on his back near the spine. Dr. Klein's initial prognosis was that even if he didn't have to amputate, Rice would probably never walk again.

A toxic compound released into the bloodstream by the burns continued to threaten both victims by attacking the kidneys. They were retaining fluids, which caused their body weight to increase dramatically.

After only a few hours of sleep, Weiner and Rice each underwent two hours of surgery early Sunday morning. Internal pressure on their leg muscles had to be released and the wounds cleaned out to prevent infection. Dr. Klein led a surgical team of five physicians, who performed a fasciotomy on the leg muscles: They cut the fascia, or lining that holds muscle together like a sleeve, and thus allowed the swollen muscle to bulge out. This, in turn, reduced pressure on the blood vessels and nerves, averting permanent damage. Once such swelling subsides, physicians repair the fascia and then graft skin over the affected areas.

◄○►

AFTER THE HELICOPTER rescue, postclimax letdown settled in among those who remained on Half Dome's summit. Everyone was mentally, physically, and psychologically spent. Crozier broke the tension.

Okay, guys, she said. It's Miller time.

After nearly seven hours of life-or-death anxiety, the fates of Weiner and Rice were in someone else's hands.

The adrenaline rush that had kept Crozier alert and focused for all those hours abruptly cratered. Weary and cold, she now had to descend the cables and Sub Dome and reunite with her hiking companions. Except for Scott Jackson, the trail maintenance employee, who offered to accompany her down, the others would spend the night on Half Dome as they had planned. Steve White and his fellow hikers offered to share with her their sleeping bags and anything else that provided warmth if she elected to stay on top for the remainder of that short night. She declined.

Crozier: "I desperately needed to get off that mountain—to get away from the edge, away from the danger, away from death!"

Before she left, she thanked those who had lent so much help and support throughout the ordeal. Everyone there felt the strong sense of cohesiveness and mutual affection that had blossomed during the long hours.

Jackson and Crozier began their journey down the treacherous slope. It was fully dark; the moon had long since set beyond the western ridge. Crozier clutched the cables as hard as she possibly could and half slid, half staggered down the slick granite. The descent, although dangerous, was nevertheless manageable at that point. The next leg down Sub Dome was definitely more perilous—there was nothing to cling to for support. The steps were narrow, uneven, and irregular. A slip and fall could prove disastrous. Jackson led the way with his dimming flashlight as the pair groped along. He would descend a short distance, stop, turn around, and illuminate the path for Crozier as best he could. To Crozier, the combination of shadows and faint light was almost more treacherous than no light at all.

Panic seized Crozier. Jackson was going too fast.

Maybe I should have stayed on top after all, she wondered. No, I *had* to get off that mountain!

They reached the final steps, then level ground.

At the base of Sub Dome, Crozier reunited with Mike Hoog, her brother Dan, Jennie Hayes, and Rick Pedroncelli. She gave them a somber update on what had transpired on the summit after Mike and Rick left, then collapsed into her sleeping bag, wrapping her chilled, depleted body tightly for as much warmth and comfort as possible. Jackson spent the night with them. But the evening's events proved too unsettling for Crozier to fall asleep quickly.

Back on Half Dome, it was 3 A.M. before Brian Cage's group crawled into their sleeping bags. Clu Cotter, whose bag had left the summit with Rice, managed to find a stray one. He didn't know whose it was. It was too small, and in the frigid night air he could barely keep warm. By morning, the water in the campers' canteens would be frozen.

The six men lay there, each trying to surrender to his exhaustion, each aware that the body of a sixteen-year-old boy was still slumped in the cave only a short distance away. Nearby, Bill Pippey and Bruce Jordan were battling despair.

◄○►

AT 6:30 A.M., the pilot of Yosemite National Park's helicopter prepared to retrieve the bodies of Bob Frith and Brian Jordan. He flew to the base of Half Dome and located Frith among the rocks, then returned to pick up Rangers Evan Smith and Dan Dellinges.

With them on board, the helo flew to a ledge at the base of Half Dome's face, right above the rocky jumble—a landing zone the park routinely used for rescues in that vicinity. In contrast to Medi-Flight's large helicopter, this aircraft was much smaller and better able to maneuver in tight places. The pilot carefully finessed the helo to the ledge and brought the front half of the landing skids down on it for stability. This enabled Smith and Dellinges to hop out. After they moved a safe distance away from the rotors, the helo lifted off, bound for the summit.

Smith and Dellinges followed standard procedure for a fatality. They took pictures and measurements, and surveyed the scene for evidence of foul play. As with all accidents, the rangers didn't want to assume anything, only to be surprised later on.

The helicopter flew to the summit to get Bruce Jordan and ferry him down to the Valley. There, a priest, Father Rod Craig, offered comfort. The teenager broke down, his pent-up emotions and sorrow finally spilling out.

He sobbed uncontrollably, asking over and over, Why him and not me? Why did I survive? Why didn't I save him?

The helicopter returned to the base of Half Dome to remove Frith's body, which Smith and Dellinges had placed in a body bag and wire rescue basket—a "wire coffin." Part of Frith's foot was missing and couldn't be found. They attached the basket to a rope lowered from the hovering helicopter, which rose and headed toward the park morgue.

After a long night and only a few hours of sleep at home, Colin Campbell—the first ranger on the scene the night before—returned to the Valley at 7 A.M. Someone told him a female hiker had brought his cowboy boots down to a ranger station in the Valley from the camp where he had swapped them for sneakers. According to the ranger there, the hiker had held Campbell's well-worn boots at arm's length. Campbell collected them and then joined the helicopter flight taking Rangers J. R. Tomasovic and Jim Tucker to the summit to prepare Brian Jordan's body for removal.

After the helo deposited Tomasovic and Tucker on top, it dropped Campbell off in Little Yosemite Valley. There he saddled up John Paul and rode down to the Valley floor. The helicopter returned again to the base of Half Dome, picked up Rangers Smith and Dellinges, and transported them back to the Valley.

On the summit, Tomasovic asked Pippey to identify the body in the cave, a standard procedure. It was a heart-wrenching moment for Pippey; he confronted the tragedy all over again. The body of Brian Jordan lay before him, more than seventeen hours after lightning had ended his brief life.

Jackson had since returned to the summit. He helped lift Jordan's body over to the helicopter landing site. One image that still lingers in his memory is that of a partial head of broccoli on the granite cave floor.

By noon on Sunday, July 28, the rangers and Jordan's body had been airlifted from the summit. The rescue mission was officially over.

◄○►

HOOG'S GROUP ROSE with the sun. They packed their gear and said good-bye to Jackson, who was heading back to the summit. The group spoke little on the way down to the Valley. Crozier mused that, during the long ordeal the previous evening, she'd never once absorbed the view from atop Half Dome, her reason for going up there in the first place. She and her companions promised themselves to return the next summer.

Along the trail, they heard hikers chattering about something that had happened on Half Dome overnight, but neither Crozier nor Hoog said a word in passing.

From the Valley floor, they saw a helicopter flying up to Half Dome's summit. The helo and speculative human buzz in the Valley about what was happening seemed eerie to Crozier, as though there were a locked room holding profound secrets and only she had the key.

The group went to the Yosemite Clinic to inquire about Rice, Weiner, and Esteban. The staff were reluctant to give out any information, saying only that Rice and Weiner had been transported to the UC Davis Medical Center in Sacramento. Crozier and Hoog didn't mention their role in the rescue.

Later, they spotted the park helicopter swooping away from the base of Half Dome with a body bag slung below. This was the image that stayed fixed in their minds as they departed Yosemite.

Cage's party packed up and left the Dome sometime early that morning. An unnamed hiker joined them on the somber hike out, relating a story about how, when the previous day's storm rolled in, he'd taken cover in a rock enclosure on Half Dome, fearing for his life.* Aghast, he'd watched five guys dance on the granite as the storm raged. Then they disappeared. He said he'd scrambled down the mountain as soon as it seemed safe to do so.

Now he knew what had befallen the dancers.

After the helicopter lifted Bruce Jordan from the summit, a solitary Pippey hiked down. Karl Buchner and Steve Ellner were there to meet him at the camping area below. The three trudged back to the Valley. Ellner's primary thought was that he needed to call his parents and tell them he was alive. He suspected there already had been publicity about the episode.

He was right.

Pam Pippey, Bill's wife, who was four months' pregnant with their first child, was driving home at nine o'clock Sunday morning from an appointment when she heard the radio report: *Lightning strike on Half Dome, five people hit, two killed.* Her first thought was that her husband was among the five, and she might now be a widow. Frantic, she raced home and called Yosemite. No one there could give her the names of the people involved. A park official she spoke with said someone would call her back. Three hours passed before anyone did, just shortly before her husband himself called.

---

* This individual's name and whereabouts during the episode have remained undisclosed. He was the anonymous observer of that striking scene that opened this book.

By noon, Pippey, Buchner, and Ellner had arrived in the Valley. Pippey immediately called Pam, and Ellner phoned his parents. When the three reached the ranger station, Mr. and Mrs. Jordan, whom park officials had contacted the previous night, were there with a stone-faced Bruce Jordan. Seeing the Jordans was more than Pippey could handle; he broke down yet again. Mr. Jordan's attempts to comfort him helped Pippey considerably.

Esteban doesn't remember much about what transpired after the helicopter evacuated him from the Dome, including whether he even slept. All he recalls is the flight down and then sunlight. That morning, rangers questioned him. Esteban briefly described the incident and what happened to each of the men in the cave.

"I didn't know there was a lightning rod there," he added, referring to the iron pipe that park officials had sawed off after the lightning incident in 1973, leaving a one-plus-inch section protruding from the granite.

A priest tried to comfort Esteban, who could think of nothing but Frith tumbling over the edge. The image terrified him. Later that morning, he passed a structure—the rescue cache building—where there were rangers and search dogs.

This must be where they took Frith, Esteban thought.

He wanted to see his friend one last time. A ranger told him that wasn't a good idea, but Esteban persisted. A body bag was inside, and to Esteban, its size and shape seemed odd. Then it struck him why. He stopped in his tracks, whispered a farewell to his companion, and left.

Esteban had placed a note on Pippey's windshield telling him to meet Esteban at the rescue cache. When Pippey, Buchner, and Ellner arrived, they were surprised that Esteban seemingly didn't have any injuries. Park officials interviewed the three men; Buchner and Ellner could offer little information about what had happened.

Word was circulating that a lawsuit would be filed.

Mrs. Jordan asked rangers, Why did the park allow my son and the others to go to the top of Half Dome if it was dangerous and there might be lightning?

Mrs. Jordan: "We hold Yosemite rangers responsible for the tragedy. They allowed the hikers to scale Half Dome despite the hazardous weather. How many city people realize the danger? They were permitted to go, so they must have figured it was safe."

That Sunday, Monroe Bridges and Brian Cage, two of Linda Crozier's helpers the prior night, lumbered into the ranger station in Yosemite Village, introduced themselves, and were escorted to an office. At the request of Ranger Tomasovic, the two men agreed to make a voluntary statement "for the record" summarizing what they had witnessed. At that point, both were physically beat, having completed the hike to the top on Saturday, helped with emergency care into the wee hours on Sunday, and after minimal sleep hiked back down to the Valley.

A ranger asked if they had seen the sign at the start of the stairs at Sub Dome. Both replied that they had. Then the ranger asked if either could recite what the sign said. Again, they responded yes, and repeated its warning. The ranger thanked them for cooperating and added that their statements could help the National Park Service defend itself in a potential lawsuit.

Cage: "That's when it really hit me. As much as this was an accident caused by a combination of Mother Nature and poor human judgment, there remained a looming wrongful death lawsuit against Yosemite National Park. I remember the ranger commenting that a big-money lawsuit could easily consume the entire budget the park allots for making Half Dome and other backcountry destinations accessible."

Bridges and Cage also told the ranger they were prepared to testify that the accident happened because the five men in the cave had been reckless. Esteban himself had stated as much.

That same day, Yosemite closed the trail to the summit until the electrical storms abated. According to park rangers, the hiking tragedy on Half Dome was one of the worst in Yosemite's history.

"Half Dome is probably the worst place you can be during a thunderstorm," said Bruce Brossman, director of Yosemite Mountaineering School. "It gets hit all the time. The skies that day were black, and it had been raining on and off for several days. These were the fastest-moving and most violent thunderstorms I've ever seen in sixteen years I've been in the Sierra. But they were predicted."

◄○►

WITH NOTHING ELSE to do in Yosemite, Esteban, Pippey, Buchner, and Ellner left. Pippey wanted to rejoin his wife as quickly as possible and begin his healing. He drove home alone and remembers little about the trip, his mind in a complete fog, his emotions swinging wildly. He knew that his sudden bout of diarrhea on the cables of Half Dome surely had saved his and Bruce Jordan's lives. But that was small consolation. With the previous day's events, he had suffered another severe setback in his young life.

Why, he wondered, do tragedy and death follow me?

His mother, grandparents, best teenage friend, and now Bob Frith and Brian Jordan—all dead. And Rice and Weiner might yet die.

Buchner also drove back alone, still speechless and distressed. He found solace in the fact that Esteban and Ellner, his two closest friends, had survived the ordeal. Ellner drove Esteban in Esteban's truck. Ellner talked incessantly on the journey home, hoping to boost Esteban's spirits.

Esteban was tremendously agitated. He and Rice had been the leaders that day. Others followed them and suffered grave consequences. The fates of Rice and Weiner still hung in the balance. He could not rid himself of the crushing knowledge that he and Rice were ultimately responsible for the tragedy. But further riling him was Rice's accusation that he, Esteban, had abandoned him in the cave. And Esteban kept telling himself he had done everything possible to save Frith.

Esteban: "The dilemma I faced: Do all I could to save someone else, and let myself possibly die, or save myself and let someone else possibly die."

In trying to rationalize his actions, Esteban wanted to believe Frith "told" him with the whites of his eyes that it was okay to leave him. He felt like their souls had touched, had connected. He thought he had had little choice but to leave Frith "in God's hands" on the ledge.

However, he also had fled the cave and sought safety for himself. Of the five hikers in the enclosure, only Esteban had endured the catastrophe with no major injuries. He should have felt thankful, and he did feel enormously thankful, but guilt nevertheless overwhelmed him. At the moment of peril, the self-preservation instinct took over.

Now self-doubt tormented him.

Ellner turned the radio on and began flipping from station to station, hungry for news. The story came on, although by now it had widely circulated: *Hikers hit by lightning on Half Dome.*

There were still many untold parts to this tale to dissect.

◄○►

LINDA CROZIER RETURNED to her apartment in Davis. She recounted for her roommates what had happened and called her parents to fill them in. That night, she still felt traumatized. Crozier could recite all the events but, at that point and for many days to come, felt no emotions tied to them.

"I was terrified up there, but I learned a lot about myself. Up on top, I kept my cool, but once it was all over, I was totally numbed. I was in mental shock for days afterward. For the first time in my life, I didn't like being alone at night."

Like Esteban, Crozier felt guilty. But the genesis of her guilt was how she had consciously avoided checking on Brian Jordan in the cave. She wondered if he might have been in a state of suspended animation rather than dead; if he could have been revived with CPR. She did some research on lightning injuries but couldn't find any definitive information.

Several months later, Crozier got a whiff of burned hair from her curling iron. The odor was familiar—and then she suddenly realized why.

"The smell rocketed me right back to Half Dome like a shock! I hadn't realized I had smelled burned hair up there until I smelled it that day in my apartment."

—◦—

AT HOME, ESTEBAN sank into deep depression. He had no one to talk to, no one to comfort him. There were nightmares about Frith toppling off the edge. The worst had Esteban letting go of Frith— who miraculously wakes up during the fall. This gruesome thought tortured Esteban. He sought comfort from a priest, who assured him there was nothing else he could have done.

Esteban wanted to feel better. But deep down, he had to battle these demons—and battle them alone.

He recalled his attitude after the lightning strike: Just thankful it wasn't me. Esteban had a keen interest in the military, and in his readings about it, he learned that his reaction mirrored that of soldiers whose comrade triggers a land mine: Glad it wasn't me. It was simply human nature to feel that way, he believed. Guilt, however, almost always followed.

By then, the press was calling for information. Esteban didn't take the calls; instead, he sought refuge at his parents' house. But reporters also called there, so he hid at a friend's place, where other friends joined him. They urged Esteban to go on TV, seeing this as an opportunity for him to gain notoriety and make money in the process.

Esteban: "Of course, these 'good friends' really didn't care about the feelings of the survivors and their loved ones. All they cared about was my fifteen minutes of fame on TV. And they hoped in some way to cash in, too."

Though Esteban was a poor communicator, he finally succumbed to an overwhelming barrage of requests and consented to be interviewed. A friend set up the first interview and started behaving as if he were Esteban's agent.

Inwardly, Esteban was looking to the media for a favorable judgment of his actions on Half Dome.

◄○►

AFTER A HASTILY BOOKED FLIGHT, Weiner's parents arrived at the UC Davis Medical Center on Sunday.

Rice and Weiner were still in serious condition on Monday. Doctors considered a kidney transplant for Weiner, whose kidney functioning had declined 90 percent. He gained 40 pounds overnight from retained fluids, his weight ballooning to 205. While Rice's kidney problems weren't as severe, his weight skyrocketed, too. Blood circulation in both men's legs was still seriously impaired.

On Tuesday, Klein operated a second time to further decompress their leg muscles. Doctors wouldn't know for several days if they had succeeded in saving the legs, or if Rice and Weiner would ever walk again.

The pair underwent frequent baths to debride (scrub) dead tissue from their burns. Such tissue provides an ideal medium for the growth of bacteria that can cause infection, one of the biggest risks associated with burns. Debridement involves an instrument not unlike a cheese grater. This procedure was "extraordinarily painful," according to Weiner, despite higher doses of morphine. Meanwhile, each man wore a device that kept a foot raised and flexed. This kept the large tendons in their legs, such as the Achilles tendon running down the back of the shin, stretched, preventing them from contracting and becoming disabled as a result of disuse.

The fasciotomies had exposed Rice's and Weiner's leg muscles, which were covered by bandages extending from their toes to their backs. Incisions beneath the bandages would remain open for weeks. When Weiner's bandages were temporarily removed for bathing purposes, exposing the damage, he experienced sheer horror. Only then did he realize the extent of his injuries. He was appallingly disfigured. Large globs of what looked like ground meat protruded from six or seven surgical sites, each three to twelve inches long. His legs were swollen to incredible proportions. It was as if two huge sausages had burst open in numerous places, their contents squeezed out under high pressure.

Linda Crozier called the hospital to inquire about visiting Rice and Weiner. No one could say when that would be possible, but on Tuesday she went to see them anyway. The burn unit nurse said they had undergone surgery earlier that day and were in bad shape.

Dr. Klein dropped by and told Crozier that, absent her care on Half Dome, both men surely would have faced amputation. She couldn't tell if he was being honest or just trying to make her feel good. In any case, the scene Crozier encountered in Rice's and Weiner's separate rooms was sobering. Their bodies had swelled so much, she could barely recognize them. Both men were under medication and in much pain. Crozier whispered to each that she was thinking of them, then left.

Crozier: "Seeing the two guys in the hospital alive is when I began to feel good again."

◄○►

AMONG THE HIKERS that day, only Pippey attended Brian Jordan's funeral. To say the event was extremely sad for the Jordan family—mother and father, sisters, and Brian's twin brother—doesn't convey the agony they endured in burying their young son and brother. Pippey shared their despair but also felt great torment, believing he had been responsible for Brian's death. Being at the funeral, he recalls, was "the hardest time I ever had in my life."

Bob Frith's funeral took place in Virginia, another emotionally devastating event. Grieving parents, six older sisters, and a brother had to lay to rest the youngest member of their family. Again, the only member of Rice's band who attended was Pippey. Frith had been Pippey's dear and important friend, someone he deeply admired and had grown to love.

Pippey gutted out the two funerals—barely. He wondered about his relationship to God and, once again, why close family members and friends had been snatched from his life.

In his fragile state, Pippey resisted visiting Rice. Dealing with any more heartbreaks would simply be too much. But after about two weeks, he forced himself to go. When he arrived at the hospital, Rice was lying in bed "all torn up, with tubes everywhere," still crippled from the waist down. In roller-coaster fashion, his weight had fallen dramatically. Seeing his good friend in that condition freaked Pippey out; he just couldn't take it on top of everything else.

He didn't visit Rice again until several weeks later, long into his recovery.

Pippey visited the Jordans every weekend, and together they grieved and supported each other. In his view, Mr. Jordan had handled the tragedy with sensitivity and class, providing tremendous comfort not only to his wife and children but also to Pippey. Pippey tried to console a morose Bruce Jordan, who seemed to be sliding back into oblivion.

◄○►

NEWSPAPER REPORTERS interviewed Esteban, who also appeared on several TV news programs.

He told one reporter: "It was instantaneous, like going from heaven to hell in a second."

To another, he said: "I know what we did was totally stupid, but we're gung-ho types. We knew the dangers, but we also knew the excitement, the thrill of a challenge. We decided we were going to go for it no matter what.

"It was the thrill of being in a life-and-death situation. It was like playing Russian roulette. There was such a rush as we were going up and saw those dark clouds. The adrenaline was flowing. There was an intense feeling that you could die at any moment."

He had nothing but praise for Linda Crozier and others who treated the victims on Half Dome.

"They saved our lives," he said. "They were really noble—full of courage and sure about what they were doing. We were all so lucky that they happened upon us."

Later, Esteban reflected on why he agreed to be interviewed.

"All I know is that I had to let people know what had happened, and in a strange way this outpouring to anyone and everyone who would listen was sort of a confession that I was hoping would cleanse away the pain and sorrow I was going through. This was one of the lowest points in my life. I felt like an outcast from my 'older brother' Tom [Rice]. Without a spouse or girlfriend to share my innermost thoughts and to comfort me, I was truly lonely. My only out was to talk about it. And once I started talking, I felt better. I was not depressed anymore. The excitement of being on five different news stations live made me forget about all my mental suffering. People wanting me gave me a sense of belonging, a positive feeling. It was a cathartic experience. In the same way Tom needed a fix of attention at the diving board, I had found my fix."

In each interview, Esteban mentioned that he hadn't been aware of the "lightning rod" near the summit cave. Its sole purpose, he reasoned, must have been to draw lightning away from people up there. He related how the pipe extended into the rock chamber.

This explanation was far from accurate. The one-plus-inch pipe stub surely had nothing to do with the lightning strike or how the blast whipped through the enclosure. The iron remnant was anchored in solid granite about twenty feet away; neither it nor any other metal pipe extended into the chamber. The stub couldn't have attracted lightning—the entire summit was available. Perhaps it had in the 1972 case, when the pipe stuck up two feet, but even that scenario was dubious. Assuming the protrusion drew lightning on that fateful day in 1972, the charge could have streaked across the wet rock and through the rock enclosure. And certainly anyone who was near the iron pipe or touching it would have placed himself at greater risk, given that any metallic object is a prime conductor of electricity. So the National Park Service was correct to whittle the pipe down. However, lightning barrages had continued to batter Half Dome every year since.

Amazingly, not one reporter queried Esteban further or verified the accuracy of his statement—which, if true, certainly cast a whole different light on the tragedy.

Esteban also put a different spin on Frith's fall from the summit. He told most interviewers that he'd held on to Frith's sweater until it began to rip from his grip, that he'd had to let go when Frith was about to tumble over the edge. Actually, Esteban was recounting how, given his weakness at that instant, he tried in vain to pull Frith up and over a boulder, then into the enclosure. He couldn't hold on to Frith indefinitely, so he released his grip—not letting Frith tumble off the ledge, as he later claimed, but rather letting him slump back onto it. There, Weiner continued to grasp Frith's sweater for a few seconds before it slipped from his grasp.

Esteban: "In my interviews, it seems that I was looking at the presence of the iron pipe as a logical reason to account for the deaths of two people and the life-altering injuries to two others. I sought some external justification for the disaster. And with my overwhelming feelings of guilt, I didn't want to admit that I chose to leave Frith on the ledge. So I described how I had to let him go. This was true, but what it doesn't say is that when I let him go, he settled back down on the ledge and did not immediately tumble over the edge. That came seconds later."

In those interviews, he also stated: "Half Dome is my spiritual place, and I must go back there."

Some of Esteban's fellow hikers and others connected to the incident didn't take kindly to his media activities. In their opinion, he was exploiting the tragedy for personal gain. Karl Buchner's father called Esteban at one point and counseled him to stop, arguing that the publicity was insensitive to the victims' families. Only then did Esteban grasp the serious implications of his actions. He canceled all upcoming interviews.

◄o►

ESTEBAN WAS HESITANT to face Rice, even though the recovery period was "when Tom needed me the most." Part of him wanted to go. And he really had no excuse for not going. Nevertheless, he remained at home or at a friend's house, where he lost himself in drink. It was pure denial—in his effort to rid himself of guilt, he wanted to believe a major tragedy hadn't even occurred.

He also didn't attend the Jordan and Frith funerals. Why? He wasn't sure.

A full two weeks passed before Esteban visited Rice and Weiner. His decision to go was partly serendipitous: One of Rice's girlfriends had called to ask if they might carpool to the hospital. She had just recently met Rice and promised to do whatever was necessary to help him fully recover. She and Esteban drove to Sacramento together.

In intensive care, hooked up to IVs, Rice was very subdued. He was still receiving morphine to kill the pain. He mumbled that he was very glad Esteban had finally come to visit him. But then Rice admonished Esteban not to talk to the media, even though he surely knew that Esteban had already done so. Apparently, Rice was telling him indirectly that he had betrayed their trust. He said Esteban's priorities were all wrong, that two people had died, that he and Weiner had nearly died, too. Esteban felt wounded. Rice was scolding him—in front of his girlfriend, no less.

Esteban: "That was Tom's style. He would rip into you no matter what the surrounding circumstances were."

Rice told Esteban he couldn't remember much about the lightning incident. He did say, however, that the second bolt delivered the major blow to Weiner. This was news to Esteban; until then, he had no inkling of the second strike hitting Rice and Weiner.

Something troubled Esteban: the possibility that Rice and Weiner, either in the cave or there at the hospital, had spoken privately about his actions on Half Dome that day. He worried that they blamed him for leaving them behind in the cave.

Esteban: "To this day I do not know what Tom and Bruce may have talked about when I was not present. I have a guilty feeling that Bruce's version of what happened afterward reflected negatively on me, that I basically left them to die in that hole in order to save myself and that Bruce saw me drop his best friend Bob to his death."

In fact, Rice and Weiner never discussed it. They occupied separate rooms in the hospital as a precaution against cross-contamination and infection. Furthermore, Weiner held no affection for Rice and had no reason to confide in him. Esteban's fear that the pair had confided behind his back was totally unfounded.

He visited with Weiner only briefly on that occasion. The next time he came, Weiner had been flown to Massachusetts.

During Esteban's second visit, Rice seemed really pissed off. He stripped off his shorts and showed Esteban his testicles, which looked like a single grapefruit.

Look what happened, he said.

Rice's tone was accusatory, as though he resented the fact that Esteban hadn't suffered any injuries.

Feeling further aggrieved, Esteban stormed out.

—<o>—

AFTER THE SECOND ROUND of surgery, some sensation and circulation returned to Rice's and Weiner's feet. But according to Dr. Klein, a specific prognosis was very difficult because their electrical injuries were still in the early stages of healing.

He said both men were extremely lucky to have survived the ordeal so well.

Dr. Klein: "Even if they both have terrible problems with both of their legs, they're still alive, their brains suffered no damage, and their heart and lungs seem okay. Each appears to have been spared serious kidney damage, a major concern in electrical burn cases. They have a lot to be thankful for."

He cautiously told Rice that once Rice regained movement in his lower limbs, he might be able to get around—but probably "won't be able to dance again." Rice retorted, half in jest, I'm going to dance on your fuckin' grave!

During the first two weeks after the accident, Weiner also had suffered pneumonia, heart problems, and several infections. Any of these problems could have proved fatal. The two men, in Dr. Klein's opinion, would require many more operations, skin grafts, and plastic surgery. Even under the best of circumstances, both faced a long road to recovery.

Weiner remained at the medical center through August 9. A constant morphine drip into his jugular vein—the only vein big enough for that large a dosage—blurred his recollection of what transpired there. Mostly, he remembered extreme pain.

Weiner's parents wanted him at Massachusetts General Hospital in Boston as soon as transfer was safe.

Mrs. Weiner: "First we were afraid he was going to die. Then we were afraid he was going to lose his legs. Then we were just afraid."

◄○►

THE NEXT TIME Linda Crozier went to UC Davis Medical Center, Weiner was gone. She promised Rice she would visit him at least three times a week.

Up to then, Crozier hadn't had any contact with the media, which reported extensively on the tragedy but didn't cite helpers' efforts in the aftermath of the lightning strike. Her dad called a TV station and relayed the story from their point of view. It sparked a media blitz that engulfed Crozier. In several interviews, she repeated the names of all those who had lent a hand on Half Dome, but, to her disappointment, the media ignored that aspect of the story. All they wanted was information about her efforts and those of Mike Hoog.

The other hikers, too, focused their praise on Crozier and Hoog.

Steve White: "They are the real heroes of this thing. I've never seen people work better under such conditions. I can't think of what would have happened if they hadn't come along."

Crozier's father proudly stated: "Our family has always been built around the kids. We told them that they can do anything if they work hard enough. Linda's always been the take-charge kind of person, from the days of Little League to today. What she did at Yosemite didn't surprise me."

She also received letters of commendation from helicopter rescue pilot Al Major, paramedic Bill Bryant, and California governor Pete Wilson.

Yet out of the spotlight, Crozier insisted that her companions deserved as much tribute. "Everybody still needs heroes in this country," she said. "These young people cared enough to get involved. They had the skills and they really saved lives. I'm very proud of them."

◄〇►

CROZIER CONTINUED to visit Rice at the hospital right up until his release three months later. She was there when he walked for the first time.

To her surprise, Rice talked excessively, bubbling over with commentary. They spent hours gabbing. Rice spoke mainly about himself—how karma had spared his life and that henceforth he must do something to fulfill his destiny, though what that might be wasn't clear. However, neither spoke much about the incident, a subject Rice clearly avoided. Nor did he say much about his cohorts, other than that he really didn't know Frith, Weiner, or Brian Jordan very well. He repeatedly beseeched Crozier to extend his appreciation to all of her Half Dome helpers.

Rice wasn't modest when it came to showing Crozier his wounds and scars. He had lost a lot of weight in the intervening weeks. He spoke at length about his family, how he was "the black sheep." It came out that Crozier's and Rice's fathers worked at the same company, Chevron.

In all of the time Crozier visited Rice at the hospital, there were never any other visitors.

—◦—

WEINER WAS FLOWN to Massachusetts General Hospital, where Dr. John Burke, chief of trauma services, treated him. He was isolated in a special room with a plastic enclosure around the bed to prevent direct human contact, an extremely depressing state for Weiner. After several days, he was moved to another room without a plastic shield and finally allowed to have some human contact. This boosted his morale tremendously.

Instead of bathing Weiner frequently (as UCD Medical Center in Sacramento did), hospital staff swaddled him in heavy layers of gauze and, around the clock, kept the gauze soaked in a diluted solution of silver nitrate, which kills bacteria. He was constantly wet from the middle of his back to his toes, like lying in a puddle twenty-four hours a day. The silver nitrate turned his toenails and fingernails black. Weiner despised these treatments.

Dr. Burke performed eight skin grafts on both of Weiner's legs and his left foot, where the lightning had exited. Initially, Burke used skin from a cadaver, which was a temporary graft, acting more like a biological bandage, and subsequently removed. In later surgeries, he lifted skin from Weiner's intact left thigh.

He commended the emergency medical technicians on Half Dome for saving Weiner. "If Weiner had stayed overnight on the mountain, he wouldn't have survived."

According to Dr. Burke's prognosis, Weiner would have sufficient strength in his legs to lead a normal life. However, some permanent loss of muscle strength was to be expected.

Weiner left the hospital on Friday, September 13, about six weeks after the episode on Half Dome. Rice remained hospitalized for three months.

—◄○►—

THE SIMULTANEOUS Half Dome and Tenaya Canyon missions carried out by Yosemite rangers on the night of July 27 and morning of July 28 involved fifty-nine park personnel in all. All of these individuals under the command of Ranger James Reilly received an Exemplary Act Award—the National Park Service's recognition for outstanding performance.

10

AFTERMATH

We are not building this country of ours for a day. It is to last through the ages.—Theodore Roosevelt, May 1903

When Weiner returned home from the hospital, he weighed 130 pounds. He was so thin, it hurt to sit on a wooden chair without a pillow. Dr. Burke instructed him to consume thirty-five hundred calories a day, almost double what an adult normally consumes.

One night several weeks after his release from the hospital, Weiner had a horrific nightmare.

"I was back in the cave and everything was happening all over again. This time, I knew we were going to be struck by lightning, but I could not convince anybody to listen. When Bob got hit and started to fall off the mountain, I could not let go of him and I was dragged over as well. I awoke screaming and my parents rushed into the room to comfort me. Even after I woke up, I could still smell burned flesh and I could still hear the screams of those around me in the cave."

In November, two months after discharge, Weiner returned to California and his job at Lockheed, determined to put his life back on track. He could work only five hours a day. Whether sitting, standing, walking, or lying down, his constant companion was pain—the "pain of healing," as he referred to it. The first thing he felt in the morning was severe pain, most likely brought on by damaged nerves attempting to regenerate.

"Sometimes it felt like there was a knife being driven to the bottom of my foot. Sometimes it felt like someone was pulling my toenails out."

He underwent physical therapy for a full year. His legs were shriveled due to the loss of muscle mass; some parts looked like raw steak. They remained stiff, causing him to shuffle around and reach with his arms and torso rather than bend his knees. He used a cane and took great care climbing stairs. He had to wear pressure bandages every day for about eighteen months; otherwise, his legs would painfully swell and the grafted skin would form into keloids, or elevated, irregularly shaped, progressively enlarging scars. For the first year, his scars were very angry looking—bright red and highly conspicuous. Several years passed before they became inert and therapy could be discontinued. To this day, the hairless scars covered by abnormal-looking skin are readily noticeable.

The accident severely scarred Weiner's mind as well. Before, he was an easygoing, affable guy who made new friends effortlessly. Afterward, he became very cautious and withdrawn. Driving made him especially nervous, and loud noises easily startled him. Expelling the Half Dome events from his mind took a long time.

One relentless torment was the image of Bob Frith slipping over the edge. It prompted him to seek professional help.

Doctors assured him there was nothing he could have done; that Frith's fate was sealed when the lightning lashed his head.

Weiner: "The first four weeks, the story ran nonstop through my mind. I visualized pulling Frith back into the chamber or Frith falling over the edge while I still held on to him. Now, months later, it's still in my mind, but I have more control over when I run the story."

During his recovery, Weiner experienced many emotional states: guilt that he survived, which others told him was a normal response; moments of elation, thankfulness, depression, despair; and everything in between. After his return to California, he was diagnosed with post-traumatic stress disorder. He tried two or three counselors until he found one he liked—a man who helped him stabilize his life.

It took a good ten years for Weiner's emotional roller coaster to grind to a halt, until a degree of equilibrium and happiness returned to his life. But issues lingered. It's still difficult for him to establish new relationships. He has made few new close friends and shies away from being fully open with anyone other than close family members.

Weiner remained at Lockheed for almost two years before he left in September 1987 to join InSystems, another Bay Area company, where he worked until late 1991. Then he returned to Massachusetts to take a position with Image Engineering Corporation in Somerville. Although he worked there during most of the 1990s, Weiner began transitioning to a more helping profession. Before Half Dome, material values hadn't really driven him; they were even less important afterward. Instead, he wanted to contribute to others in some way, to be proud of his work and feel fulfilled. As early as 1994, Weiner had started doing volunteer work at an animal hospital. He continued volunteering over the next several years at various veterinary agencies. Meanwhile, he enrolled in the School of Veterinary Medicine at Tufts University in 1995. In spring 1998, he began working full time at a veterinary clinic, thus ending his long career in engineering. He received his veterinary degree in May 2000.

Throughout his long recovery, Weiner has endured constant physical discomfort. Now, twenty years later, he still doesn't have much feeling in his feet. Pain shoots through them, then travels up his legs—a result, he explains, of severed leg nerves still trying to regenerate. The pain and suffering have made him a more tolerant and grounded person. He's more appreciative of his life and tries to express that to others. On the other hand, he is less patient when someone uses his time unnecessarily, as if he realizes the preciousness of each minute and doesn't want to waste it.

As a veterinarian, making a difference in peoples' lives and those of their animals brings Weiner pleasure and reward. His own experiences as a patient have helped him be a more caring vet. One of the things that disturbed him most in the hospital was a sense of dehumanization: Staff seemed to ignore his wants and wishes. They bathed, fed, disturbed, awakened, or left him alone at their own convenience and paid very little attention to his emotional and spiritual needs. Doctors and nurses treated him like a large burn, not as a human being with injuries. Weiner realizes as a vet that even though his charges have a physical ailment, he must treat their entire being. Before treating an animal, he always spends a few minutes just petting and calmly talking with it. He thinks this helps.

◄○►

WITH ONLY A FEW exceptions, Rice remained adamant about not discussing the Half Dome episode. However, he did communicate at length with Linda Crozier while hospitalized, and the two corresponded in the months following his discharge in November. Those exchanges revealed a sentimental and receptive side to Rice that others rarely saw. Crozier respected Rice's strong desire for privacy, but she did reveal some of his sentiments to others to illustrate how the tragedy had affected him. His experiences served as a kind of instructive mirror.

After his discharge, Rice really zeroed in on earning a college degree. He enrolled at Chico State University in Chico, California, studied diligently, and kept to a tight schedule, often remaining at the library until it closed at midnight.

Physical rehabilitation was almost as intense a pursuit for him as academics. Once he was able, he began biking, hiking, swimming, skiing, and lifting weights.

In letters to Crozier, Rice shared his thoughts and detailed his progress toward full recuperation. "I'm still dancing," he wrote. He charted that progress using the Half Dome hike as an analogy and baseline. In one letter, he drew a diagram for her depicting the trail and how far his recovery had advanced along it, with an arrow labeled I AM HERE pointing to the spot. It would be great fun, he mused, to visit Yosemite with her, though "most of the park rangers probably think that I'm a cross between a stupid idiot and a crazed maniac."

Rice also expressed interest in meeting Linda's brother, Dan, but acknowledged that "I know he probably isn't too anxious to meet me." The couple of times Dan Crozier had seen him, "I was either burnt to a crisp cluttering up one of the most beautiful places on earth or stark naked around his sister. Not a good first impression."

In a rare reference to the episode, Rice described his feelings on his helicopter flight down from the Dome: "I probably would have been scared to death flying down the face of the dome if I was all there. As it was, a blur of noise and stars and then awesome, almost breathtaking silence (though I had not much breath to take), and a beautiful, calm, peaceful feeling... floating... floating... until we landed!!! Then it was time to find out if I was going to live or die. You see, being sober in an accident for the first time I finally felt the feeling of death trying to fill my body. It had already crept through my left leg and was emptying the life out of the bottom half of my body." Rice confessed that the episode had given him greater faith: "You know, it is just amazing how many wonderful stories have been written depicting the power of faith. But for a stubborn man like me it takes the pleasant shock of reality to drive the message home."

That faith reemerged in a letter he wrote to Crozier in spring 1986:

"I am very thankful for my health, the fact that I was just alive has never been enough for me and I think God knew this. Though it has been a long hard road toward recovery, I feel good, real good. My legs are getting stronger and stronger, ankle not up to par yet but I am starting to hike.... I'm starting to enjoy progress at a slower pace now. Before it was flying off of cliffs, instant gratification, standing in the winner's (he-man's) circle; basically having to satisfy my ego so I could temporarily lose that scary feeling of insecurity. But now I'm finding I am slowing myself down, gaining more over a longer period of time by steadily working toward a goal. Granted the limelight doesn't come to swoon me away; but, I feel good within myself... I can go off by myself on a nice hike, swim, workout... and feel good. This freedom is wonderful. I can feel God with me and I don't feel alone."

Rice added that he hoped "happiness has found you and spring is in your heart."

◄○►

THE VERY NEXT SUMMER, Esteban, Rice, Pippey, and a companion returned to Half Dome's summit. Rice may have undergone a personal transformation in the preceding year, but some things hadn't changed. Once again, he was the prime organizer and motivator, demonstrating that he still lived by his *face-your-fears* credo, the lightning episode notwithstanding.

We have to prove to ourselves we can do this, he preached.

The group called itself the "Get Back on the Horse Society."

Esteban: "Rice was still assertive and our recognized leader. Because of all the medical operations, diet, and therapy, he was much thinner than before, but he appeared to be in excellent shape. He had curbed his drinking and indulged in wine instead of beer, even diluting the wine with water. He showed no interest in partying. He was more health-conscious than ever. The only thing that showed he was ever in the accident were long black elastic stockings he wore over his feet and legs to hide the scars, which he seemed very self-conscious about, and to provide support for his calf and back-leg muscles. He had to stretch his legs every morning and before any strenuous leg activity. He followed a very rigorous routine that had been developed especially for him while he was recovering in the hospital. He said he had to do this every day for the rest of his life so he wouldn't lose the flexibility of his leg muscles and possibly the use of his legs.

"Looking back at that return trip to the Dome, I remember we were all feeling very special about the whole thing because it was the first time we had been back since the accident. I was partly scared and very excited to climb Half Dome once again. We brought flowers to leave inside the cave to honor Bob and Brian, and when we reached it, we all gathered and gave a eulogy and toast for our fallen comrades. I said how we were sorry and that we missed them and if I had to go I would like it to happen at Half Dome. At that moment, I felt a real sense of loss, how sad and useless it was for both of them to die so young."

—◄o►—

THE TRAGEDY GAVE ESTEBAN a new outlook on life: "I realized how short and precious life is and how quickly it can end. It was the first time I had seen death up close and personal."

The lightning jolt knocked much of the thrill-seeker out of Esteban. Before, he had been nonchalant about life, taking stupid chances without giving them a second thought. Now his attitude was: "It's not worth the risk. Nothing is."

He often returned to Half Dome in subsequent years. The tragedy hadn't detracted from its beauty, and going there continued to serve as a barometer of his physical well-being. The rock chamber, however, became for him a sacred place not to be disturbed.

Esteban: "At times, I still acted impulsively. But after a trip to the Dome, I grew more reserved and reflective. In being there, it seemed like everything was put back into perspective, that life is really not as complicated as we all make it out to be. Living and working in Silicon Valley is very stressful, but for one day I can escape all of that by going back to the Dome, where I could always find a certain peace of mind."

Life was a gift, he now realized. And he resolved to live it to the fullest.

"You only live once. If there is something that you really want to do or try, then just do it—you may never get another opportunity."

When Spectra Physics was bought out in the late 1980s, Esteban, who was twenty-seven years old by then, faced a deteriorating work situation. New management demanded higher performance. So, true to his newfound doctrine about seizing opportunities, he decided to fulfill a lifelong dream and enlisted in the U.S. Marine Corps.

Esteban: "Surviving the lightning strike gave me the spark to join the corps. All our previous trips up the Dome created a mindset to continue in the face of adversity, so on that July day in 1985, that's what we did. Even though it turned out to be a disastrous decision, I nevertheless retained the inner fire not to let obstacles deter me from going after a goal. I long wanted to join the Marine Corps. It was time to pursue it."

Like Half Dome, the marines dramatically changed Esteban's life. He enlisted in the Marine Corps Reserves instead of combat infantry—his earlier goal when he was young and more gung-ho about the military. As a reservist, he kept his job in the laser industry. The corps taught him to overcome his greatest weakness: lack of discipline. It shaped his core values and beliefs about loyalty and camaraderie. In 1985, he had been a follower mostly; in the marines he learned how to lead.

He designed a tattoo for his upper arm that celebrated more than just his status as a U.S. Marine. USMC was emblazoned beneath a big scorpio eagle whose claws gripped a red lightning bolt. In his mind, the two events—the lightning episode and becoming a marine—had merged.

Esteban served in the reserves for ten years, earned the rank of staff sergeant, and held many different jobs. The one he loved the most was military policeman. With the expert training, experience, and contacts he gained, he thought he would be a shoe-in to get hired as a police officer—his occupational goal upon leaving the corps. But when asked in a job interview if he had ever used cocaine, Esteban responded yes, believing that honesty was the best course. Instead, he was rejected. He returned to the laser industry, enrolled at several community colleges, and eventually earned an associate of arts degree in laser technology. In 1998, he enrolled in Phoenix College and, two years later, received a bachelor of science degree in business management.

◄○►

THE HALF DOME TRAGEDY impacted—and in some cases shattered— many lives. It had driven a wedge between Esteban and Rice.

Esteban: "The Half Dome brotherhood that we felt toward each other changed in the horror of the calamity. The long-standing mutual trust and loyalty we shared were gone, and they did not return."

Ironically, Esteban and Rice became relatives. Esteban's female cousin lived in Hawaii, and on a backpacking trip Rice and Esteban took there in 1986, Rice's nephew joined them. He met and fell in love with Esteban's cousin. The two later married. While surfing and hiking there, Rice wore long socks. Whenever anyone asked about his scars, he jokingly referred to them as an old football injury. Throughout the trip, neither Rice nor Esteban mentioned the Half Dome episode. There was an underlying friction between them that sparked little arguments over trivial things. According to Esteban, the two men "never got anything out in the open."

For months afterward, Pippey's emotions were erratic, intense, and often self-destructive. The lightning strike obliterated his tight circle of friends. The estrangement between Rice and Esteban, and Bob Frith's death, left him without a hiking clique. His backpacking treks dwindled, causing his physical condition and spirit to deteriorate. He began drinking heavily again and abusing drugs. He clung to his marriage and job by a thread.

Also dashed were Pippey's onetime hopes that nature would be a therapeutic force in the lives of the Jordan twins. Bruce Jordan seemed unable to cope with the death of his brother and withdrew into a shell.

Pippey: "It's as though he descended into a darkness, where morbidity and a Gothic-like fascination with death and the occult reigned." (Bruce Jordan chose not to contribute to this book.)

"For me, nothing good came out of the tragedy. It was all just sad and terrible."

Pippey held considerable admiration for Rice's drive to enroll in college and pursue a degree. When Pippey visited him at Chico State, Rice was in great physical shape—even better than before the lightning strike. However, Pippey also noticed that Rice hadn't changed in some respects. For example, on a whitewater rafting trip together, they entered a dangerous rapid, out of control. Amid the mayhem, Rice and others tried to throw someone overboard in reckless horseplay. It was too much for Pippey, who demanded to be put ashore. On another backpacking trip, Rice hiked for a day and a half in the nude. Rice's exhibitionism, it seemed to Pippey, was even more pronounced than before.

For Steve White, the days following Half Dome were filled with deep sadness.

White: "I would go to work, close the door to my office, and think of how tragic it was for the two who lost their lives, and for their families, especially the sixteen-year-old twin who died and his twin brother. I've gone back up to Half Dome many times since. It has a spiritual nature for me now because of what happened there. I've never been back into the cave and don't want to go back in. Even though all of those trips have been with big groups who are thrilled to be there, I always take time to sit alone and remember. Sometimes I tell the story but tend not to because it has become more personal. I keep two pictures of Half Dome hanging in my office.

"I secured my EMT certification as a result of my involvement in the tragedy and my admiration for Linda Crozier and the other EMTs that night."

A large framed picture of Half Dome being whipped by lightning hangs in paramedic Bill Bryant's office along with the front-page story that appeared in the *San Francisco Examiner* the day after the incident.

Mike Hoog proposed to his girlfriend, Louisa Munger, atop Half Dome. Their wedding cake featured a representation of it.

Hoog: "I wanted to bring her to the Dome because that was a part of me and my life. I have a lot of wonderful memories of Yosemite and Half Dome, and also some intense ones because of the lightning strike, and I wanted her to experience the things that I did so that she could understand. When we went to the Dome for our 'dare the Dome in a day,' it was like filling her in on my experiences. I guess in a way the Dome is like a sacred place, a vortex for me. I knew that I would propose to her on the Dome."

Because of her efforts that night, Linda Crozier frequently was asked to teach emergency medial technician classes in which she recounted her experience and outlined the steps that should be taken in such situations. She met and ultimately married another EMT instructor, Mark Ghilarducci, who led search and rescue operations.

◄○►

ON JULY 28, 2001, Peterson High School in Santa Clara held a "Super Reunion" for all eleven classes that had graduated before the school closed in the 1980s as a result of district consolidation. Among Peterson's graduates were Rice and Esteban.

Coincidentally, the Super Reunion coincided with the sixteenth anniversary of the Half Dome calamity, almost to the day. On a whim, Esteban contacted Rice before the event and asked if he planned to attend. Rice wasn't sure, due to job commitments. But when the reunion rolled around, Rice was there.

Esteban: "He was the same old Tom, the best I had seen him since the accident. As usual, he was the center of attention, dressed to kill in some outrageous black leather pants and custom shirt with hair slicked back, looking like a model out of *GQ*."

The Half Dome epic, which had widely circulated during the intervening years, bestowed celebrity status on Rice and Esteban. Reuniongoers were curious: Had they really been involved in such a tragedy? Esteban, always willing to play second fiddle, just sat back and listened as Rice rattled off his typically quick and superficial account:

We were up there hiking, went into this cave when it started raining, and it was just very unlucky that a lightning bolt hit us.

Rice said he recalled very little about the accident and rescue; he had been hospitalized for four months, he hated the whole time he was in there, and he was lucky to be alive. Rice also praised Esteban: If he hadn't left the cave before the second bolt struck, and come back afterward, "we would all probably be dead."

"Esteban," he said, "saved my life and was the hero of the whole thing."

It was the first time Esteban had heard Rice talk so expansively about the incident. It was also the first time he had cast Esteban as the hero. Later that night, the two had a heart-to-heart talk. Esteban really had saved his life, Rice explained, because if he hadn't fled the granite enclosure, the second lightning bolt probably would have incapacitated him, too. Consequently, no one else would have known their whereabouts on the summit or that they were in dire need of help, without which Rice and Weiner surely wouldn't have survived the night. Rice, aware of Esteban's tremendous guilt about having abandoned his buddies in the chamber, said that in fact he was grateful to him.

Rice gave Esteban his blessing to tell their story in a book but said he wouldn't participate. And whatever bad feelings there may have been between them, real or imagined, he was willing to consign to the past and move on.

Esteban: "I think neither one of us wanted to face the severity of what had occurred, and neither of us wanted to take responsibility for the death of two human beings. And finally, over time, we just let the hurt in us die to the point that everything now was just an afterthought and we could finally acknowledge that we were happy to have survived. We never really talked about who was to blame for this."

—◄○►—

DESPITE THE JORDANS' initial threat to sue over the death of their son Brian, they never did. However, legal action regarding two other lightning-related incidents—the one in 1975 on Moro Rock and the other in 1990 on Mount Whitney, both in Sequoia National Park—shed important light on culpability in such cases.

The 1975 event spawned two lawsuits: one by the wife of the deceased, Lawrence Brady, and a second by Edward Schieler, who incurred extensive, life-altering injuries. Both plaintiffs alleged that the National Park Service "failed to provide any warning, guidance, or supervision with respect to the danger of being struck by lightning atop Moro Rock, or of the fact that such a storm was impending, and further failed to provide and maintain reasonable or any safety devices to de-electrify the observation area."

The court dismissed their claims. It held that:

... the National Park Service has broad discretionary power to regulate the parks in such a manner that the scenery and natural and wild life in the parks are preserved unimpaired so that they may be enjoyed presently and in the future. Placing signs throughout every area that might be potentially struck by lightning, or subject to any other dangers, such as rock slides, certainly would impair the scenery and naturalness of the parks. And, before this lightning strike on Moro Rock, there had been no prior record of lightning striking it. No injuries from lightning ever happened there before.

The outcome of several lawsuits filed against the National Park Service after the July 1990 lightning strike on Mount Whitney was quite different. (In addition to the fatality, two people were injured, one seriously.) Plaintiffs won damages totaling $1.7 million. The judge was very disturbed by the five-year history preceding the accident, beginning with an event in 1985 in which several hikers who had sought shelter in the Smithsonian Hut on Mount Whitney's summit were injured by lightning. In 1986, the safety manager for Sequoia and Kings Canyon prepared a plan for installation of lightning protection on the hut, and the park superintendent approved it. Implementing this plan, however, was a low priority for the next safety manager. Lightning struck the hut again in 1987, 1988, and 1989.

In early 1990, the National Park Service moved forward with its lightning protection plan but chose not to install warning signs until the protective equipment was in place. Thus, when lightning struck in July of that year, killing one and injuring two, the warning signs were stashed in a ranger station at the bottom of Mount Whitney.

The judge found that "the actions of the Park Service over the period 1985 to 1990 constituted a willful failure to guard or warn the public."

Given the findings in these cases, the Jordan family would have had great difficulty winning a lawsuit. In Yosemite, warning signs were posted both at the bottom of Sub Dome and at the top of the cables on Half Dome. Furthermore, Esteban and his companions had stated that they were aware of the dangers and chose to ascend Half Dome regardless. Other hikers, too, were prepared to testify that the men who took refuge in the granite chamber behaved recklessly and irresponsibly.

—◄o►—

MEDICAL KNOWLEDGE about lightning injuries has increased considerably since 1985. In 1992, Dr. Mary Ann Cooper and colleagues co-edited a text, *Lightning Injuries: Electrical, Medical, and Legal Aspects*, that had its roots in the late 1970s, when Dr. Cooper treated a lightning patient in the emergency room at a Cincinnati hospital. She discovered there was little information about such injuries in medical texts. Her text was an effort to pull together what medical professionals knew about lightning injuries up to that point. Today Dr. Cooper is the first to admit that much has changed since her text was published.

Based on her own extensive research, Dr. Cooper has concluded that substantial quantities of lightning probably do not enter the body. That's because, contrary to common belief and the way people speak or write about lightning, it isn't a simple, unidirectional force comparable to a bullet. Rather, lightning is a very complex wave-and-current phenomenon that behaves more like a wave washing over, around, and perhaps through some portions of a fairly large area. A lot of evidence suggests that much, if not most, of lightning energy doesn't even enter the body. It creates a flashover effect instead. This is why Dr. Cooper dismisses as inaccurate the terms *entry* and *exit*—words applied in the field of electrical burn treatment—when describing the flow of lightning. More accurate terms, she says, are *source* and *ground.*

Experimental evidence suggests that a fast flashover apprecia-
bly diminishes energy dissipation within the body, thus producing
the low percentage (10 percent) of lightning fatalities. Current
may flow internally for an incredibly short time—thousandths of
a second. When it does, it can cause the heart, respiratory centers
in the brain, and the autonomic nervous system to short-circuit,
and spark spasms in arteries and muscles. Such injuries can be
severe and in some cases fatal.

From her studies, however, Dr. Cooper has found that lightning current seldom results in significant burns or tissue destruction. A heat source must be in contact with skin long enough to
burn it. Lightning's exposure time is so brief, it can't cause substantial skin burns. Those that do occur are mostly secondary.
They happen when sweat or dampness from rain vaporizes and
the resulting steam causes red burns and blisters. Clothing, such
as a jacket, or a backpack may trap the steam, which enables it to
inflict more damage. The conversion of moisture to steam and the
resulting vapor "explosion" can blow clothing and shoes off someone's body. Metal, which holds lightning heat longer, can burn
nearby tissue. But the direct burns from the lightning current are
generally quite minor and superficial.

◄○►

A LONG-OVERDUE BAN on overnight camping on Half Dome took
effect in 1993. The unlikely impetus for this action was the rare
Mount Lyell salamander, an endangered species. Quantities of
human waste under the summit rocks and the many rock shelters
built there by campers were threatening the salamander's survival.
Clearly, humans' impact on the summit had become widespread
and destructive. Only one of seven trees that populated the summit for many years remained; the others became firewood.

Tens of thousands of hikers tramp about Yosemite and thousands hike to Half Dome's summit every season. So many were
cramming into Little Yosemite Valley to camp overnight that the

park began requiring reservations. The hordes on and around Half Dome can make the journey, as Brian Cage complained, "more like a trip to Disneyland than a solitary refreshing backcountry experience." The constant foot traffic widens and churns trails into dust and degrades the land. For those same reasons, Mount Whitney limits the number of hikers, a possible restriction that looms for Half Dome, as well.

The cables that put Half Dome within reach of countless persons wouldn't be installed if the decision arose today, given the current priority to keep national parks as natural as possible.

Twenty-five years have passed, as of this writing, since the adoption of Yosemite's master plan, yet implementation has occurred at a glacial pace, principally due to the park's tradition of administrative gridlock, competing interest groups, and political seesawing. Nonetheless, in 2004 Yosemite finally embarked on a $440 million plan to limit or change human activity in the park consistent with the 1980 master plan. As Park Superintendent Michael Tollefson put it, "the goal is to have a smaller human footprint." This ambitious undertaking may take two decades to complete. It involves demolishing a parking lot near Yosemite Falls; replacing another one with a grassy pedestrian promenade; rebuilding and rerouting trails near waterfalls; razing a dam on the Merced River; moving some employee housing outside the park; eliminating about 250 campsites, including those along the Merced River; limiting the number of day-visitor cars to 550 (additional visitors will have to ride buses into the park); and launching extensive remodeling projects.

Despite objections to the plan from some quarters, a broad coalition of organizations supports the overall plan as a sensible approach to preserving the natural wonders, historical values, and sublime beauty of this national treasure called Yosemite.

EPILOGUE

Think like a mountain.—Aldo Leopold, *A Sand
County Almanac*

In the annals of hiking tragedies caused by lightning, July 27,
1985, ranks as one of the most calamitous dates of all time. By
all accounts, the storms in the Sierra Nevada on this day were
exceptionally violent; when combined with human misjudgments,
this proved a formula for disaster. All told, three people in two
close-by national parks were killed. These occurrences in eerily
similar circumstances were most startling, like the night in the

1960s when grizzlies killed two hikers in different locations in Glacier National Park.

Three other hikers on Half Dome were stricken in 1985, with two sustaining life-altering injuries. It could have been even worse, because other hikers and rock climbers also were in extremely high-risk circumstances in Yosemite on this day.

Twenty years later, those who were involved in the episode reflect on its meaning and aftermath.

◄○►

LINDA CROZIER FOUND HERSELF primarily responsible for the emergency medical treatment of two individuals for over five hours. All of the other helpers that night looked to her for leadership.

"I've always marveled at the raw power of nature and am amazed when people make careless, at times reckless, decisions in the outdoors. Our natural world can at one moment be beautiful and serene, and in the next violent and terrifying. It gives warning signs—hints of what's to come—but people sometimes ignore the signs or are simply unaware of what those signs are saying. What individuals don't realize when they act irresponsibly and put themselves in a high-risk position in the outdoors is that they are also risking the lives of those who have to rescue them. I have the deepest respect for the men and women in the search and rescue community who put their own lives on the line to save others.

"On that July day in 1985, some of us rested and stared in awe at the sights, sounds, and sensations of the most intense electrical storm I have ever seen, while at the same time that very storm was taking the lives of two men and injuring three others. From this experience, I learned to love and respect nature even more, and expand my own knowledge about the outdoors. I joined a volunteer search and rescue team. I learned more about wilderness medicine and, in turn, passed along what I have learned to hundreds of others through classes and lectures. It is my hope that recounting this story will do the same."

—◄○►—

BILL PIPPEY WAS AS emotionally affected as anyone by the episode, both at the time and afterward.

"What was revealed to me was how everybody deals with tragedy differently. That night, several courageous persons stepped up and kept it from being an even worse catastrophe. Others turned away and seemed concerned only about themselves. Some used the tragedy to make something of their lives, to chart a new direction, to finally live their dream. One devoted himself to helping others. Another retreated into a shell and allowed his life to deteriorate. One creep who wasn't even involved in the incident saw it as a chance to make money. One thing is true: No one was the same afterward and no one looked upon the other person in the same way as before. No one seemed interested in rekindling old ties.

"I took it as a major defeat, a crushing setback. I slipped back into my heavy drinking and drugging once more. I barely hung on to my life and my wife. Then one day in the mid-'90s, I woke up. I discovered Jesus Christ and became a devout, born-again Christian. I stopped abusing my body with substances. I refocused on my family, and in my work I became a laser engineer, which surely must surprise many of my old Hayward buddies."

—◄○►—

BRUCE WEINER LIVES with the effects of the lightning strike each day of his life. It caused him to see firsthand how fragile life really is, and that it takes very little "to totally screw up one's life."

Weiner: "Going to the top at that time, I know now, was a stupid decision, but I didn't know then that it was a stupid move. How can you say you'll risk your life just so you can reach the top of a mountain twenty minutes early? That's beyond stupidity. That's just a total lack of brains. What we didn't know at the time, though, was how reckless it was to go to that cave during a raging holocaust, that we were playing with our lives.

"A big part of our decision was that we [Frith and I] were following the two leaders, Rice and Esteban. We trusted their knowledge and judgment. After all, they had been doing this hike for years and were seasoned veterans. They believed that we'd be fully safe once in the cave.

"Am I bitter about what happened? On one level, yes, I am very bitter. Rice and Esteban led us into a totally unnecessary disaster that cost my best friend his life and me my health. I guess the question is, When should one trust a 'leader' and when should one not? I'm sure there are times when one must absolutely follow a leader in dangerous situations, when he possesses the expert knowledge and skill. But this was not one of those times. There was counterinformation from real authorities staring us in the face, and still we chose to go up.

"So, in retrospect, I feel I really have nobody to blame but myself. We passed signs that gave specific warnings about not going to the summit when there are signs of a thunderstorm and not taking cover in a rock enclosure. Frith and I were adults capable of thinking for ourselves, so we had little excuse for our own actions. We were the only ones with college degrees, for God's sake! But maybe that kind of learning doesn't matter in the outdoors, when it comes down to common sense and reasoned judgment. It's a valuable lesson why someone should not give in to the pressures of the moment, to group pressures, if one's own thinking and intuition say it's not right. One always needs to think for himself—in effect, not to relinquish control over his own destiny and allow someone else to determine it for him."

◄○►

ADRIAN ESTEBAN HAS CARRIED around the tragedy in his head and heart for more than two decades and is willing to be as honest as he can in terms of confronting his role in the calamity and talking about it.

Esteban: "I can now look back and feel totally responsible and not hide from the fact that I found the cave, and that it was my idea to bring everyone else on this trip. I did not force anyone to climb the cables to the top, but Tom and I were the leaders and they were just following us. If Tom and I did not make the climb to the top, then Bruce, Brian, and Bob would not have been there and all our lives from that day on would be different.

"The thing is, Tom and I really believed that facing and overcoming your fears was the right principle to follow. For 99 percent of the time, it's a sound approach in life for realizing your potential, succeeding, progressing. It's just that it failed us that one time on the top of Half Dome. With something as powerful and unpredictable as lightning, we should have understood that sound judgment had to be part of the equation.

"Despite the enormity of the tragedy, my feelings toward Half Dome remain the same, only now they are more profound. It is still a special place for me and, if anything, the entire incident was almost like my destiny. It served as a catalyst to motivate me to do something good with my life. No matter how difficult or bad things could get from that moment forward, all I have to do is look back at the accident and remember the clarity of the actions of the many people who helped us and I gain once again the proper perspective on life. In times of distress, I have used it to help me get through and overcome tough times—for example, when my father died in 1993 and when my mother came down with cancer. The most important thing is to never give up.

"Half Dome forced me to really turn inward and find a purpose for why I am here. Because of the person I am, being very deeply involved in natural wonders and having a spiritual outlook on life, everything about the strike at Half Dome has deep meaning for me—the place where it happened, the way it happened, the time in my life when it happened, the different ways it affected people.

"I think everyone, if they live with awareness and become wise enough, will recognize some event, incident, or chance happening in their life that transforms them and drives them to live life the very best that they can from that time forward.

"For me, it was that moment."

APPENDIX

———◄◦►———

Safety Guidelines for Lightning

Of all the weather-related phenomena, lightning kills and injures more people than any other, with the exception of floods. As seen in the tragedies on Half Dome and in Kings Canyon on July 27, 1985, persons tend to seek shelter when caught in a thunderstorm and driving rains. They may also believe it's safer to be under some cover, such as rock enclosures or a tree, than out in the open if lightning strikes. (Golfers are particularly prone to do this.) But small caves, tall trees, rock enclosures and outcroppings, "chimneys" located on rock walls—each can become a death trap if lightning strikes in the vicinity. (A large cave can offer safety but only if you stay in the middle, away from the walls.) It's far safer to stay out in the open and get wet.

Here are some additional crucial safety principles:*

All thunderstorms produce lightning and are dangerous.

The outdoors is the most dangerous place to be during a lightning storm. At the first indication of an impending storm, go inside to a completely enclosed building (not a carport, open garage, or covered patio) or into a hard-topped vehicle.

Lightning can strike as far as ten miles away from any rainfall, and can travel sideways for up to ten miles.

---

*These principles of Lightning Safety are mainly those of the National Weather Service (NWS).

If you hear thunder, you are in danger from lightning.

If the air starts buzzing and your hair bristles, you are in immediate danger and should adhere to the principles below.

If caught outdoors, *seek* the lowest point and *be* the lowest point. Do not be the tallest or second tallest object during a lightning storm. Avoid tall trees (be at least twice as far from a tall tree as the height of the tree). If in an open area, crouch down on the balls of your feet.

Avoid being near or touching any metal.

If you're with a group, stay several yards away from other people.

Get out of water, and out of small boats and canoes. If you're caught in a boat, crouch down in the center of the boat away from metal hardware. Don't stand in or near puddles of water.

Wait at least thirty minutes after the last clap of thunder before leaving shelter, even with blue sky and sunshine.

The safest measures to follow with lightning are awareness and prevention. Avoid being caught in precarious circumstances.

—◄o►—

IF THE HIKERS IN Yosemite and Kings Canyon that day knew and followed the above principles, their calamities most certainly would have been avoided.

ACKNOWLEDGMENTS

———◄○►———

I AM ENORMOUSLY GRATEFUL to all those persons who helped me complete this book, from the first stages of research to the final phrasing. First I want to thank each of the individuals who played a role in the events and who assisted me in telling their story. They are: Adrian Esteban, Linda (Crozier) Ghilarducci, Bill Pippey, Bruce Weiner, Mike Hoog, Rick Pedroncelli, Dan Crozier, Karl Buchner, Steve Ellner, Brian Cage, Steve White, Monroe Bridges, Paul Kolbenschlag, Zip Cotter, Clu Cotter, Ken Bokelund, Rob Foster, Al Major, Maggie (Newman) Dias, Bill Bryant, Colin Campbell, Scott Jackson, Jim Reilly, Gary Colliver, John Dill, Ron Mackie, Scott Emmerich, Dan Horner, Paul Ducasse, Mike Mayer, Dan Dellinges, Jim Tucker, Jennifer Corcoran, Marvin Talbert, Steven King, Debbie Bird, Robert Hensel, and Dr. Howard Klein. I also wish to express my deep appreciation to all those who provided information and/or critiqued what I wrote. In no particular order they are: Jim Snyder, Dr. Mary Ann Cooper, Paul Engstrom, Rick Donker, Bob Kinkead, Jim Mongillo, John Little, Jennifer Madgic, Dr. Marsh McLean, Dave Cone, Dr. Phil McLean, Jeff Rennicke, Randall Boone, Sally Howell, Liana Holmberg, Mary Heldman, John Nagle, Kris Fister, Don Coelho, Edward Schieler, Dolores Schieler, Alyza Salomon, Mike Peckner, Richard Keady, Charles R. "Butch" Farabee Jr., Mike Harding, Karen Little, Sarah Madgic, Richard Kithil Jr., Dr. Rob Hamilton, Jason Thrasher, Dave Toal, Felicia Eth, Howard Boyer, Darryl Brock, Lydia Bird, Sherry Symington, Bill Contardi, Walt Simmons, Mike Acker, Marilyn Young, Ruth Rowe, Ed Robertson, Diana Thrasher, Doug Madgic, Liz Robbins, Royal Robbins, Jim Erickson, Art Higbee, Ron Schultz, Phil Pochoda, Kirk Madgic, Richard Baumann,

Marc Soares, Jed Mattes, Linda Eade, Leonard Coyne, Buck Tilton, Sarah Rabkin, and of course my wife, Diane, who as always provided supportive companionship and sage counsel at every step of this journey.

Lastly, I wish to express my gratitude to the publisher, Peter Burford, who quickly saw the power of this story and who has been a delight to work with. I doubt an author could find a more encouraging and supportive publisher.